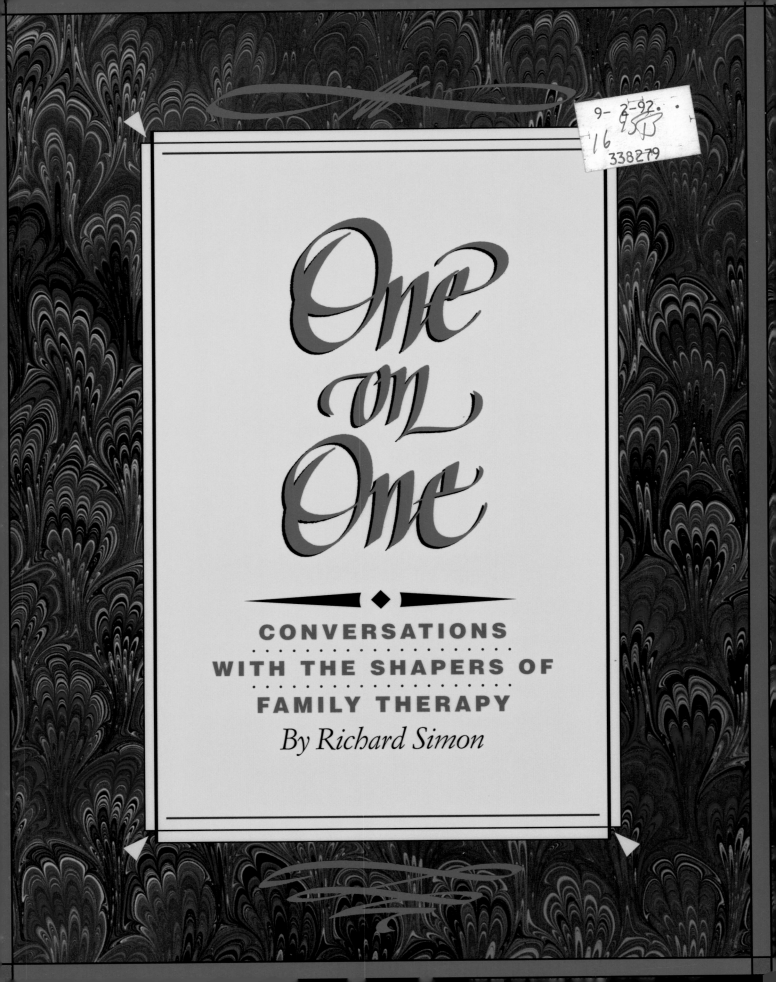

One on One

on One

CONVERSATIONS
WITH THE SHAPERS OF
FAMILY THERAPY

By Richard Simon

ONE ON ONE

ONE ON ONE

CONVERSATIONS WITH
THE SHAPERS OF FAMILY THERAPY

By Richard Simon
Editor, The Family Therapy Networker

THE FAMILY THERAPY NETWORK
Washington, DC
THE GUILFORD PRESS
New York · London

© 1992 THE FAMILY THERAPY NETWORK
7705 13th Street, N.W.
Washington, DC 20012

Copublished with
THE GUILFORD PRESS
A Division of Guilford Publications Inc.
72 Spring Street, New York, NY 10012

Printed in the United States of America

This book is printed on acid-free paper

Last digit is print number: 9 8 7 6 5 4 3 2 1

Library of Congress Cataloging-in-Publication Data

Simon, Richard, 1949-
     One on one: conversations with the shapers of family
therapy/by Richard Simon
        p.   cm.
Contents first appeared in The family therapy networker.
ISBN 0-89862-254-9 (hardcover)—ISBN 0-89862-269-7 (pbk.)
1. Family psychotherapy.   I. Family therapy networker.
II. Title
RC488.5.S543 1992   91-43238
616.89'156—dc20   CIP

Cover and book design by Jann Alexander
Cover calligraphy by Julian Waters
Typesetting by Wordscape
Copyediting by Karen Craft
Printed by Maple-Vale

Contents

Introduction

TWENTY YEARS AGO, WHEN I STARTED graduate school in clinical psychology, it was—at least as far as I was concerned—still the heyday of the encounter group, and I wanted to be the next Fritz Perls. My picture of a therapist then was of an intuitive, inscrutable guru, intolerant of phoniness and game playing, confidently guiding clients in the quest for the real, the authentic, the true. I had read Perls and R. D. Laing and understood that therapy was about peeling off the crust of self-deceit and stripping the ego of its defenses in order to uncover the core self. And I accepted the idea that the therapy group was the preferred arena for making that happen. There, in the company of strangers who had gathered for the same purpose, it was possible to find liberation from the lies and unexpressed feelings that were at the root of human misery.

Clearly, one's own family was not the place where one looked for this kind of healing experience. In fact, as a good child of the '60s, I knew the family was what you needed to escape from in order to find out who you really were. After all, wasn't that why people went away to college? To my ears, the term "family therapy," which I first encountered in graduate school, had the disturbing ring of an oxymoron, like "Peacekeeper Missile." My classmates apparently shared my distrust of family therapy—it was the least-requested course in our training program that year. So, as a first-year student with the lowest status, unable to get into the group therapy course, I found myself assigned family therapy instead. I became a family therapist by default.

Fortunately, my graduate program had a one-way mirror and an observation room, and my family therapy supervisor had a new convert's enthusiasm. Each week a bunch of us watched one another repeat the phrases he phoned in to us, shamelessly pretending a calm and a worldly wisdom none of us possessed, to the succession of surprisingly compliant families who had come to the university's mental health clinic. And, in spite of our fumblings and posturing and crude mimicry of the techniques we picked up watching videotapes of the "masters," our families seemed to change, often dramatically. Each case became its own engrossing story, filled with angry standoffs, tearful

reconciliations and some sublime moments of laughter and kindness.

Sometimes, in supervision, our teacher would show a video of a family's first session and then run another taped several weeks later. And there it was, in how people looked and talked, and, of course, in how they sat. (We were all taught to attach tremendous importance to the cryptographic significance of who sat next to whom.) We could *see* change taking place. That course reordered my therapeutic pantheon. Irascible Fritz Perls was expelled, to be replaced by the family therapists whose workshops and videotapes made such an impression on me.

Many young therapists in the '70s, members of the baby-boom generation who swelled the ranks of the therapy profession during that time, had experiences that echoed mine. Family therapy, in its rebellion against psychiatry and medical-model thinking, in its optimism about human nature, in its conviction that there had to be a better way, seemed to reflect the countercultural values that these young therapists had already imbibed on their college campuses. For us, family therapy was more than just another technique that required larger offices and more chairs. It was the first cinemascope therapy, a panoramic vision of human relationships that promised to revolutionize not only the way therapists did their jobs, but the way schools, hospitals, courts and, indeed, the world worked. There was a great buzz of excitement over the dizzying implications of finally grasping the relationships between apparently disconnected phenomena and understanding families as multigenerational pageants that explained much of the mystery of human personality.

But new ideas—as visionary as they seemed—were only a part of the appeal of the family therapy movement. In large part, the popularity of family therapy was the result of the personalities of what long-time family therapist Lynn Hoffman has called "The Great Originals," the charismatic crowd pleasers who demonstrated the family approach in live interviews before large workshop audiences of therapists around the country. Here were clinicians so supremely self-possessed, so sure of the power of their methods, that they were willing to regularly put their work on public display and take on whatever unpredictable challenges a family could present. Even more than the provocative papers and books about systems theory and therapeutic strategy that were

being published during this time, these clinical demonstrations triggered the field's rapid growth and the therapists who conducted them became both the legends and the great recruiters of the family therapy movement.

By 1982, there were dozens of family therapy training institutes, a national family therapy professional association with nearly 10,000 members, and packed family therapy workshops taking place around the country. That year also marked the debut of *The Family Therapy Networker*, a bimonthly magazine that purported to cover the latest developments in a young, fast-changing field. But the interviews with the new field's practitioners and thinkers were the *Networker*'s main attraction in its early years.

By the time these interviews began to appear, there was plenty of literature explaining the theories and techniques of family therapy. The *Networker* interviews attempted to do something else. They were an opportunity to steer the field's leaders away from familiar themes and have them address topics they had never previously discussed. The interview is an especially intimate journalistic form. It allows large numbers of people to listen in on a one-on-one conversation, and the *Networker* interviews were often unusually personal, probing the mysterious relationship between the personality of the therapist and the particular form of his or her work.

Three of the most popular *Networker* interviews were with Salvador Minuchin, Carl Whitaker and Virginia Satir, probably the most admired—and most imitated—therapists in the history of family therapy. In countless training tapes and workshop demonstrations, these celebrated clinicians had brilliantly handled the most sensitive clinical situations, sweeping aside resistance and using both their techniques and the force of their personalities to open new worlds for clients bogged down in hopelessness and despair. Readers welcomed the opportunity for a close-up conversation with these giants of the field, to hear their personal stories, trace the course of their careers and see how they reacted to challenging questions. These interviews gave family therapy's almost mythologized figures a chance to reveal their humanity and close the gap between themselves and a field caught up in hero worship.

As the interviewer, closing that gap with these famous people who had been my role models was an important growing-up experience for me. Only a couple of years

before, I had been an awestruck attendee at their workshops; now I didn't have to compete for attention with others in a crowded audience or stand awkwardly in a post-workshop huddle, silently preparing for the moment when it would be my turn to ask a bright question. At the same time, I felt the immense responsibility of having to come up with The Question that the *Networker*'s readers would want me to ask. Sometimes, sitting in a hotel room during an interview, I imagined a grandstand full of family therapists outside the window, keeping track of how the conversation was going.

My first *Networker* interview was with Jay Haley, who holds a central position in the development of family therapy. Haley's biting irony had made him the field's foremost polemicist, its point man as it challenged the mental health establishment. During the 1950s and 1960s, as one of anthropologist Gregory Bateson's collaborators in his famous research project on human communication, Haley helped formulate some of the earliest theories about the relationship between family interaction and individual symptoms, including the famous "double-bind" hypothesis. For much of the '60s and '70s, he also was the foremost student of the field, chronicling the many diverse developments during that exciting time when the field was first taking shape.

Haley was the historian of the early family therapy movement, and in the interview he seemed more interested in talking about the work of other contributors than about his own. He was a walking encyclopedia of anecdotes about the development of family therapy, and I remember thinking, as he kept drawing on his vast store of information about the field's pioneers, that the *Networker* seemed to be picking up on a task he had begun.

Haley is still probably best known for popularizing the work of his mentor, the brilliant hypnotherapist Milton Erickson, and extracting therapeutic principles from Erickson's seemingly intuitive approach that became the foundation of many of the most influential developments in family therapy, including Haley's own strategic method. While Erickson died before the birth of the *Networker*, the profile of Erickson included in this collection attempts to capture the sense of creativity and personal commitment that were his legacy to a field to which, during his lifetime, he insisted he did not belong.

This book includes interviews with two other prominent non-family therapists who nevertheless helped create the cultural climate that spawned the family therapy movement. By the time most young clinicians of the '70s and '80s decided they wanted to be family therapists, they had probably already read Thomas Szasz and R. D. Laing, in books like *The Myth of Mental Illness*, *The Divided Self* and *The Politics of Experience*, which took a buzz saw to psychiatric orthodoxy and the medical model. In approaching both Szasz and Laing, I had assumed that they would find common cause with a field so obviously in line with their values and beliefs. Instead, both men expressed grave misgivings about what family therapy had become and the harm it was doing. These interviews turned out to be troubling reading for a field used to seeing itself as the good guy, and offered a painful lesson in what it was like to be on the receiving end of an iconoclast's rebuke.

The *Networker* interviews soon went beyond examining family therapy's origins to focus on the field's continuing ferment during the '80s. Three themes stood out during this period. Perhaps the most influential was the profound impact of feminist thinking. I still remember the heart-thumping tension in the audiences at the large conferences where feminist presenters first began delivering ringing indictments of family therapy. At the plenary session of one such meeting, a witty and playful woman friend of mine grimly denounced the legacy of patriarchy, decried the oppression of women, and attacked family therapy for its sexism. Up at the podium, she had become a stranger, bearing no resemblance to the kindred spirit I was used to kibbitzing with. Listening to her, I felt that all men, including me, were on trial. The rhetoric about patriarchy and oppression sounded overblown, but my friend was so brilliant and her argument about how the cultural laws of gender shape families so compelling that I found myself recognizing that something very important was being said.

Since that time, the feminist critique has transformed the theory and practice of family therapy. Probably the most influential figures in bringing about this revolution have been the Women's Project in Family Therapy—Betty Carter, Peggy Papp, Olga Silverstein and Marianne Walters—a group of four widely respected clinicians with differing theoretical orientations who joined together to challenge the unacknowledged

sexism in many family approaches and to offer clinical alternatives. I approached the 1984 interview with the Women's Project as a bit of a tightrope act. Here I was, a young man, interviewing four prominent women on a subject about which even an interviewer could not pretend neutrality. I survived by acknowledging my own confusion, which, it turned out, was shared by much of the field. The interview wound up offering one of the most accessible early statements of the feminist critique, laying out issues that family therapists have been struggling with ever since.

Despite the male domination of the family therapy field in its early years, during the '80s women were at the forefront not only in the examination of gender issues but in experiments with new and unconventional clinical techniques. Two of the leading clinical innovators of the past 10 years have been Italian psychiatrist Mara Selvini Palazzoli and strategic therapist Cloé Madanes. As the central figure of the famous Milan Group and first author of the classic *Paradox and Counterparadox*, Palazzoli captured the imagination of the field with her operatic use of ritual and therapeutic paradox. Even though at the time of the *Networker* interview, Palazzoli had renounced her earlier work with paradox in order to experiment with a procedure called the "invariant prescription," she approached her new work with the same intensity, the same fascination with detail and the same absorption in deciphering the inner politics of the family. While for Palazzoli, everything seemed high drama, Madanes, known for ingenious interventions relying on play and pretending, found it hard to take anything seriously, including herself. Watching both of them go through a day of treating families was a hypnotic experience in which every other concern receded and became a mere distraction. The power of their approaches seemed to emerge not only from their technical methods but from their tremendous power of concentration and their ability to make solving the riddle of the therapy session unfolding before them the only thing in the world that mattered.

In the latter part of the 1980s, family therapy appeared to approach a crossroads as critics began to ponder the basis of the therapist's authority, openly questioning the directive tradition established by figures like Erickson, Haley and Minuchin, and challenging some of family therapy's basic premises. A Chilean biologist named Humberto

Maturana, who, one noted family therapist claimed, "has made a breakthrough in understanding living systems which . . . is comparable in magnitude to Einstein's theory of relativity," became a leader of a movement called "constructivism," which declared all our so-called objective truths to be merely a function of human subjectivity. The *Networker* interview with Maturana, and a later conversation with Lynn Hoffman, author of *The Foundations of Family Therapy* and veteran observer of the field's trends, raised the question of whether the family therapy movement had finally spent itself and it was time for a new cycle of theory and clinical innovation to begin.

Today, allegiances to the various schools that family therapy's charismatic founders established—structuralist, strategic, systemic, etc.—figure less prominently in the field's debates. The leadership in the field is in a process of transition. With the passing of giants like Virginia Satir and Murray Bowen, and the aging of others, the inevitable process of the changing of the guard has begun in earnest. A new generation of therapists has entered the field, and for them, the once-revolutionary ideas of family therapy are the commonplaces of everyday practice.

For this younger generation, this collection may serve as a kind of genealogy of their professional family, showing the roots of its assumptions and practices, revealing how the seeds of the field's future were planted in the past. For those who have lived through the field's mushrooming growth over the past 20 years, this collection may serve as an old home movie, showing the way we were as well as offering an opportunity to reflect on the contributions of the field's great innovators. No longer so dazzled by their originality and the power of their presence, we are now in a better position to see their contributions in perspective. These master clinicians still have much to teach us about the wedding between an individual's personality and his or her therapeutic theory and method. Their productive careers offer us all lessons about how to remain creative through the full course of a professional lifetime. This gallery of idiosyncratic and gifted therapists voicing so many different theories and styles provides a role model for every taste.

RICHARD SIMON

BEHIND THE ONE-WAY MIRROR

AN INTERVIEW WITH
JAY HALEY

THERE IS A STORY THAT CLOÉ MADANES LIKES TO tell trainees at the Family Therapy Institute of D.C. to illustrate the complexities of human communication. The story is about her husband, Jay Haley. Every morning he drives their youngest daughter, Magali, to school, and every morning as they are going out the door, Madanes says, "Magali, take your jacket." The child answers that it is not cold, her mother insists that it is, and the discussion prolongs the moment of separation. Haley patiently waits at the door until he finally ends the bantering between mother and daughter. Winking at Magali, he says, "Your mother is cold today, you'd better take that jacket." Magali smiles back and, dragging her jacket behind her, offers her cheek for her mother to kiss as she goes out the door.

With a sense of humor tested by thousands of hours of watching other families enact their rituals, Haley manages to side simultaneously with his wife and his daughter and do it in a spirit of playfulness that appeals to both. If Haley has been less successful in appealing to all the factions in the "family of family therapists" (an expression he abhors), it is not

for want of a sense of humor. Rather, for much of his career, Haley has seemed far more intent on stirring things up than on gaining allies. For more than 25 years, he has been family therapy's foremost provocateur, returning again and again—sometimes with delicious irony, sometimes with biting sarcasm, always with great lucidity—to one of his favorite themes: the self-serving tendency of professional helpers to rationalize what they do and overcomplicate what is going on right before their eyes.

Haley has been so successful in setting the terms for how we think about therapy and change (whether one agrees with him or not) that it may be hard to understand what the field of psychotherapy was like before he began commenting upon it. No one has ever accused Haley of a reluctance to stake out a clear position. From early on in his career, his work has served to furnish a compass bearing that has enabled others in the field to establish more clearly what their position was. Even if you found some of his ideas totally wrongheaded—like his view of the role of power and control in the therapeutic relationship (important), or the therapeutic value of

expressing feeling (not important)—his writing usually roused you to respond in a way that the ordinary professional literature did not. Probably more arguments about therapy have started by invoking Haley's name ("You know what Haley would say about this, don't you?") than that of any other figure in the field.

When, as a member of anthropologist Gregory Bateson's famous research project, Haley first got involved with the field of psychotherapy in the early 1950s, the Freudian model was in its ascendancy as the dominant thera____. At that time, before the developm____es or behavior thera____ there simply was no a____ was *the* vehicle for cl____ Haley about this era, ____ the "strange philoso____ lievers seemed to be ____ them out at a party because, whatever you said, they would interpret it," recalls Haley. "And whatever they said, they'd stop and wonder, 'Why did I say that?' By that time, there were people who, after years of analysis, couldn't enjoy sex without wondering, 'Why am I enjoying sex?'"

Even though he had been a coauthor and editor of "Toward a Theory of Schizophrenia," the Bateson project's celebrated paper on the double-bind hypothesis, the first publication that established Haley's special identity in the field was a hilarious dissection of the Freudian method called "The Art of Psychoanalysis," published in 1958. "The Art of Psychoanalysis" took the position that, far from providing a "pure" scientific method for unearthing the profound truths lurking in the unconscious, the analytic method was actually a brilliantly disingenuous way of placing clients in an unwinnable bind that they could escape only by being cured.

It was in "The Art of Psychoanalysis" that readers first encountered the ironic voice one finds in so much of Haley's best writing. Haley wrote in a way that was utterly free of technical jargon, with an irresistible appeal for anyone who enjoyed the spectacle of professional pomposity being mocked with wit and subtlety. Haley seemed to say to the reader, "What you always suspected is true. It's all not really as obscure and convoluted as the experts are trying to make it."

HALEY'S FIRST BOOK, *STRATEGIES OF PSYCHO-therapy,* was an elaboration of the ideas implicit in "The Art of Psychoanalysis." In *Strategies,* the struggle between analyst and patient became only one example of the ongoing struggle in human relationships to see who was in control. Throughout, Haley offered the argument that symptoms could best be understood not as expressions of inner conflict but as interpersonal power maneuvers and that the therapist's job was to render these maneuvers ineffective and thus introduce the possibility of change.

Strategies established Haley as the most accomplished hit man in family therapy's assault on the mental health establishment. But it did something else that strongly influenced the course of the early family therapy movement. As a result of the success of *Strategies,* Haley began receiving speaking engagements to talk about therapy. Coming at the same time that he became the first editor of *Family Process,* this opportunity made it possible for Haley to make direct contact with family therapists all across the country. From this time until the late 1960s, when he got involved in developing a model of family therapy training based on live supervision at the Philadelphia Child Guidance Clinic, a major part of Haley's professional energies was invested in traveling around the country observing family therapists at work, collecting papers for *Family Process,* and tying together developments in family therapy. Throughout this period, Haley was less interested in fostering a particular point of view about how to work with families than with serving as a synthesizer and developing an overview of the field.

[handwritten margin note: symptoms – interpersonal power maneuvers, not expressions of inner conflict]

Because so much of Haley's impact during this period was behind the scenes, its importance may be lost on younger family therapists today. One enduring product of this phase, however, which reflected Haley's interest in the various practical methodologies for working with families that were just being developed during this time, was *Techniques of Family Therapy*, which he coedited with Lynn Hoffman. *Techniques* featured conversations with each of five different therapists about how they conducted a particular therapy session, all of which were subjected to an extraordinary amount of scrutiny. Carl Whitaker remembers that Haley spent more than 20 hours talking with him about a family session. Another pioneering therapist who discussed his work with Haley in *Techniques* was Frank Pittman, now in private practice in Atlanta. Pittman remembers his contact with Haley during this period as "one of the greatest experiences of my life." As Pittman recalls it, "Between 1965 and 1966, Jay came to watch me work several times. During his visits he would tell me what every family therapist in the country was doing. Throughout that whole period, he did an amazing job of making people aware of each other and letting them know who they should be contacting. The thing that most struck me was that he was not so much trying to sell his own stuff . . . as exciting everyone with his discoveries about what worked and what didn't and what was happening in the field."

From the time the Bateson project disbanded in 1962 until about 1969, Haley's primary interest was in family research and the observation of therapy. He had himself stopped doing therapy in 1962 once he had become established in a full-time research job that enabled him to give up the private practice he had been conducting since the mid-'50s. Haley's shift into focusing on supervision, the activity for which he is most noted today, came only after he joined Salvador Minuchin at the Philadelphia Child Guidance Clinic and the two organized the Institute for Family Counseling (IFC), a project training people from the Philadelphia ghetto who had no formal education beyond high school to be family therapists. The procedures for live supervision that later became the basic elements of Haley's training model first developed out of a concern that client families would need to be protected as they worked with beginning therapists.

In Frank Pittman's view, it was through his work at IFC that Haley "differentiated himself out" and moved from the position of being an observer and commentator to having a particular approach of his own to offer. The widely read books that he has written since that time—*Problem Solving Therapy*, which drew on much of the teaching material he had developed at IFC, and *Leaving Home*—have established Haley's position today as probably the leading representative of the "strategic school." Not surprisingly, in his latest professional incarnation, Haley has managed to fuel every bit as much debate and activity within the field as in his earlier endeavors.

TALKING WITH HIS STUDENTS, HALEY SOMETIMES gives himself as an example of how a person's position in a system determines how he thinks. Entering the field of mental health without proper clinical credentials as part of a vaguely defined research project, Haley began as an outsider. Being an outsider, he believes, gave him a freedom to challenge accepted ideas because "I didn't think like the insiders."

To some colleagues, however, Haley's "outsider" status has been as much a liability as an asset. According to Fred Duhl, director of the Boston Family Institute, Haley's work "demonstrates the difference between the therapist as healer and the therapist as outsider and commentator. He teaches a distance therapy that is brilliant for issues of hierarchy and power, but limited, I think, in dealing with the real pains and pleasures of living in the middle of life."

To some, even the accessibility of Haley's writing

has been a double-edged sword. Describing Haley in a *New Yorker* article about family therapy that appeared some years ago, Janet Malcolm wrote, "Haley's style is so lucid, his tone so natural and agreeable, his wit is so nice, his language so unpretentious and untechnical, that he invites mistrust: If it's that easy, it can't be sound."

The more one speaks to therapists outside the orbit of structural/strategic thinking, the more one does encounter a certain mistrust of Haley, a belief that he represents a kind of heartlessly efficient way of producing changes. In part, this view may have something to do with the fact that Haley himself has remained a bit of an enigma. More than any other major figure in the field, he is someone who is known primarily through his writing. While one can readily see videotapes of people like Minuchin, Whitaker, Satir and Bowen actually at work with families, Haley has remained a somewhat mysterious figure behind the one-way mirror. As Minuchin, his colleague for 10 years, explains it, "Jay has a public persona created in his writing and a private persona. In his writing, he presents himself in an adversarial position, as an iconoclast against the established therapeutic modalities. He has a writing style that becomes sharper in confrontation. Because of that, people who read Jay imagine a particular kind of person. Actually, he is really a rather shy person and very respectful, particularly of students. But it is almost as if Jay is reluctant to be seen in this light—it would break his image. People can become prisoners of their image, and I think this may be what has happened to Jay."

Something else has been happening to Haley in recent years. As many of his ideas about therapy have attracted more and more adherents, Haley, the iconoclastic outsider, has found himself getting perilously close to becoming an insider. Some of the traditional thinking, which he took on so deftly in his article "Why Mental Health Clinics Should Avoid Family Therapy," has begun to shift. Many of the same clinics Haley satirized a few years ago are now being staffed and even administered by therapists trained in his method. Haley's own institute, for example, has trained truckloads of therapists at every level of the Maryland mental health system under a multiyear contract with the state Department of Mental Hygiene.

Like it or not (and he clearly does not), Haley has come to be venerated as (to quote Frank Pittman again) a "cult leader." Placed in such a bind, the determined outsider has few choices but to put as much distance as possible between himself and his overzealous devotees. A sense of humor helps, but even there, admits Haley, there are problems. "It used to be that when I said something funny, people used to laugh. Now they take notes."

In the interview that follows, Haley offers his views on the more than 25 years of family therapy history that he has observed and helped create.

Q: *You seem to have found your way into the field of psychotherapy by a rather circuitous route. I understand that as a young man your great ambition was to be a writer.*

HALEY: Well, yes. I started writing short stories when I was about 18. While I was an undergraduate at UCLA, I sold a short story to *The New Yorker*. I thought that I was on my way. I began to think of myself as a writer and a playwright and changed my major to the theater. But after that first story was published, I didn't sell another one for six years. In the meantime, I spent a year in New York, almost eight hours a day writing without any success. Then my father died, and I went back to California to settle what had to be settled and ended up staying there and going to graduate school in English at the University of California.

Q: *I know you have a master's degree in something, but no one has ever been able to tell me what it is in. Is your degree in English?*

HALEY: Oh, no. While I was in graduate school, I

had to get a job, and so I got a B.L.S., a librarian's degree. After that, I went to Stanford and worked as a reference librarian while getting a master's in communication. That's where I met Gregory Bateson.

Q: *How did the two of you actually meet?*

HALEY: We really got to know each other because we were both interested in popular films. In my last year as an undergraduate, I had heard a social psychologist ask the question, "Why do people go to the movies?" I had never thought about that before, and I got interested in the question. At that time—this was about 1948—there were five million people who saw every movie released, I mean, they went day and night. Of course, this was in the days before TV. Now I suppose those are the same people who watch TV 12 hours a day. Anyhow, I started analyzing movies to see what was in them that was so appealing, and I later went to Stanford to continue to study films. I first met Bateson because he was one of the few people who was interested in analyzing movies at that time. He had analyzed German propaganda films, and I went over to talk to him about films. We got in an argument about a Nazi film because I didn't think his interpretation was Freudian enough—there was a whole castration theme in the film that I didn't think he appreciated. He decided to hire me to work on his project on communication. The project was not a clinical one at that time; it was on films and animal behavior. John Weakland, who had been studying Chinese films, was also hired on the project.

Q: *So up to that point, you had no interest in mental health, certainly none in doing therapy with families. How did you get interested in family communication?*

HALEY: Back then we were interested in studying all kinds of communication. Bateson's project happened to be housed at the VA hospital in Palo Alto, and one day a psychiatric resident said to me, "If you're interested in communication, you should talk to this patient I have." Actually, the resident was leaving, and he wanted someone to take this guy on

in therapy. The patient, who had been hospitalized for 10 years, had first been sent to a state hospital, where he wouldn't give his name; he said he was from Mars. Then, after he gave an Army serial number, they put him in the VA, and he had been there ever since. I talked to him, and I was impressed with his tremendous imagination and use of metaphor. So I started recording our conversations, and Bateson got interested. As a result of listening to this man, we began to think about schizophrenia as a confusion of levels of communication. Soon after that, we started a survey of schizophrenics in the VA and began interviewing them to examine their strange styles of communication. Don Jackson was hired to supervise our therapy with schizophrenics. When Bateson came up with the double-bind hypothesis, he had never seen a family. He developed it in 1954, and we didn't see a family until about 1956 or 1957. We wrote the double-bind paper in June 1956; it was published in September 1956—the fastest journal publication ever done, I think.

Q: *Did you ever meet with the family of the patient who first got you interested in all of this?*

HALEY: No, but I saw him for one hour a day for five years.

Q: *For five years? What did you do for all that time?*

HALEY: Just whatever we were doing in those days for therapy. Mostly I interpreted to him. We had a theory at that time that if you made the right interpretation, a guy would be transformed into normality and go out and get a job. This man had been a migratory worker, and it was difficult to track down his family. I finally did locate them, and he went to see them. Just before he arrived, his mother died, and somehow he got put into the hospital in Oregon. So I went up there, met his father, got him and took him back to the VA in Menlo Park. Finally, he did get out of the hospital and back home with his family, but it took a long time. He had been locked up so long when I first took him outside the hospital, he had never seen a car without a clutch—

and they'd been around for 10 years—he had never even ordered dinner in a restaurant.

Q: *So what was the first family that you actually interviewed?*

HALEY: It was the family of a guy who had a theory that he had cement in his stomach. He was about 40 years old, and his parents were in their seventies. Every time they would visit the hospital, he would start to walk across the grounds with them, and then he would fall down and insist he couldn't get up because his stomach hurt so much and he was so anxious. Then an aide from the ward would come over and say, "Get up," and the guy would get up and go back to the ward.

I was seeing this man about three times a week, interpreting oral issues related to his stomach, I think. Anyhow, he wanted to leave the hospital, but he could not think of leaving without going to live with his parents, and he could not stand being with his parents without collapsing. So I called his parents in, mainly to see what he was so frightened about, and when they came in, the guy stood up against the wall like Jesus crucified. His parents seemed to me like nice people. I mean, they were a little weird, but nice people. I asked them to come back several times, and I recorded the interviews. It was by listening to them that we first began to see double binds in a session.

Q: *Was this the famous family in which the son gave his mother the Mother's Day card with the inscription "You've always been like a mother to me"?*

HALEY: Yes, that was the one. Up to that point, we had this great idea of the "double bind," but we couldn't actually find one. Everything was hypothetical about the childhood of the schizophrenic; it had nothing to do with current life. In fact, John Weakland and I talked about writing a musical with a song called "The Search for the Double Bind." But once we began to see how these parents and their son were behaving with one another, we began to realize that double binds were really all over the place. We especially saw them in hypnosis.

Q: *I've heard that your work with hypnosis and your interest in the issues of power and control in human relationships sometimes put you at odds with Bateson.*

HALEY: Bateson was an anthropologist to his soul, and an anthropologist doesn't believe you should tamper with the data or change in any way. The task of an anthropologist is just to observe. For Bateson, the idea of stepping in and changing something was kind of personally revolting. After I met Erickson and began to go into a very directive style of therapy in which you produce a change, Bateson got more and more uncomfortable, particularly when I began to describe the therapy relationship as a struggle for control or power. Actually, he didn't mind it as a description of what therapists were doing—he minded it as a product of *his* project. So someone like John Rosen would say, "You've got to win the struggle with a crazy patient. If he says he is God, you've got to be God and say, 'Get on your knees to me.'" Now, Bateson wouldn't mind that, but he would mind it if it was connected with his project. But he was in a funny position. He was against hypnosis, he was against psychotherapy, and he didn't like psychiatry. Yet his project was on hypnosis, psychiatry and psychotherapy. So he had a problem. Even years later, after we were no longer working together on the project, people kept bringing up the issue of therapy with him and implying that he was connected with my description of therapy in terms of power and hierarchy. By then he had gone off to study animals—he had gotten tired of people—and he did not like my work being thrown up to him. So more and more, he just stepped aside from it.

Q: *Can you tell me something about your personal relationship with Bateson and what kind of man he was?*

HALEY: He was an English intellectual to his soul and probably the major social science thinker in the country. He had an amazing ability to draw from so many fields—biology, chemistry, anthropology, even mathematics. We got along very well, at least for the

first eight years of the project. I named my son Gregory after him. Bateson was my teacher; a tremendous mind. He was the kind of person to whom you could go when you were stuck for an idea. He could always stimulate you to think about a problem in a different way, which is something so valuable in a research project.

When that project started, he was a well-known scientist, and both John Weakland and I were at the graduate student level. As the project continued we shifted up to where we did our own writing and began to move into a more professionally equal status with him. In that kind of small research group, a shift like that is really a tremendous change. Bateson had to deal with it and accept it, and we had to deal with it and accept it. It was a struggle, but it pretty well worked out. One of the ways we began to handle it was by dividing up the work. So I headed up a family experiment program, and John headed up a family therapy training and research program, while Bateson went off on whatever his interests were.

Q: *How did the Bateson project end?*

HALEY: We were together on the project eight hours a day for 10 years. Can you imagine that? We were dealing with very hot, personal material because it was about people going mad, therapy and the rules of human relationships. It was not easy stuff to deal with and talk about. Still, we stuck it out for 10 years, but by the end of it we had had enough of each other and were ready to go our separate ways.

Q: *You had begun to work with Milton Erickson in the early 1950s. How did what you were doing with him relate to your work on the Bateson project?*

HALEY: I had learned hypnosis from Erickson in 1953 at a workshop. Hypnosis then became part of our research in the Bateson project. John Weakland and I began to visit periodically with Erickson, spending a week audiotaping him talking about hypnosis. Then Weakland and I began to teach a class in hypnosis to local psychiatrists, but they

began to say, "It's awfully interesting, but I don't want to really do it. Why don't you take this patient on?" I had no degrees and qualifications for it, but Don Jackson persuaded me to start a practice. So I started a little practice about 1955 or '56, and when I began to do that, I realized I didn't know enough. That's when I started going to talk to Erickson about therapy. I soon began to find that producing very rapid changes in people upsets their families. I'd change a wife, and the husband would come to see me. It took me a while to realize that it was because I had changed the wife that the husband came. I was learning a lot about families in my private practice at the same time we were getting interested in studying families on the Bateson project.

Q: *So you began to look to Erickson to discuss your therapy. What was the style of supervision with him? Did he ever observe you at work with a client?*

HALEY: No, he never watched me work. It never occurred to me to ask him to watch me with a patient. His style of supervision was to tell stories. If you asked him about a case you had, he would tell you a story about a case *he* had. Although he could be very straightforward about telling you what to do, he was always unexpected. I had a woman who lost her voice; she couldn't speak. So I asked Erickson, "What would you say to this woman?" He said, "I would ask her if there was anything she wanted to say."

Q: *You've written about how Erickson was always working on the people around him—friends, students, patients—everyone. As his student, did you ever get some clear sense of what he was trying to do with you?*

HALEY: Not really. Usually, if you figured out what he was doing, you soon realized he was actually doing something else. So I never bothered. But the first time I came to consult with Erickson about cases after I began my own practice, I sat down and he said, "What is it you *really* want to see me about?" I said, "Well, I have some cases I want to talk about." And he said, "Alright." But he was

letting me know we were going to talk on two levels: we were going to talk about me and about cases.

Q: *Did you start noticing changes in yourself that seemed to arise spontaneously after you began to have contact with him?*

HALEY: I don't know, because I was going through so many changes. I mean, I was having kids, getting promoted, doing interesting research, going into practice—so much was happening in my life.

Q: *Erickson impresses me as being such an awesome human being, but it sometimes seems to me that his genius may have made him a rather lonely man. Did he ever acknowledge anyone as being on his level? Did he have a peer?*

HALEY: I think Erickson defined every hypnotist in the world as his student. I remember once he was talking about himself as a poor hypnotic subject, and he said, "I've repeatedly tried to go into a trance for one of my students and I wasn't able to." He just didn't think of anybody as his peer.

Q: *You would think somebody who was as flexible as Erickson and able to talk to so many people at so many different levels would have this very wide experience of the world, but that wasn't really the case, was it?*

HALEY: Well, Erickson had two subjects: hypnosis and therapy. I mean, he knew quite a bit about various issues, various cultures, and so on, and he traveled some, but the man worked 10 hours a day, six or seven days a week, doing therapy. He would start at seven in the morning and he often quit at 11 p.m. at night. Every weekend he was either seeing patients or he was on the road teaching.

Q: *How would you describe your relationship with Erickson?*

HALEY: He was a man you enjoyed. I enjoyed having dinner with him. He was funny when telling stories. But at the same time, he wasn't a pal kind of a man with me. A few of the old-type hypnotists, I think, were pals of his. But I started as such a student to him that I was never in that relationship. By

the time I got on more of a peer level with him, he was old. It was very hard on me seeing him so old. In his work, Erickson felt what was most important was his ability to control his voice and to control his movement. But as he got older and more paralyzed, he lost articulation in his speech, he got double vision, and he could not fully control his movement. So it was sad to see him toward the end of his life. Of course, he did extraordinary things, given what he had, right up to the very end. But compared with what he could do before, it was such a contrast, and it was just distressing to me to see him.

Q: *If he were alive today, what do you think he would say about live supervision and this whole technology for doing training that we are developing now?*

HALEY: I'm trying to remember if I talked to him about it—I think I talked to him about it. I believe he would do a much more personal supervision. He would get bored with the one-way mirror, for one thing, and be doing things with the people behind the mirror all the time. But I think he would teach more by having somebody sit in, or he would demonstrate. His reaction to one-way mirror supervision might have been like Minuchin's. Sal can't stand being out of the room, so he developed a theory of supervision where he has to go in the room. But when you watch him behind the mirror, he's bored; he paces up and down. I think Erickson would be the same way. Unless he was in there doing the maneuvering, he would be bored. You have to really rule yourself out of going in if you wish to stay out of there, and someone who is really a clinician to his soul, like Minuchin or Erickson, can't stay out of there.

Q: *As long as we're on the subject of the one-way mirror, do you know how its use began?*

HALEY: I think the one-way mirror originated with Charles Fulweiler in Berkeley, California. He was across the bay from us when I was studying the different methods of therapy on the Bateson project. When we began to work with families, I heard

about Fulweiler, who was with the juvenile department in Berkeley. I went over to speak with him and found that he had a one-way mirror because he was teaching psychologists how to do testing, and he wanted to watch them test. He was really offering live supervision on how to do psychological tests. I found out that since 1953 he had been seeing families using the one-way mirror setup. He would observe them from outside the room, come in, make a comment, and go out again. When I found him in 1957, he had that method well established. He may very well have been the first family therapist.

Once I got to know him, I found that I enjoyed watching behind that one-way mirror because we could observe and talk about what was happening while it was happening. Fulweiler would come out, have a cup of coffee, talk about the family, go in and make an intervention, come back out, and we would chat about it. I believe, but I am not entirely sure, that it was only after finding out about Fulweiler's setup that we put in our own one-way mirror at the Bateson project. Once we started using a one-way mirror and got more into family therapy, people from all over the country began to visit us at the Bateson project. They thought that having one-way mirrors was a great idea and just considered it part of family therapy. So they went back and put in one-way mirrors, and then everybody had them. But I think it was Fulweiler who started it all.

Q: *How had Fulweiler gotten the idea for using the one-way mirror with families?*

HALEY: He told me that the first family he saw in that way came to him because the 16-year-old daughter, who had run away and gotten picked up in a bar with a bunch of bums, had been sent to him for testing. She tested in the normal range. So he turned her loose, saying whatever psychologists say when they mean, "Go forth, and sin no more." In a few months, she was back. She had run away, and she had been picked up in a bar again with a bunch of bums. So Fulweiler tested her again, and again she

came out in the normal range. Being a psychologist, this, of course, was a great puzzle to Fulweiler. So for the first time he got interested in what this girl's home situation was like—was there something at home that she was running from?

At the time the girl came for testing the second time, the parents hadn't seen their daughter for six weeks. So Fulweiler arranged to have them visit her in the one-way mirror room, where he could watch what happened. He put the girl in there and the parents came in. They said, "Hello," and she said, "Hello." Mom said, "How are you?" and she said, "I'm fine," and the mother said, "How are the people here? Do you get enough cigarettes?" or something. Fulweiler got mad—he is a very intense guy—and he went around and knocked on the door and asked the father to come into the hall. He said to him, "Do you love your daughter?" The father said, "Sure," and Fulweiler said, "Then you go in there and tell her so." The father went in there and got up his courage, and after a while he said to his daughter that he loved her. The girl began to cry, the mother began to cry and said, "We were so worried about you." The father began to cry. They all had a big emotional session. Fulweiler was so pleased that he asked them to come back the next week and do it again.

He started seeing that family over a series of sessions, each time pulling a family member out in the hall and talking to them and sending them back in again. Finally, he started going in himself. He developed a method in which he introduced the room to the family, said that he would be behind the mirror, gave them a little speech about being the best therapists for each other, and said, "Why don't you bring me up to date on your problems?" and walked out of the room. Then they would start to talk. Soon they would get uneasy in this situation and, naturally, start to attack the problem kid—that's what he's there for. The kid would look unhappy, and Fulweiler would come in and say, "It looks like you need some

help in improving your communication," or whatever, and they would say, "Yes, we do." And he would say, "Why not try it this way?" and he would go out again.

I spent about 20 or 30 sessions behind the mirror with him. When I first began, Don Jackson used to come over and watch also. I spent my time trying to figure out why Fulweiler went in the room when he did. This was an interesting problem to me because Fulweiler himself couldn't say. Eventually I began to realize what he was doing, although it took a while. At first I thought he was going in to support the father or to interpret something to the mother, but I began to see that what he was really doing was breaking up sequences. That is why it was so hard to see why he went in when he did, because he did it at different times. That is, the sequence would be: father would pick on the kid and the kid would begin to weep, then mother would pick on father. So father would say, "The kid shouldn't be doing what he is doing," and retreat. Then in a few minutes, the father would pick on the kid again, the kid would begin to weep, the mother would jump on the father, the father would say the kid shouldn't do that, and he would back off. Fulweiler would come in at different points to break up that sequence. He might come in right before the kid folded. He might come in and jump on the father before the mother did. Or he might come in after mother spoke, before father could back down. Watching him, you couldn't figure out why he was going in if you didn't know the sequence.

Q: *Where is Fulweiler today?*

HALEY: He still has a practice in Berkeley. His method is effective. Many therapists get uncomfortable with it, though, because being out of the room so much makes them feel unnecessary, and they don't like to do it.

Anyway, we started using a one-way mirror in the Bateson project after observing Fulweiler. We got together a whole group of psychiatrists and gave them supervision in return for their interviewing the sample of families we were studying. I can remember being behind the mirror and seeing what a dreadful job somebody was doing and not interrupting or intruding. At that time, the mirror was just something to use to observe. The supervisor did not intrude into the therapy, even if something awful was happening.

I can remember supervising a psychiatrist at Stanford treating a kid who had just come out of a state hospital. The kid was improving in an open ward at Stanford and was about to be discharged. Before the session the psychiatrist said to me, "You know what is going to happen, don't you? Those parents are going to be upset with this kid coming out of the hospital, and they are going to want to put him back in the state hospital." I said, "You're right." He said, "I am not going to let them do it. I am going to hold the line because Stanford is an open ward, where he can go in and out. There is no reason in the world to put him on a closed inpatient unit. I am going to have to get the parents past this." So he started with the family, and they began to complain about the problem with this kid. By the end of the interview, the psychiatrist had agreed to put the kid back in the state hospital. When he came out of the session, I said to him, "How could you do a thing like that?" He said, "What?" I said, "Put the kid back in the state hospital. You said at the beginning you weren't going to do that." He said, "I did?" Being in the session had given him amnesia. What impressed me even more was that I stood behind the mirror watching and just let it happen, because I did not challenge the unwritten rule that the supervisor shouldn't intrude.

Q: *So when did you actually begin to do live supervision?*

HALEY: I think it was after I went to the Philadelphia Child Guidance Clinic in 1967.

Q: *How did that move come about?*

HALEY: That goes back to my first meeting with Minuchin when he was at Wiltwyck in the early

'60s. I was traveling around watching therapists and collecting papers for *Family Process*. So I went to visit Minuchin and Braulio Montalvo, who was working with him, and I liked them both very much. Still, coming from the West Coast, I did think their therapy was a little conservative. I observed a session with an unmarried mother and her three delinquent kids. The mother, who had no front teeth, seemed very shy, and she kept covering her mouth while struggling with the kids. Minuchin would talk to the kids and then talk to the mother, then put the kids behind the mirror, and then put the mother behind the mirror, and so on. Finally, they asked me what I would do, and I said, "Well, I would say to the kids that I thought they ought to earn some money because their mother was so embarrassed by not having front teeth. They should sell newspapers, or do something honest, to raise some money to get her a bridge made." I thought the kids would do that, and it would be a way of organizing the therapy around the kids' helping their mother in a different way than by being delinquent. Sal and Braulio thought that was a strange idea. But I was only describing a typical Erickson procedure.

So I returned to California, and soon afterward I heard that Minuchin was moving to Philadelphia. Then one day he called me and said he wanted to come out to visit me. I said sure, and that I would meet him at the airport. So I met him and I took him home, which is not what I usually did with visitors. I kept my private life and professional life pretty separate. What I didn't know was that Sal had come out to offer me a job.

We got to talking about his taking over the Philadelphia Child Guidance Clinic. You see, he and Braulio had gone there and turned a traditional child clinic into a family therapy place and lost 95 percent of the staff. Sal and Braulio had to start over, and they were looking for company. I made a deal with Sal that if I didn't have to apply for grants—I was sick to death of going after grants—

and if I could get a salary and be allowed to do whatever I pleased, I would be happy to go with him. And he agreed to that.

The first couple of years, that's what I did, researching what interested me, until he began to say, "You should do something more practical than you're doing." Minuchin had thought of taking a mother or father in a poor family that had done well in therapy and having them be therapists for another family. So instead of teaching middle-class people what it was like to be poor, the poor would be trained to be therapists—which is something nobody had thought of doing up to that time. From a quite different perspective, I had been interested in training lay therapists. I had thought of taking mothers or fathers in families of schizophrenics who had done well in therapy and have them do therapy with other families of schizophrenics. The two of us got to talking about the similarity in our ideas, and in the process Minuchin said, "I think we can get a grant and train some of these people." As the idea developed, we stopped talking about parents from families that had been in therapy, and it became people from the community with no formal education beyond high school. The project was called "The Institute of Family Counseling," and it involved putting therapists who had never interviewed anybody in the room with families. We started off believing that we had to protect the families being seen. So we developed a live-supervision procedure for calling the therapist on the phone, guiding them, pulling them out of the room when necessary. Actually, they did very well. We worked with them in live supervision, 40 hours a week for two years. Nobody has ever been trained that intensely.

Q: *The period that you spent in Philadelphia was a very important one for family therapy. In Minuchin's book* Families and Family Therapy, *he credits much of his work to the daily conversations that went on in the commuter pool that you, Salvador Minuchin and Braulio Montalvo set up. Tell me about that.*

HALEY: Well, in the clinic, we were all very busy in different enterprises, and during the day we would only meet in formal sorts of meetings. But the three of us lived in the same neighborhood, which was 45 minutes to an hour from the clinic. So we had a car pool and took turns driving. Montalvo, Minuchin and I would get in the car in the morning and spend 45 minutes talking shop all the way down. Then, in the evening, we would spend the 45 minutes driving back either talking about cases or talking about people we knew or places we were visiting. It was like having almost two hours a day just to sit and chat about the field. We got together on a lot of things doing that.

Q: *No wonder people have so much trouble trying to figure out what are the differences between structural and strategic therapy.*

HALEY: It puzzles me how people can confuse the two. To me, "structural" is a way of describing a family. The term "strategic" defines a way of doing therapy in which you plan what you do, in contrast to other therapies where you just respond to what happens. So I don't see how one can confuse the two, because they are two different issues.

Q: *But certainly there are different tactics associated with each approach. If you watch somebody who is trained by Minuchin seeing a family, it is a different ballgame than watching a strategic therapist that you have trained.*

HALEY: I think the way that Sal and I describe a family is very similar in terms of its organization and structure. I mean, we worked it out for 10 years together. I tend to think that the '50s was the time for focusing on an individual unit; the '60s, the dyadic communication unit, and the '70s was when the whole structural, hierarchical thing came in. Sal, Braulio and I were together when that came in.

The biggest difference I see between what Minuchin does and what I do is that strategic therapy has an absolute focus on the symptom. Everything in the therapy should be related to the symptom. If a therapist is talking to a couple about their sex life, I think the therapist should be able to defend how that is related to the problem they come in with, or they shouldn't be talking about it. I believe that the symptom is the lever that changes the family. The cases where Sal tends to work that way is when there is a life-threatening symptom, like anorexia. With that, he absolutely focuses on the symptom, makes the parents make the kid eat, and so on. In that, there is no difference between his approach and mine.

Q: *About 1976 you began to disengage from the clinic and started developing your own institute. How did this come about?*

HALEY: Around then I had begun to get dissatisfied with the clinic because it was getting so big. When I had started, there were 12 people on the staff, and when I left, there were about 300. What can you do in a giant place like that? Also, I didn't approve of having an inpatient arrangement. So I decided that I would like to try doing it differently. About that time Cloé [Madanes] and I were talking about getting married. She was teaching at the University of Maryland Department of Psychiatry and at Howard University Hospital, doing live supervision. I began to do that, too. We decided to start our own institute in the Washington, D.C., area. At first, it was a day or two a week, but it did so well that we expanded it.

Q: *For almost 30 years now you have been observing therapists at work. How have you tried to create the kind of environment at your own institute for teaching the skills of being an effective therapist?*

HALEY: One of the things that is special about this place is that the live supervision focuses on planning a specific strategy for each family. Our trainees also see just about every age range and type of problem.

Q: *It is one thing to criticize individual therapy after sitting down with a guy one hour a day for five years at a VA hospital in Palo Alto. It is quite another to do that without having had that experience. One criticism that I*

hear about your trainees—as well as the trainees from other institutes—is that their training becomes a kind of orthodoxy that can become every bit as confining as the unthinking belief in psychoanalysis that you have been so successful in challenging. Does it ever worry you that strategic therapy may become the new orthodoxy?

HALEY: Oh, certainly it does. One thing we try to make clear to our trainees is that you don't do the same thing in every situation. We are trying to teach a strategy that is different for each family that comes in. Trainees often don't like that. I mean, who would? They prefer a method which they can learn quickly and then make everybody fit that method. So there is always a tension between our desire to have each case treated differently and the student's desire to know the "method" to make sure that he or she is doing it right. Over time, I think they get more innovative so that they don't do the same thing with each family.

We do teach standard procedures that are effective with many families—like putting the parents in charge of someone coming out of the hospital. But when this procedure does not work, or when the supervisor can think of a better, more economical strategy, a new procedure is introduced. An example is a strategy that Cloé Madanes is developing in which the children are put in charge of the parents. Compared with almost any other therapy, we try not to have set procedures that are always followed. If you do the same thing every time, you cannot deal with the complex differences that come in. You have to adapt what you do to the people who come to you.

Q: *I would like to go back to Erickson for a moment. So much of your own work developed out of his, I'm curious to know what he had to say about what you were doing as you became less a student of his and more of a contributor in your own right.*

HALEY: I never talked to him about my work. He did like what I had to say about him; he bought the books I wrote about him.

Q: *Did he have much sense of what your contribution was, separate from him?*

HALEY: I don't know. I never even thought about it. He was so wrapped up in his own work, and so was I, that he didn't talk to me about my contribution. He might talk to somebody else about what I was doing, but I cannot conceive of him talking to me about it.

Q: *You've said a great deal about the impact that Erickson had on you, in what ways do you think you had an influence on him?*

HALEY: Thinking back now, I realize that he depended on John Weakland and me more than I understood at the time. We brought the world of new ideas to him more than other people did because we were involved in so many schools and ideas about therapy back then. I didn't think of that at the time, naturally. But as we would ask him a question, we would say, "Well, so-and-so would do it that way." I played him a tape of John Rosen once, and he said, "There is a guy who works very similarly to the way I do," but he would have never had access to a tape of Rosen if we hadn't presented it to him. So I guess we brought to him quite a bit of the changes happening in therapy.

But, you know, the real tragedy with Erickson was he spent so much time over the years teaching hypnosis when he had a whole new school of therapy to offer. People did not recognize the significance of his work until he was too old to really demonstrate it.

Q: *You regularly give workshops around the country on an approach to therapy that jars a lot of traditional ideas in the mental health field. At least it was an approach that many people used to find jarring. What kind of reception are you getting these days?*

HALEY: The audiences are quite respectful. I think the mental health field has changed. Cloé and I have found that people are more interested in a directive brief therapy approach. There was a time when people were more attacking, especially those

who felt there was a mystique about therapy that needed to be preserved. People like that seemed to consider a strategic approach superficial and rather banal. Some objections I hear now about strategic therapy seem to come from people in private practice because, for them, there is a practical problem. They wonder if they can survive economically doing brief therapy with a rapid client turnover. Typically, it is the people in public agencies, with more clients than they know what to do with, who are more receptive to a brief therapy.

Q: *I don't know whether you are asked this at workshops, but a criticism I often hear about your approach is that it's authoritarian and overly concerned with issues of power and control. What is your response to that?*

HALEY: I think power is at the center of psychopathology, and the best way to think of symptoms is as an expression of a power struggle. But that doesn't mean that the therapist has to be authoritarian and give orders.

In fact, at times, one of the most useful things a therapist can do is to be helpless. Of course, being helpless doesn't mean that you're not in charge. You can be authoritative without being authoritarian. Obviously, if being authoritarian is the only thing you can do, you'll lose most of the time. It does seem to me, though, that once you accept the idea of hierarchy in social organizations, you begin to see how the struggle for status, and the question of who is going to be in charge, is basic to human relationships.

Q: *The point you're making right now is one that has been challenged quite a bit recently, especially by some of the authors who have been writing about the epistemological assumptions in family therapy. In particular, the idea of the therapist serving as a kind of power broker has been criticized as being linear and nonsystemic.*

HALEY: Systems theory tends to be a theory of how things remain the same rather than a theory of change. You might be able to understand what keeps a man drinking by looking at how his wife provokes him and see how she provokes him because he drinks. But it is very difficult to see in that description anything that helps you make an effective therapeutic intervention.

If you take systems theory far enough, you can even decide that nobody has any individual responsibility or can be blamed for anything. How can an individual criminal be blamed for his acts if whatever he does is a product of input from others which drove him to do what he did? That might be an appropriate view to a systems theorist, but if you're living in society, it's disastrous. There are just a lot of guys out there that ought to be put away, whether they are driven by others or not, because they are going to kill you if they get half a chance.

Being a therapist means not just looking at why things are what they are but taking a position of responsibility about things being one way or another. If you can stand behind a one-way mirror and watch parents beat up on a kid every three and a half minutes or a kid beat up on parents every three and a half minutes, and not intervene, then you're a true systems theorist. But if you have some responsibility within the family to see that they don't beat up on each other, then you can't stand back and just watch it happen. You have to think about how to intervene so that it doesn't happen. That requires, I think, a different theory than just the theory of why they are beating up on each other. I think it requires a theory based on ideas about power and hierarchy.

Q: *So what, then, is your view of the attention being devoted in the journals these days to epistemological questions?*

HALEY: When people don't know what to do in therapy, they become philosophers. A big problem with talking about epistemology, I think, is that most of the discussion is irrelevant to doing therapy. To be helpful to a therapist, a theory has to be simple enough so that it can help him think about what he actually needs to do with his clients. Philosophizing about epistemology just isn't helpful in that way. I

do think, though, that the attention the writing about epistemology has gotten does say something about what is missing in the field. Many people are looking for a new conceptualizer—a careful, solid thinker—who can point the field in some new direction. He could be called "The Messiah."

Q: *What is your guess about what this direction will be? In other words, are there important unanswered questions that will shape family theory in the years to come?*

HALEY: I don't know what will come, but perhaps someone will integrate the ideas of hierarchy, systems and individual responsibility and put them in some unified theoretical framework.

Q: *Before going on, I'd like to ask you about another kind of objection that is raised to your therapeutic approach. Therapists influenced by the work of someone like Virginia Satir, who places so much emphasis on the therapist helping family members to establish intimate, loving relationships with each other, seem to look at your therapy as cold and technical and feel that it misses the point in not dealing with the central emotional issues of family life.*

HALEY: Virginia and I have always represented different schools of therapy. She comes out of a tradition that says that you shouldn't focus on the symptom but should focus on the relationships within the family. I think that it is when you focus on the symptom, and in the process deal with problems in the area of power and control, that the family is able to go on to develop more intimate personal relationships.

Q: *It occurs to me that you probably consider a lot of the criticisms of strategic therapy to be misinterpretations of what you are doing. What do you think are the most common misinterpretations of strategic therapy?*

HALEY: I don't find myself correcting misinterpretations of strategic therapy much these days. Most people seem to know what it is and want to learn more about it. At one time, there were objections about deception and manipulation. I don't think

you can do therapy without manipulation—depending, of course, on how you define "manipulation." You can sit and do nothing, and let all the therapy be spontaneous, but that would still be manipulation. Once you accept the idea that what the therapist does is part of the process and that he's being paid to get somebody over something, then manipulation has to be involved. But deception is not necessarily part of that. For example, many people believe that in order to do a paradox, you have to deceive, and I don't think so. When I was in practice, professional people would come to me and say, "I have a symptom, would you do a paradox on me?" So, to an experimental psychologist, I might propose something paradoxical within a framework of aversive conditioning which he would find acceptable. Now, that's not the way I would think of it, but it's the way he would. Someone hearing me offer a rationale to a paradox like that might think I was being deceptive, but I would just consider that a way of joining with him. I don't believe in lying to people or tricking them. I do believe in offering a rationale that will help them cooperate with what you are trying to do.

Q: *What's your reaction to the criticism that your kind of therapy is a "cookbook approach," a kind of technique-for-any-occasion form of treatment?*

HALEY: Actually, I wish I had such a cookbook. The more techniques we learn that are successful, the better it will be for the people in distress. But sometimes you do something with a case, and that is what people think you do every time. If you encourage a symptom, people think that is all you do. The problem is that clients just won't fit into a single standard procedure. The task of strategic therapy is to make a unique plan for each case, each particular situation.

Q: *In light of the popularity of your writing, do you ever find yourself being held responsible for saying or for supporting things that you think distort what you really believe? Do you sometimes find yourself thinking,*

"Oh my God, that's really not what I meant."

HALEY: Well, there are people who, after reading *Leaving Home,* go out and tell families that the problem is that their kid needs to "leave home" and even that the parents should expel them. The fact that I say at least 10 times in the book that a therapist shouldn't say that does not seem to make any difference. Sometimes what you write for therapists spills out into the community in unfortunate ways, and then you're sorry you ever wrote it.

Q: *Of all the things you've written, the most moving for me was the ending of* Uncommon Therapy. *You describe a case in which Erickson goes to great lengths to help an elderly stroke victim and does some incredible things but finally tells the man's wife that nothing more can be done. It's the only case in the book in which Erickson says anything like that.*

HALEY: Perhaps one of the reasons the ending is sad is because Erickson always expressed hope, and for him to give up on someone is sad.

Q: *That ending made me think about your approach to therapy and your belief in focusing in so tightly on the symptom. Is that a matter of ethical belief about what a change agent should do, or does it have more to do with the idea that therapy is a limited tool that really can do only so much?*

HALEY: A little of both. Therapy was oversold years ago. People thought that if you put somebody through intensive therapy when they were in their late teens or early twenties, they would never have a problem the rest of their life. It was thought that you were clearing everything up, which justified it being so long and so expensive. But the problem was that, very often, they weren't even getting people over symptoms. I think if you get people over symptoms, you're doing very well—that's difficult enough—but there's something else as well. I think you have more success if you deal with what people are interested in. If someone comes in to me with a symptom and they're told, "I'd much rather talk about problems with your family relationships," they

begin to lose interest, and then you begin to have more difficulty.

Q: *Most of what you've written has been for a professional audience. The one book that you really wrote for the lay public, I guess, was* The Power Tactics of Jesus Christ.

HALEY: Yes. The publisher thought it was going to be a best-seller and it wasn't, although it sold a lot of copies over the years. I'm thinking of publishing a new edition of that now.

Q: *Reading the title essay in that book, you can come away with the idea that Christ was a pretty good hypnotist, next best thing to Milton Erickson. You don't seem to give much credence to a spiritual dimension in working with families, but do you have some sort of hidden set of spiritual beliefs? I know at one time you were interested in Zen and Alan Watts.*

HALEY: I never thought of Jesus being like Milton Erickson. Erickson was not an organizer. He really didn't recruit a following, an organized following like Jesus. Jesus was a mass-movement leader, which Erickson never would have been. It's Erickson's followers now who have been trying to make him a cult leader. But in terms of any spiritual interest, no.

Zen had a big influence on me, because it was a set of ideas about change that was an alternative to the ideas of Western psychiatry. Until the 1950s, there was no ideology in Western psychiatry that allowed you to do brief therapy and not insight therapy, at least until behavior therapy developed. Even there, all you had was learning theory, which wasn't very helpful. But Zen has had 700 years of experience with one person sitting down with another to bring about change. It reflects a lot of experience and wisdom about people. I think what drew me to it was that it was anti-insight in the sense that it was, I think, partly designed to help young Japanese intellectuals recover from being intellectuals. So it had a set of procedures for getting out from under excessive self-awareness.

Q: *Are you saying that you have no spiritual beliefs?*

HALEY: I still incline toward Zen, which has no beliefs, just the contemporary experience.

Q: *The world is as you create it?*

HALEY: Sure, or as you find it.

Q: *But you also create it. Certainly yours is a therapy of creating beliefs that enable people to change.*

HALEY: I don't think people change on the basis of a change in beliefs. They may accept what you say and do what they're told because you offer them a rationale which they can believe, but I think beliefs are a product of a social situation more than the reverse. Also, I think we have the illusion that we create things when circumstances do. I mean, I'm not sure how much I have innovated, if you look at it that way, and how much just happened. At one time I thought I had more freedom because I was an outsider: I didn't have to think in a restricted way, like the insiders. Then I realized I was not free because I was not allowed to think like an insider if I was to be on the outside. Still, I do think we need to have the illusion that we are innovating and causing things.

Q: *What else do you want to accomplish in this field? What's ahead for you that is a critically interesting area you might explore?*

HALEY: I am accomplishing what I want to in various areas. I've been defining myself as a teacher the last 10 years, and Cloé and I have founded a successful training institute. We also are producing books and films. Cloé, whose first book was successful, is writing a second one, and I have finished a book on the use of ordeals in therapy. I am also working on a book with a different perspective on Erickson. But in terms of ideas, I would like to go to another sort of theoretical dimension.

Q: *What sort of theoretical dimension?*

HALEY: I have stayed involved in therapy over the years believing that it is in the process of change, that new ideas about man and his systems will be generated. It is not in analyzing problems but in observing things as they are changing that you can see what's there. The clinical field has been the most interesting place if you are interested in social behavior. But, at the same time, I have become so wrapped up in the technical and practical aspects of doing therapy that I have not gone any further with some of the larger questions. At this point I'm beginning to move back to thinking about larger systems, but I haven't gotten far. I'm still struggling with ideas about the small unit of the family network and the social situation of a family rather than larger issues of social change. I tend to think that whatever happens in a pattern is replicated in all kinds of places. So if you see one sequence in a family, you'll see it in another part of the family or in the larger sequence of the family. I am sure that's true of large social groups. I think there are some rules of social systems that you can tease out in working with a family in therapy that will apply to larger and more significant enterprises. I'd like to get to that someday, but I am not there yet.

Q: *Do you have a sense that you have a social mission in your work?*

HALEY: No.

Q: *That's what Whitaker has said about you, that you are "interested in solving the culture's problems," and that, unlike him, you are interested in "service."*

HALEY: I think we have an obligation to get people over the problem from which they are paying us to recover, and in that sense I am interested in "service." I think to establish ideas and training procedures that are effective in the field of therapy, which is the field of helping people in distress, is a service to society. But as far as reforming the culture, I don't have that in mind.

Q: *I did an interview with Minuchin a couple of years ago in which I asked him what was the biggest lesson for him in working with families. What has been the biggest lesson for you, as far as your way of working with families?*

HALEY: I think it's been a greater concern with how family behavior is generated by the therapy. I

keep seeing that in different areas. It used to be that families were classified as schizophrenic because of their strange and amorphous behavior. It didn't occur to us that they behaved that way because of the strange and amorphous ways that therapists were dealing with them. If you take the approach of saying to the parents, "Take charge of this kid," and so on, you don't get that behavior. The families aren't any different, I don't think. They just behave differently in therapy because the therapist behaves differently.

Q: *What do you consider your most important contribution to the field of family therapy?*

HALEY: Bringing some clarity to the issues. ■

See references, page 173.

STILL R. D. LAING AFTER ALL THESE YEARS

AN INTERVIEW WITH R. D. LAING

IN THE FAMOUS FINAL PASSAGE OF HIS 1967 BOOK *The Politics of Experience*, R. D. Laing wrote: "If I could turn you on, if I could drive you out of your wretched mind, if I could tell you, I would let you know."

These words were a call to revolution for college students in the 1960s, and in the jacket photo that looked out from his books during that era, Laing seemed as if he was ready to lead one. Fiercely intense, a little haggard, brimming with angst, he had just the right measure of brooding, Byronic good looks that one would expect in the leader of a revolution to transform Western Consciousness.

But what was it that he could not quite manage to tell us then? And today, at a time when our minds seem shaped by things like *People* magazine and TV commercials, is Laing still hoping to turn us on?

IT IS LATE JANUARY, AND R. D. LAING IS SITTING IN a large New York City hotel ballroom in front of a crowd of 60 attendees at this year's Eastern Regional Conference of the Association for Humanistic Psychology. At 55, Laing seems to have less the intense manner of an angry Jeremiah and more that of an amiable English gentleman who, at the moment, is trying to cater to the needs of the unwieldy social organism before him. He is nothing if not painstakingly solicitous of his audience. Would they like the chairs to be rearranged in a circle? What would they like to talk about? Would they mind if he smoked?

The first 20 minutes or so of the workshops are taken up with these matters, culminating in an elaborate discussion on the subject of breaks. How many should there be? How long should they last? When should they be taken? Is 90 minutes long enough for lunch?

Eventually the audience manages to make it clear that there is nothing in particular they wish to hear—they just want to listen to R. D. Laing say whatever he wants to say. So Laing begins to do what he claims he typically does "at these types of things"—he begins to "voice my thoughts as they occur to me."

Soon he is telling a story about a teenage anorectic whose parents had brought her to see him. "The girl was very bright, very knowledgeable about

anorexia," Laing informs the audience in his rich Scottish burr. "She told me flat out, 'I'm not an anorectic. I'm on a hunger strike against my parents.'" Laing's eyes crinkle up in amusement as he describes the girl's feistiness. Smiling, he continues, "So I made it clear to her that that was perfectly okay with me, and I had no intention of making her eat. I did tell her I would meet with her again if she wished, but she decided not to come back."

The story seems over as far as Laing is concerned, but someone in the audience wants to know if his approach with this girl is typical of what he does with anorectics. "I have no specific approach," Laing replies. "I just try to stay out of the power game." He pauses for a moment and then adds, "I don't think I have any authority that entitles me to get people to comply with the way I see things."

For any fan of Laing's enormously popular books of the 1960s—*The Divided Self, The Politics of the Family, Knots,* as well as the apocalyptic *Politics of Experience*—just hearing this fragmentary reaffirmation of the laissez-faire attitude toward abnormality that those books celebrated is enough to set off a rush of old associations. Most of the audience seem entranced with what is happening, almost if they are listening to a snatch of a fondly remembered old tune.

ONE WOULD BE HARD PRESSED TO NAME ANY psychotherapist since Laing who has been able to occupy a position in the culture at large comparable to the one he held in the '60s and early '70s. College students in that era didn't just read Laing's books, they used them as guides for discovering secret dimensions of themselves that no one had ever talked about in quite the way that he did: "We have our secrets and our needs to confess. We may remember how, in childhood, adults at first were able to look right through us, and into us, and what an accomplishment it was when we, in fear and trembling, could tell our first lie, and make for ourselves the discovery that we are irredeemably alone

in certain respects, and know that within the territory of ourselves there can be only our footprints."

With writing like that, Laing established an intimate connection with a vast readership. His books became icons of the counterculture, right up there with Beatles albums and Kurt Vonnegut novels.

Since then the ethic of personal freedom and letting people "do their own thing" that Laing and others helped popularize has come to be sneered at as the self-indulgent excess of the Me Generation. But to appreciate what Laing's work has meant, one must recognize that he first came to prominence in a very different cultural context than the one we know today. To a post-World War II society that had been dominated by an ideology of adjustment and conformity throughout the '50s, Laing proposed a radical shift in understanding the age-old struggle between the will of the individual and the demands of the social world. It was a shift perfectly suited to the rebellious temper of the '60s.

Speaking with the authority of his experience as a psychiatrist, Laing argued that the turmoil most of us undergo in becoming a productive cog in the social wheel—the kind of distress that typically brought people into the offices of people like him—was not so much an indication of an individual's psychological infirmity as a consequence of the twisted and distorted values dominating modern life. In such a world, Laing insisted, it was impossible for health and authenticity to emerge.

Laing's version of sanity and craziness was a stunning inversion of the assumptions that lay at the foundation of traditional psychiatric thought. Like his American counterparts in the family therapy movement at that time, Laing rejected psychiatry's diagnostic system and most of its treatment procedures. But Laing went further than his American colleagues in defining the struggle with psychiatry as one involving not only treatment philosophy and clinical technique but politics as well.

As the acknowledged spokesman for something

R. D. LAING

ROBERTA RUSSELL

that came to be called *antipsychiatry*, Laing cast psychiatrists, and the mental health establishment they represented, not in the role of healers (albeit misguided ones) but as agents helping to maintain a repressive social order. From the viewpoint of antipsychiatry, the problem therapists needed to address was not the pathology raging inside people's heads but the pathology raging in a social and political system that drove people crazy.

L AING'S CRITIQUE OF MODERN SOCIETY WENT beyond the social and political order into something even more fundamental—the nature of contemporary consciousness. As Laing put it, "There is something deeply wrong with the Western mind." In his view, what passed for our normal, workaday state was actually a trance from which few of us ever really awaken. As he described it in *The*

Politics of the Family: "Hypnosis may be an experimental model of a naturally occurring phenomenon in many families. In the family situation, however, the hypnotists (the parents) are already hypnotized (by their parents) and are carrying out their instructions, by bringing their children up to bring their children up . . . in such a way which includes not realizing one is carrying out instructions: since one's instruction is not to think that one is thus instructed. This state is easily induced under hypnosis."

Here, as elsewhere in Laing's writings, the social institution that inspires his harshest expressions of outrage was the primary molder of the mind—the contemporary family. When Laing looked at the family, he seemed to see not a humanizing, nurturing haven that prepared people to assume responsibility for their lives, but rather something more like a cluster of storm troopers living uneasily under one roof, policing each other's thoughts and feelings, desperately defending the status quo. To Laing, the typical bond keeping families together was neither love nor fondness nor even force of habit; it was, by and large, the fear of psychological violence—the kind of terror that only intimates could inspire in each other: "A family can act as gangsters, offering each other mutual protection against each other's violence. It is a reciprocal terrorism with the terror of protection—security against the violence that each threatens the other with, and is threatened by, if anyone steps out of line."

In one of the most memorable sections of *The Politics of Experience*, Laing offered what is probably his most damning account of how the family shapes a new being: "From the moment of birth, when the Stone Age baby confronts the twentieth century mother, the baby is subjected to those forces of violence called love, as its mother and father, and their parents and their parents before them, have been. These forces are mainly concerned with destroying most of its potentialities and on the whole this enterprise is successful. By the time the new human being

is 15 or so, we are left with a being like ourselves, a half-crazed creature more or less adjusted to a mad world. This is normality in our present age."

Laing depicted the family as the most reactionary of social organizations, dedicated to guarding against any awareness of possible experience beyond its own narrow boundaries. Over generations, the family creates an ongoing drama providing roles to preoccupy and define the family members/players— literally entrancing them. They become captives in a cosmic con game whose overriding purpose is to keep them from plumbing the deeper mysteries of human existence: "The family's function is to repress Eros; to induce a false consciousness of security; to deny death by avoiding life; to cut off transcendence; to believe in God, not to experience the Void; to create, in short, one-dimensional man."

THERE ARE NOT MANY FAMILY THERAPISTS TODAY who look upon Laing as one of their own. The whole tone and emphasis of the current family therapy movement, with its essentially benign view of the family and its emphasis on the pragmatics of treatment, has moved in a different direction than that presented in Laing's work in the '60s. Fifteen years ago, Laing's writing was anthologized in some of the early family therapy compendiums. Today his name is rarely invoked within the field.

Nevertheless, Laing's influence on the development of family therapy should not be underestimated. Certainly no one has done more to popularize the idea that the individual's apparent pathology is best understood as serving a function in his family. As much as anyone, Laing challenged traditional psychiatric procedures and diagnoses in a way that created an intellectual climate in which alternative models like family therapy could be taken seriously.

The fact that it is difficult to categorize Laing's contribution to something like the growth of family therapy also suggests what has been unique about his appeal. Laing's writing has always been a curious mix of poetry, clinical observation and existential philosophy. He has had little interest in setting forth a specific approach to family treatment or in propounding a fully developed theory. Rather, his primary concern has been in evoking the inner world of the individual and the family with a dark power that no one in the mental health field, let alone the field of family therapy, has been able to approach. While others may have been able to formulate more carefully their observations about fusion and enmeshment in families, no one could match Laing's gift for conveying the experience of what it is like to live in such families.

With *Knots,* a collection of poems about the intricate puzzles found in human relationships, published in 1970, Laing's work began to take a new direction. At that point, he seemed to be losing interest in the clinical realm and in addressing his readership as either a psychiatrist or a revolutionary. His work began to take on the form of a personal meditation. During the '70s and '80s, he seemed to slip out of the popular consciousness. As Laing puts it, some people believe that "I'm in some sort of semiprofessional retirement or that I've bombed out."

In fact, Laing continues to write and is hard at work in his private practice. His most recent book, *The Voice of Experience,* was published this year. He is active in operating several London households modeled after Kingsley Hall, the therapeutic community for schizophrenics that he set up in London in the late '60s to provide an environment largely free of rules and regulations where, as he puts it, "people could be people with each other."

Laing's work is best characterized by the play of its contradictory currents. His pessimistic view of the knotty complexity found in human relationships rests alongside an almost mystical faith in the ability of even the most troubled psyche to heal itself—if given the freedom to do so. His fascination with the emotional intricacies of family life is set off by a belief in the inevitable isolation of the individual.

For a man who achieved great fame for his writing, Laing seems profoundly skeptical of the ability of language to convey the heart of his view of people and their process of change. Consequently, his style has always been cryptic and elusive, his appeal more to the imagination than the rational mind. But every age looks for different qualities in its spokespeople. The very style and sensibility that struck responsive chords in the '60s seem no longer attuned to the concerns of these more cautious, more down-to-earth times. If this is true, reading Laing today may tell us more about what once turned us on than what could possibly accomplish such a feat today.

A FRIEND OF LAING'S ONCE WROTE: "LAING IS A very moody man, in a unique sense. Indeed his repertory of moods is so vast that he is always upsetting even the most benign expectations. Furthermore, whatever mood he is in he seems astonishingly unafflicted by any degree of self-consciousness. In a single evening I have seen him run the gamut of human emotions, taking on one distinct persona after another, even changing sex, and in each one appearing to be wholly himself. This is quite a performance."

As might be expected, this aspect of Laing makes getting him to sit down for an interview a somewhat arduous business. After a couple of false starts during the two days of his workshop, I was reluctantly granted what I was plainly told would be a one-hour interview on the following day. Five minutes before the interview was to end, the time was extended, with the proviso that I absolutely had to go in a half hour. For the rest of the afternoon, deadlines kept being reiterated and then somehow forgotten. As a result, the one-hour interview turned into a five-hour conversation, excerpts from which are reported below.

During the course of that afternoon, Laing's moodiness and changeability made him seem extraordinarily accessible. He offered no fixed wall of a public persona against which to batter. Instead, there was a completely disarming acknowledgment of ordinary fallibility occasionally superseded by an unexpected display of intellectual arrogance. Throughout, there seemed to be an unspoken invitation to engage him on any topic, even the most personal. As a result, I found myself asking questions I never expected to ask.

In what follows, Laing offers his views on his writings about the family, his reactions to the family therapy movement today, and some comments on the peculiar role of culture hero that he has occupied for the past 20 years.

Q: *Back in the '60s you wrote, "The family is the usual instrument for what is called socialization, that is, getting each new recruit to the human race to behave and experience in substantially the same way as those who have already got here." For many people, one of the compelling things about your writing in the rebellious '60s was the way you challenged the family's traditional authority. You likened the family to a "protection racket" in which the members are held in place by bonds of "reciprocal terrorism." For a generation eager to reject their parents' values and way of life, you elevated their struggle to break away into a kind of holy search for authenticity. Do you still take such a dim view of the family and what it stands for?*

LAING: I was writing then mainly about unhappy families. I was trying to describe the family "mangle," the way families can manufacture pain for their members. You might say that my writings have been biased in terms of addressing myself to the misery and unhappiness that can occur in families, but I never felt that was the whole story. I do think most people would agree that the family is a system going through a tremendous amount of tossing and straining. In some upper-middle-class sectors of Europe, in fact, the family has largely evaporated in the contemporary world. But in looking into what happens in families, I saw myself as making a contribution to happy families—if that doesn't sound too naive.

Q: *While you are saying that, it seems to me that in books like* The Politics of Experience *and* The Politics of the Family, *you weren't very interested in distinguishing between the pathological family and the normal family. In your writing, all families sound pretty pathological. But I also understand that at one time you did an extensive study contrasting normal families with those containing a schizophrenic member.*

LAING: For six years, back in the '60s, I did have a full-time research fellowship to do a social-phenomenological investigation of the families of schizophrenics. I published a group of those studies in a book called *Sanity, Madness and the Family,* which I did with Aaron Esterson. We also did a study of some so-called normal families, which was never published. I still have hundreds of tapes and piles of analyses laying around somewhere from that.

I should say that, although we were interested in contrasting the two different sorts of families we were very scrupulous in not framing the question in the form of "Is the family a causative agent in the generation of schizophrenia?" Instead, the schema of the project was this: "Given that these people—X—have a diagnosed schizophrenia in their family and these people—Y—do not, is there a difference one can make out in the variables of their family?" To answer that question, we did things like trying to identify double binds, paradoxes and tangential communications from tape-recorded interviews. We had a lot of trouble getting reliability in the measures, but eventually we convinced ourselves that there was a lot more of that sort of communication going on when there was a diagnosed schizophrenic in the family.

Q: *But you never published the part of the study about the normal family. Why not?*

LAING: I found that, by and large, interviewing the normal families was a more grueling experience than speaking with the families of schizophrenics. They were just so dead and stifling, and at the same time, it was hard to describe what the deadening

was. So it was difficult to say what the difference between the two was except that in the normal family, nobody had cracked up.

Let me give you an example of the kind of thing we encountered. Here's a normal family we interviewed. They live in a suburb of London. The father is the assistant manager of the local butcher shop, who had come to London from Liverpool after the war. So I asked him why he came down to London, and he said, "Because I wanted to he nearer the center of reality." So I said, "What's the center of reality?" And without a moment's hesitation, he said, "The center of reality is the changing of the guard at Buckingham Palace." So I asked him, "How often do you visit the center of reality?" (He lived in a district of London called Mussell Hill, from which it would take about 45 minutes to get to the center of reality.) "Well, actually, never," he said. "I've never seen the changing of the guard at Buckingham Palace, but I like to feel I can any Sunday morning."

Q: *That sounds like the same sort of thinking that keeps people living in places like New York City.*

LAING: Absolutely. It's also the main determinant of property values in London. It's exactly the same sort of thing that goes on in any primitive tribe. People like to feel they are close to the center of the world pole.

Q: *But what's the connection between what this man told you and your not publishing your study of normal families?*

LAING: Well, as I was saying to you, I found normal families even more oppressive than the families with schizophrenics. At least in them you could have a laugh with the schizophrenic, but in a "normal" family there was just no one. But how do you talk about that? There are all these social workers out there trying to promote normal families. If you make a statement, as I once did, that if you tried to manufacture schizophrenia instead of normality we'd all breathe a bit freer, all sorts of people will misconstrue what you're saying. If you start talking

like that, the only way you can speak is ironically, as Kierkegaard did. But for people to pick up an ironic message, they have to have irony within themselves. Otherwise, there's no point in speaking ironically. It's like when the best friend of a tap dancer gives him encouragement as he goes out on stage by saying, "Break a leg." I mean, you've got to be on the right side of that statement for it to work.

Q: *Certainly, people don't think of you as a researcher in any conventional sense but as someone who created a darkly intimate poetry about things like the schizophrenic state of mind and the craziness found in families. What do you think there was about the period in which you began writing that made it possible for you to offer the perspective you did on people's experience of alienation and longing for wholeness?*

LAING: I think that the late '50s and '60s were a kind of watershed era in the modern world. Before World War I, and even afterwards, divorce still was a taboo thing in the so-called respectable world. There's an interesting historical fact about that that many people don't realize. The expectancy of both parties in a marriage in mid-Victorian England living more than 20 years was very poor. There was almost a 100 percent expectancy that one party would die in that period. "Till death do us part" had a very different connotation in that world. So when people ceased to die so early, they had to begin getting divorced in order to separate. One historian of the family once wrote that divorce is a rather poor substitute for death in that regard.

The marriage by choice that we take for granted is really a rather recent phenomenon. It didn't become prevalent until late Victorian times. That's only about three or four generations back. Even today, marriage by choice is still largely unknown in a place like India. There marriages are still arranged, usually after consulting the stars and matching horoscopes. Some time ago, I discussed the whole matter with a number of very sophisticated Indian women at Benares University who told me that they really couldn't understand why their Western sisters would actually want to go out and hunt for men. They said that it's much better, if you have a friendly relationship with your parents, to leave it to them to fix it up for you. You tell them what you want, and they hunt for you.

Of course, an important development that marked the '60s was the end of the constraints on sexuality. The Pill didn't come in until 1961 or so, and then it completely changed sexual mores. When I was growing up, if a boy and girl went together and the girl got pregnant, the boy was expected to be a gentleman and marry her. Today there's hardly a lady I know under the age of 26 who hasn't had an abortion. But when I was 26, there was hardly anyone I knew under the age of 26 who had had one. So the nature of the bond between people in getting married in the first place and the nature of the bond between parents and children underwent a total transformation around the late '50s and '60s and '70s to get us where we are now. I mean, I now live in a world where everything I was taught was wrong happens as a matter of course.

Q: *You've been talking, more or less, about the sociological shifts in the family over the past 20 years. But the special domain that you've staked out in your writing is the odd logic of people's inner world. What about the changes in the inner experience of family members that go along with these social changes?*

LAING: Obviously, the only way I can respond to that is with some generalizations, but one thing that does stand out is that the aura of God and his commandments behind the patriarchal family has evaporated. People today see their relationships as much more secular than in the past. But even now the word "marriage" to many people means a vow, a promise. I think it's very important psychologically if you take a vow or take an oath and then break it. And, of course, if you had a promise made to you which has been broken, that affects you. I mean, to take an oath on the Bible before God—"I take this

man . . ."—and then break it is a very bad idea.

Mostly we seem to have put that aside. To experience today what it was like to feel the presence of God in the family, you must listen to a person like Mother Teresa. Some time ago I heard her give a talk in St. James's Church in Picadilly in which she said that the main problem in the present world is abortions. She said that while women kill their own flesh and blood even inside their own bodies, there can be no peace in their heart and no peace in the world. In such a world, it's even blasphemous to pray for peace.

Q: *Besides proposing a kind of laissez-faire approach with schizophrenics, there is little mention of treatment approaches in your work. You have contributed some wonderful descriptions of what goes wrong in families, but nowhere have I found you saying anything about how to change them.*

LAING: I really stopped writing about families about a dozen years ago, after I finished *The Politics of the Family.* The reason was that I didn't want to pass along any more information to the people who were beginning to develop careers in family therapy. In places like Britain and Europe, most of the family therapists are state employed. In that kind of social context, the effectiveness of a therapist in changing a family is an index of the accruing power of the state.

In this, I've got to make a distinction between the United States and most of the countries in Europe. In your country, family therapy is free-lanced to a great extent; it's more part of the private sector.

Q: *Yes, we're quite an entrepreneurial bunch.*

LAING: I think that's marvelous and as it should be. But when family therapy is applied in a communist or socialist country, it becomes a very dangerous thing. It becomes more like an offer you can't refuse. In a country like Italy or Sweden or Switzerland, where the family therapists are empowered by the powers that be, it is very difficult for them to restrain themselves from trying out anything on people. The people themselves can't stop you. They

have no choice. So in "helping" a family, you might decide to break the front door down, drag someone off, and the people couldn't stop you.

Q: *Are you saying that if you had been working in the United States, you might have written more about family treatment?*

LAING: I might have, but it would have been parochial and wrong for me to do so because the stuff I write is circulated all over the world. Sometimes it appears in 12 different languages before it gets published over here.

Essentially, writing about therapy is a very poor way to convey ideas about it. Words have no tone of voice on the printed page, so they're read by people in their own tone of voice and construed in their own way. Since my words on the page have to do with changing the way people actually read the words, I have no control whatsoever. They can read what I say and construe it in the exact opposite manner of what I'm trying to express.

Q: *Given that, this might be a chance for you to correct a misimpression I've developed about what you've written. So much of family therapy as practiced in this country involves the therapist developing a working alliance with parents. But your work conveys such an intense empathy for children in pathological families, as the victims of the psychological violence directed at them by their parents, that it sometimes appears you have little sympathy with parents.*

LAING: I'd like to put a footnote to that. Maybe I haven't been as explicit about the kind of psychological violence children can direct at their parents, but some 3-month-old babies can drive their mothers mad better than their mother can drive them mad. I mean, if someone is going to live with me, he's going to toe my line. I'm not going to live with anyone who is absolutely insufferable, whether it's a 3-month-old baby or a 30-year-old baby that's driving a 60-year-old mother around a bend.

Q: *A favorite theme of yours is the mystification and deception that go on in families as people battle each other*

to maintain their particular view of the family reality. But perhaps the most influential development in family therapy over the past 20 years has been the growing popularity of strategic therapeutic methods that seem to rely on a certain amount of deception or, at the very least, control of information for their effectiveness. I was wondering whether you disapproved of such therapeutic tactics.

LAING: I think it all depends on the spirit in which the method is employed. Now, Gregory Bateson took a very disapproving view of family therapy. He was totally disenchanted with it and regarded it as a case in point about what happens when you release too much information and people begin to use it for their own power trips.

In that light, Bateson had an interesting view of Milton Erickson. He was amused and somewhat instructed by Erickson but seemed to regard him as a mild, white edition of a shaman. You know, every shaman is a bit of a trickster who employs outrageous tricksterism to so confuse people that they deconfuse themselves. So the person either goes crazy or wakes up, either goes to sleep or becomes more alert.

Although I never met Erickson, it seems to me that to do what he did required a very buoyant sense of humor. He was ready to smile back at anyone who was able to see the joke in what they were doing to themselves. It's very important for the therapist to be able to see the joke. I worry about therapists using any kind of technique when they cease to be able to see the humor and become deadly, heavily serious about what they're doing. That usually means the context has enclosed them, and they're no longer able to get to a metalevel beyond it.

Q: *Are there certain people in the field with whose work you feel a particular kinship?*

LAING: I have a very close kinship with Ross and Joan Speck, Virginia Satir, Salvador Minuchin, the Haleys. I don't think there is a major figure in the field of family therapy with whom I don't feel some kinship.

Q: *No one?*

LAING: Well, certainly there are people who look at therapy in very different ways than I do. Of course, my differences with the traditional psychoanalysts are quite well documented. Aside from that, I once had the opportunity to interview Carl Rogers, and during the interview I asked him, "What's your personal experience of evil?" He said, "I have no experience of evil in my whole life. I know nothing about evil. I've never had an evil thought, an evil imagination. I've never done anything evil in my whole life." So I said, "How do you connect with your clients?" And he said, "I sit and listen to them and learn about evil from them."

He told me about a meeting with Martin Buber in the late '40s in which he told Buber that schizophrenics were the most evil people. Buber was very much in agreement with that and told Rogers that schizophrenics are incapable of an I-Thou relationship.

Some time later, Rogers did expose himself to a therapeutic relationship with a schizophrenic lady that drove him over the edge. He went completely crazy himself but had the social prudence to get out. One day he got in his car and disappeared from his family and his practice and drove up to Canada. It was three months before he found his balance again. When he came back, he decided to never, ever listen to a schizophrenic again.

Q: *Aside from the perils of therapy with schizophrenics, I'd like to find out more about how you would compare your work with some of the people you mentioned earlier. For example, at the conference you spoke at today, you described working with an emaciated young woman who insisted that she wasn't anorectic but was on a hunger strike against her parents. You told her you could accept that and certainly wouldn't force her to eat or to continue to be in treatment with you. That hardly sounds like a session with Salvador Minuchin.*

LAING: There's a book written by a 16th-century warrior named Musashi that was the standard textbook on the samurai and is now read by all the

Japanese businessmen. In that book, Musashi says that the way of the warrior is death. In the middle of a battle when the mist comes down and you can't see and you don't know whether you're standing north, east, south, or west and you don't know where people are coming from, either you just wield your sword at anyone who comes toward you, friend or enemy, or put your sword down and do nothing. Those are the only choices under the circumstances.

That is often the position of the therapist in family therapy. So when Salvador Minuchin or Jay Haley or Virginia Satir and I are talking between each other, we often admit we just don't know what to do. We may do this or we may do that, or we may do nothing or we may do something. Now, the type of line we might take as expressed in writing or as codified in a textbook for the guidance of other people might appear to be diametrically opposite advice, but at the level on which we have this camaraderie—on my part and, I think, on their part—we recognize that the first principles are the same. It's just that we have different styles and ways of appealing to different people's temperaments under different circumstances.

Q: *So you are saying that you feel you have the same core set of beliefs, even if you can't quite put them into words or even if your methods might appear very different.*

LAING: That's right. John Rosen is another case in point. I once sat in on a session in which Rosen was breaking down a schizophrenic and destroying some of his delusions, which is something I would never really do to anyone. He was working with this guy who said he was the Pope. So John brought in a couple of his assistants to force this guy down on his bended knees while John stood in front of him and said, "I'm the Pope. Kiss my feet, I'm the Pope." Well, I would never do that, not that way, anyway; I might do it another way. I don't like that way.

Q: *But you felt in agreement on first principles.*

LAING: Yes, I think it serves that guy right. I mean, it serves him right if he doesn't wise up to the joke. If he is prepared to be put through that ceremony in the name of therapy, then it serves the patient right, and it serves John Rosen right for doing that.

Q: *Of all the family therapists you've mentioned feeling kinship with, the only one that doesn't surprise me is Virginia Satir. She is the only one who seems to share your concern with finding the "true" self or even to consider such a discovery possible. It seems to me that you had so many readers in the '60s because of the intensity with which you described the search for authenticity played off against all the social forces that can alienate people from that. The temper of the '80s is very different. Many people today tend to scoff at words like "authenticity" and phrases like "search for oneself."*

LAING: Those expressions do sound very dated now, as if they were from a sort of period language. The favorite word now is "pragmatic"; we've all become pragmatists. Nevertheless, whatever you call it, I think there is still a major issue here in everyone's life, all the time. It's the issue of what is the correct way to live. All the time-honored, ethical considerations haven't been wiped out by the metaphor of computer programming, which has become so popular. You know, the idea that we're all just biocomputers that can be programmed this way and that, and that is all there is to it. I think that God is as much in his heaven as he ever was and he's not a passing fancy, although the way one talks about him certainly has to be a passing idiom.

Q: *It does seem that in the social sciences in the '50s and '60s, there emerged a group of people from different fields who began to use the same idiom and to share a similar vision of human behavior. I'm thinking of you, Gregory Bateson, Jay Haley, Erving Goffman, Jules Henry and in some ways, Thomas Szasz. As far as I know, only Haley and Bateson actually worked together, but you were all very influential in challenging traditional ideas about psychopathology and, among other things, paving the way for family therapy. In that group, I think of Goffman in particular as having an affinity with you.*

His The Presentation of Self in Everyday Life *is a kind of companion volume to your* The Divided Self. *There is a quote of his that you seem fond of using in your books: "There seems to be no agent more effective than another person in bringing a world for oneself alive, or, by a glance, a gesture, or a remark, shriveling up the reality in which one is lodged." I read recently that Goffman had died. Did you ever meet him?*

LAING: We had only one meeting, which went on for about six or seven hours. We never actually crossed paths again, although we could have. He was a very, very lonely spirit. We met either in 1961 or 1962. I can't remember whether he had written his book *Asylums* by then. He proposed that we meet in a sort of milk-shake bar in a suburb of Berkeley.

It was one o'clock in the morning or so when I found my way out there. Although we had never met or seen photos of each other, we recognized each other immediately. He was carrying on like a very frisky dog—very vibrant, very conscious, very alert. He wasn't particularly frightened of me, I don't think, but was maintaining a sort of courageous terror in the face of the horror that was his main vision of things and his despair at not making any difference to it. With Goffman there was no consolation in the possibility of transcendence. It was if he was saying, "It might be all right for God in his heaven, but it's not all right for me."

In that respect, he was like Jules Henry, whose *Pathways to Madness* is one of the best books ever done on schizophrenia. Henry died a few years after writing that book. As part of his research, he went to live with a number of families with a schizophrenic in them. Doing that seemed to immerse him in the horror of the way people destroy themselves and reduce their lives to emptiness and misery and all that sort of stuff. Henry was shocked by that but seemed to conclude that, given the socioeconomic macro-context, any efforts to change it were likely only to perpetuate it.

Q: *What about your meeting with Goffman? Did anything come out of it?*

LAING: In some ways, we both saw the same sort of things: what goes on at the interface between people without their consciousness, how the contextual web in which they meet governs their slightest eye movement. In view of that, apart from exchanging anecdotes, it was a bit boring.

Q: *It sounds like something out of* Knots. *You knew that he knew, and he knew that you knew that he knew.*

LAING: Oh, certainly. He did say to me that he thought that I'd give another twist to my thinking if I got myself admitted to a mental hospital as a patient incognito and really lived out a change of roles in practice. I told him I was far too frightened to take that suggestion. He himself had never done that, although he had been a junior physical therapist at St. Elizabeth's Hospital. I didn't feel any desire to pretend I was a patient and didn't think I needed to. I told him to do it himself if he wanted.

There was a very curious postscript to the meeting when I heard a few months later that his wife had committed suicide by jumping off the Golden Gate Bridge. Carl Jung talks about marriage as always being a relationship between a container and a contained. One person is contained by the other either emotionally or intuitively or intellectually or spiritually. Goffman was such a brilliant frame analyst that anyone living with him had to feel caged in by his ability to be meta to whatever was going on. You know, he was someone who was always outside things, who could sort of put his frame on whatever was occurring. But he and I found ourselves completely relaxed with each other although, as I said, we had nothing very much to say to each other.

But Goffman was only one of a number of what you might call kindred spirits that I met in the '60s. Gregory Bateson was one, of course, and also Don Jackson, who was one of the first family therapists. Jackson was an incredibly perceptive and competent man, but he got worked up.

Q: *Worked up?*

LAING: Yeah, he got worked up about things. I think it was Oscar Peterson who used that phrase talking about Dave Brubeck, when they used to follow each other around the jazz concert circuit. Peterson said it was a terrible thing to play a piano after Brubeck because he'd always find about a dozen strings broken, and the whole piano would be out. He explained that Brubeck got "worked up." He'd go in, get worked up, and go off in those big Beethovian and Goethian rages.

And, of course, then there was Bateson. I didn't particularly like Gregory. I mean, I respected him and loved him, but I wouldn't say I particularly liked him. At the end of his research project at Palo Alto, he came to some of the same conclusions about schizophrenic families as Jules Henry did. He just got out of the whole business with them and what he called their "dumb cruelty." Toward the end of his life, he was terribly bored by it all. At the very end he developed an interest in Zen. He knew a Tibetan monk who believed himself to be the reincarnated form of some ancient being. This Tibetan friend once asked Bateson if he would agree to take a vow to come back in another life in bodily form, and Bateson said, "No, thank you. I've done my bit, and this time I hope it's the last."

Q: *Of the group of social scientists we've been talking about, you are probably the most well known to the general public. During the '60s you were one of the great culture heroes. With books like* The Divided Self *and* The Politics of Experience, *you entered into an intimate relationship with hundreds of thousands of people, like myself, for whom you seemed to evoke a secret level of mind. In some ways, it was like the aspect of Erving Goffman you described just now, his ability to stand apart and observe, to go meta to whatever presented itself to him. Very few people in our field have evoked the kind of mass response that you have. How have you managed to handle it?*

LAING: Well, the way you see me handling it.

Q: *What I saw today as you were doing your workshop was that you seemed bored. Were you?*

LAING: Yes, deeply.

Q: *You seemed to me as if you weren't present and were off somewhere else. That disappointed me.*

LAING: I was present.

Q: *Really? But you seemed so bored with what you were saying.*

LAING: That's the way I was present. There was no one else present enough to engage me in ordinary conversation. I have concluded that the best way I can convey to other people how I handle my position in the scheme of things is to expose myself to them as much as I feel like doing.

Now, if you ask me to express that in intellectual terms, as you're doing now, I would say that the way I handle it is by realizing I'm not a human being as well as being a human being. The difference is that only a few human beings in any generation realize what the human condition is. If we get down to that sort of discussion, I do meet only a few people in my life with whom I can talk on equal terms.

Q: *In the '60s, you seemed to discuss your particular version of the human condition on what at least sounded like equal terms to hundreds of thousands of people in this country. It seems to me that your following has shrunk vastly since then. Would you agree that your cultural role has changed?*

LAING: I think at the moment the role that I have in the social, cultural, professional scheme of things is really up to other people.

Q: *It always was, wasn't it?*

LAING: Yeah, always was. At the moment, people don't know what to make of me. They think I'm in some sort of semiprofessional retirement or that I've bombed out. But that's not the case. I continue to write books. It's just that people in America no longer read them.

Q: *Is it different in other countries?*

LAING: Oh, yes. My most recent books, *Do You Love Me* and *Conversations With Children*, which

practically no one in America has read, are best-sellers in Italy, West Germany and Switzerland. My recent work is regarded as having immediate contemporary relevance all over Europe. Someone told me recently that I'm on every European student's bookshelf right between Karl Marx and Carlos Castaneda.

Q: *So why is it that people in this country aren't reading your most recent writing?*

LAING: The way I continue to express myself as a writer lost any widespread appeal in this country after *Knots* appeared. At that point, I moved from trying to describe what I saw to trying to depict it. I wanted to depict the territory instead of drawing a map of the territory. The reason why people in the United States haven't picked up on the whole recent genre of my writing is that they are so estranged from the territory that they can't follow the depiction. They prefer maps anytime. Someone suggested to me that the best way for me to restore my popularity in this country would be to write a textbook.

Q: *So where to from here? Textbooks?*

LAING: Oh, no. The *Memoirs of the Making of a Psychiatrist.*

Q: *An autobiography already?*

LAING: No, no. Just an interim report on the particular zone I happen to be in right now.

Q: *Let me ask you a little more about that zone. The picture you painted earlier of the later stages of the lives of Erving Goffman, Gregory Bateson and Jules Henry—your colleagues in the avant-garde of the social sciences—is rather grim. These were all men of tremendous sensitivity and vision, but from what you said, it seemed they somehow reached an intellectual or spiritual plateau that they couldn't get beyond. What about you?*

LAING: Don't include me in that, because I have nothing to do with that.

Q: *Well, how have you managed to keep from being captured by your own celebrity and success?*

LAING: I don't know—the Grace of God. You see, I'm a great admirer of Noel Coward, who has a lot to teach about taking delight and pleasure in success.

Q: *How do you keep your work fresh?*

LAING: For me, there's no accumulation in experience. I've got to start from scratch all the time. So it's just as much an adventure now as it was 30 years ago. It's just as fresh, just as puzzling, just as enchanting, just as enjoyable. It's more enjoyable than it was.

Q: *As we've been talking today, I've had the odd feeling of going in circles, futilely asking questions without being quite sure whether you've answered them or not.*

LAING: What you are referring to now is a problem Gregory Bateson used to speak to me about a great deal. He kept trying to find some way of conveying to people the way he saw it and finding that there was no way except by his transformation and theirs. There was no way he could convey how he saw things to people, who would take what he said and receive them in their own terms. I think he died both defeated and reconciled to his failure. He deeply felt that he hadn't been able to make his point and he understood. The only way he could be understood would be for people to change the way they saw things.

Q: *So it's as if he concluded that only a certain small part of human experience can be communicated through the tools available to the rational mind.*

LAING: Perhaps. The second to the last time Bateson visited with me, I asked him what he would call a saint. He replied without a pause, obviously having thought about that question before and told me, "A saint is someone who sees things as they are and doesn't get angry about it." Bateson certainly got angry about things. He didn't think he was a saint. Neither do I. ■

ERICKSON'S WAY

A PROFILE OF
MILTON ERICKSON

LATE THIS NOVEMBER, AS MANY AS 2,500 THERA-pists are expected to gather for the Second International Congress on Ericksonian Approaches to Hypnosis and Psychotherapy, a meeting devoted to the therapeutic methods developed by Milton Erickson. Some clue to the lure of this event was offered in Jay Haley's keynote address at the 1980 congress, held shortly after Erickson's death. Haley, whose writings first made Erickson into a kind of folk hero for many therapists, told the story of how Gregory Bateson first arranged for him to attend an Erickson workshop back in the early '50s. "Bateson called Erickson at his hotel in San Francisco (we were in Menlo Park) and asked if I could attend the workshop. Erickson said I was welcome. They chatted awhile, and Bateson hung up the phone and said, 'That man is going to manipulate me to come to San Francisco and have dinner with him.' Interested in manipulation, I asked, 'What did he say to you?' Bateson replied, 'He said to me, "Why don't you come to San Francisco and have dinner with me?"' Even straightforward statements by Erickson were suspect with Gregory Bateson and

with other people who feared his power."

The very view of Erickson that aroused Bateson's wariness is part of Erickson's appeal today. Shaped by Haley's accounts of therapeutic success stories in *Uncommon Therapy* and any number of recent books detailing Erickson's intricate command of multilevel communication, the image of Erickson that has emerged in the field is of a therapeutic wizard possessed of an overwhelming personal power. Mind researcher Robert Masters has called him "probably . . . the greatest psychotherapist of our time and quite likely the foremost authority too on both verbal and nonverbal communication."

Yet, despite all that has been written about him, and the diligent efforts of so many to understand just what Erickson did in therapy and why it worked so remarkably well, an air of mystery still surrounds his work. As Haley, a student of Erickson for nearly 20 years, remarked at the first Erickson congress: "Not a day passes that I do not use something that I learned from Erickson in my work. Yet his basic ideas I only partially grasp, and I feel that if I understood more fully what Erickson was trying to

explain about changing people, new innovations in therapy would open up before me."

As we try to penetrate the mythic aura that has grown up around him and assess the substance of Erickson's contribution and its implications for our own practice, the basic irony of Erickson's situation confronts us. In so many respects, Erickson was vastly more limited than practically any of us struggling to uncover the roots of his power. He was dyslexic, tone deaf, and color-blind. He was stricken with polio as a 17-year-old Wisconsin farm boy and, in an extremely rare medical occurrence, again when he was 51. For the last 13 years of his life, the period during which most therapists learned of his work and in which many of his well-known students first met him, he was confined to a wheelchair. As he tried to model the flexibility and subtle verbal methods he had spent a lifetime developing, he did so with partially paralyzed lips, a dislocated tongue and half a diaphragm.

Erickson's first attack of polio left him almost completely paralyzed. If the stories told about his recovery can be trusted, he seems to have approached his illness with an uncanny presence of mind and an imperturbable determination to rehabilitate himself. Instead of crushing him, the experience of such a physically debilitating illness created an unlikely learning laboratory for Erickson in which he began to perfect many of the skills that were to make him so effective as a therapist—his extraordinary powers of observation, his precise understanding of the microprocesses of learning, his ability to tap normally overlooked personal resources.

In the forthcoming book *Healing Through Hypnosis,* Erickson's student Ernest Rossi describes the almost scientific detachment with which the young Erickson dealt with his condition. Rossi details how the paralyzed Erickson discovered "for himself the basic ideomotor principle of hypnosis . . . exercising the thought or the idea of movement could lead to the actual experience of automatic body movement

. . . Milton foraged through his sense memories to try to learn how to move. He would stare for hours at his hand, for example, and try to recall how his fingers felt when grasping a pitchfork. Bit by bit, he found his fingers beginning to twitch and move in tiny uncoordinated ways. He persisted until the movements became larger and until he could consciously control them."

Erickson would spend hours observing his baby sister, Edith Carol, who was just learning to walk. Years later, Erickson recalled these painstaking hours of observation in this way: "I learned to stand up by watching baby sister learn to stand up; use two hands for a base, uncross your legs, use the knees for a wide base, and put more pressure on one arm and hand to get up. Sway back and forth to get balance. Practice knee bends and keep balance. Move head after the body balances. Move hand and shoulder after the body balances. Put one foot in front of the other with balance. Fall. Try again."

Eventually Erickson recovered sufficiently to move on crutches and later to get by with a cane. But throughout his life, he was prone to periods of vertigo, disorientation and severe debility. As Rossi puts it, "However well he might be feeling, there was the ever-present possibility of pain and disability."

What seemed to forever set Erickson apart after his polio attack was not simply a stoical ability to go on in spite of his disabilities, but a belief that limitations were largely a mental construct. Somehow his physical ordeal seemed to awaken him from the oblivious trance of everyday life that usually circumscribes our sense of our own possibilities. In making his recovery, Erickson seems to have developed a view of life as a continuing experiment in which the most seemingly insurmountable obstacle became a challenge to his resourcefulness, creativity and iron will.

It was as if the young Erickson's illness, in forcing him to retrain his senses, gave him a glimpse into the superstructure of subjective reality. He became intimately familiar with some of the fleeting, typically

MILTON ERICKSON

PETER BERNDT

sort, particularly in the field of psychogenic disorders; a disruption of this pattern can be a most therapeutic measure and it often matters little how small the disruption is, if introduced early enough."

After his recovery, Erickson enrolled as an undergraduate psychology student at the University of Wisconsin. There he became fascinated with hypnosis, an interest that offered him an opportunity to further develop his already considerable powers of fine-tuned attentiveness. It also allowed him to apply what he had learned about controlling his own inner processes to influencing the behavior of others. Erickson approached learning hypnosis with the same single-minded drive he had shown in his self-rehabilitation. Over the course of his undergraduate years, he hypnotized several hundred different subjects. As he gained more experience, Erickson's close observations taught him that altered mental states and trance were very much a part of everyday functioning. "This understanding," writes Ernest Rossi, "formed the underlying principle for his later studies of psychopathology as well as for his development of the naturalistic and utilization approaches to hypnotherapy."

ignored processes that give the world its apparent solidity. He discovered that most of the "rules" of life prescribing human limitations were arbitrary beliefs, not facts. As he put it many years later, "Human beings, being human, tend to react in patterns, and we are governed by patterns of behavior . . . You don't realize how very rigidly patterned all of us are." Unless, perhaps, you are Milton Erickson.

It could be said that the course Erickson followed in his own recovery became the blueprint for some of his most effective interventions. The awareness he developed of his own minute muscular movements made him exquisitely sensitive to the psychological meanings of even very subtle movements in others. Certainly, the parallels between his own experience and his notions about therapy are apparent in his statement that "maladies, whether psychogenic or organic, follow definite patterns of some

ERICKSON SPENT THE NEXT 50 YEARS DEVELoping an enormously subtle therapy of multileveled pattern recognition and interruption that was almost totally at odds with the mainstream therapies of his day. From his earliest experiments with hypnosis onward, the thread that runs through Erickson's career is his almost complete absorption in this work. As Haley has commented, "Erickson had two subjects: hypnosis and therapy . . . the man worked 10 hours a day, six or seven days a week, doing therapy. He would start at seven in the morning and he often quit at 11 p.m. Every weekend he was either seeing patients or he was on the road teaching."

The personal descriptions of those who knew Erickson emphasize the difficulty of distinguishing

the man from the therapist. Unlike most of us, he did not seem to have a separate working and off-hours self. "He wasn't the kind of person you would just sit down and chat with," recalls Erickson's student Jeffrey Zeig, now president of the Milton H. Erickson Foundation. "He was consistently working, consistently being Milton Erickson, which entailed having the most profound experience that he could with whomever he was sitting with. In that sense he was constantly hypnotic, constantly therapeutic, constantly teaching."

Clearly, for Erickson, work was a way of life. Accordingly, he developed a concept of therapy that did away with what he considered some of the arbitrary boundaries of professional practice. What distinguished Erickson's approach to therapy as much as anything was the lengths he was willing to go to in order to help a client. "The thing that was so impressive about Erickson was the time and energy he was willing to put out," says Zeig. "Once he took somebody as a patient, he would literally do anything he possibly could to help that person."

Erickson's willingness to extend himself with a client and his ability to adopt whatever role he considered necessary is particularly striking in the case of a withdrawn 9-year-old girl that Erickson described to Haley in *Uncommon Therapy*. Whenever questioned by her parents about her increasing problems in school and her avoidance of social contact, the angry little girl would tearfully insist, "I just can't do nothing." Concerned with their daughter's school problem, the parents got in touch with Erickson. His attention was soon drawn, however, to another matter, the little girl's ineptness on the playground. The following account of how he handled this case may be especially illuminating for those who think of Erickson's approach to brief therapy as offering an easy shortcut to change or for would-be Ericksonians overly attached to the outer forms of professional decorum: "Since the girl would not come to the office, I saw her each evening in her home. I learned that she didn't like certain girls because they were always playing jacks or roller-skating or jumping rope. 'They never do anything that's fun.'

"I learned that she had a set of jacks and a ball but that she 'played terrible.' On the ground that infantile paralysis had crippled my right arm, I challenged her that I could play a 'more terrible' game than she could. The challenge was accepted. After the first few evenings, a spirit of good competition and rapport developed, and it was relatively easy to induce a light-to-medium trance. Some of the games were played in the trance state and some in the waking state. Within three weeks she was an excellent player, though her parents were highly displeased because of my apparent lack of interest in her scholastic difficulties."

Erickson extends his challenge to the girl to include other sports, and in the course of a few weeks, she not only becomes adept at roller-skating and rope jumping but even begins coaching her crippled psychiatric playmate in these skills. At this point, Erickson ups the ante:

"I then challenged her to a bicycle race, pointing out that I could actually ride a bicycle well, as she herself knew. I boldly said that I could beat her; only her conviction that I would defeat her allowed her to accept. However, she did promise to try hard. She had owned a bicycle for more than six months and had not ridden it more than one city block.

"At the appointed time, she appeared with her bicycle but demanded, 'You have got to be honest and not just let me win. You got to try hard. I know you can ride fast enough to beat me. I'm going to watch you so you can't cheat.'

"I mounted my bike and she followed on hers. What she did not know was that the use of both legs in pedaling constituted a serious handicap for me in riding a bicycle; ordinarily, I only use my left leg. As the girl watched suspiciously, she saw me pedaling most laboriously with both feet without developing

much speed. Finally convinced, she rode past to win the race to her complete satisfaction.

"That was the last therapeutic interview. She promptly proceeded to become the grade-school champion in jacks and rope jumping. Her scholastic work improved similarly.

"Years later, the girl sought me out to inquire how I had managed to let her excel me in bicycle riding. Learning to play jacks, jump rope, and roller-skate had the effect of bolstering her ego immensely, but she had discredited those achievements considerably because of my physical handicaps. The bicycle riding, however, she knew was another matter. She explained that she knew me to be a good bicyclist, was certain I could beat her, and had no intention of letting the race be handed to her. The fact that I had tried genuinely hard and that she had beaten me convinced her that she 'could do anything.' Elated with this conviction, she had found school and all it offered a pleasant challenge."

One wonders what this little girl made of this peculiar adult so willing to enter into her world, so dogged at getting her to expand the range of possibilities she saw for herself. Perhaps she would have agreed with Jeffrey Zeig, as would many of those Erickson treated, that "when you were a client of Erickson, you just felt he was totally focused on you." However remarkable were Erickson's skills of influence and persuasion, no small part of his impact must have been his ability to make his clients feel that they had never been so thoroughly attended to or so thoroughly understood.

TOWARD THE END OF ERICKSON'S LIFE, HIS ILL health restricted his professional activities to meetings with various groups from around the country who came to the seminars he gave at his home in Phoenix. Even working with a number of people at one time, Erickson had the ability to establish an eerily intimate connection with each of them. At such times, this connection may have had less to do with Erickson's familiarity with a particular set of people and more with his ability, in the words of Robert Masters, to be "totally present—something few people achieve in the course of a lifetime." The following account of a seminar with Erickson by family therapist Neil Shiff conveys something of what it was like to be in the presence of this seemingly sickly old man:

"I noticed to my immediate right, sitting impassively in a wheelchair gazing out the window at I knew not what, a small, wizened, white-haired man with a neat mustache, dressed in what looked like purple pajamas. I was shocked. I moved quickly to a chair and sat down. A few minutes later, the figure in the wheelchair suddenly came to life. Cackling and obviously enjoying himself enormously, he asked a question and then innocently added, 'What's the matter? We're all enemies here.' He did not seem like the same man who only moments ago had been shriveled in the wheelchair.

"The seminar began. No one introduced themselves. Erickson passed a sheet of paper to me and asked me to provide some simple biographical information. Sitting on a wooden chair, I was still recovering from the shock of encountering this unusual man when I heard him very clearly make a statement that I immediately knew was a reference to me. Yet he did not look at me when he made that statement. In fact, words did not even seem to issue from his lips. Rather, the remark seemed to descend from midair into the center of the room. It was an extremely peculiar and unsettling experience. New to the whole scenario, I kept my mouth shut and looked around the room. The remark had been made in the form of a question which no one appeared to be answering. During the next 15 minutes, I believe he read my mind. He may have been doing the same to other seminar participants, too, although I never asked. In the context of statements he was making, he detailed several significant facts of my life. He went on to make several statements

revealing my thoughts the night before, some of them a bit unsavory. Totally absorbed, impressed and amused, I listened for four and a half hours while he spoke."

IN THE FAMILY FIELD TODAY, ERICKSON'S INFLUENCE has been most directly felt in the various strategic therapies that emphasize the importance of a carefully conceived therapeutic plan. This view of Erickson as the consummate therapeutic tactician is the focus of Jay Haley's *Uncommon Therapy,* although Haley also emphasizes that "Erickson has no set method . . . If one procedure doesn't work, he tries others until one does."

In his later years, however, Erickson himself downplayed his reliance on conscious planning. What seemed to delight Erickson about doing therapy was the unpredictable, moment-by-moment aliveness of it. This is what he emphasized to his students, advising a stance of heightened receptivity uncontaminated by formulaic preconceptions. "Too many psychotherapists try to plan what thinking they will do instead of waiting to see what the stimulus they receive is and then letting their unconscious mind respond to the stimulus," he once said. "I don't attempt to structure my psychotherapy except in a vague, general way. And in that vague, general way, the patient structures it. He structures it in accordance with his own needs."

Part of the puzzle of Erickson's work is how such an exactingly orchestrated approach to therapy could appear so intuitive and spontaneous. "Although I knew Erickson was very meticulous in what he did, early in my studies with him, I thought he worked very intuitively," recalls Jeffrey Zeig. "Then I heard Carl Whitaker say that 'Erickson must have had some left hemisphere.' The more I came to understand Erickson's work, the more I realized that was true. But the thing that made Erickson seem so intuitive was his sensitivity to the quality of his relationship with whomever he was working. Technical or overly tactical descriptions of his work just miss how attuned he was to that."

What emerges again and again in reading accounts of Erickson's work was his ability to tune in to the unique subjective world of the particular person or persons he was treating. "The first consideration in dealing with patients," he told his students, "is to realize that each of them is an individual. There are no two people alike. No two people understand the same sentence the same way. So in dealing with people, you try not to fit them into your concept of what they should be . . . you should try to discover what their concept of themselves happens to be." With his great acuity, he was able to discern the foundations of the distinctive pattern of reality underlying a person's behavior.

TYPICALLY, ERICKSON WOULD QUICKLY BEGIN TO speak and act out of a similarly patterned reality. This is what is often referred to as Erickson's ability to "speak a client's language." Of course, appreciating the uniqueness of the person with whom one is working is an idea that most therapists would endorse, but actually doing it, especially when a client's world seems very different from one's own, is something else again. It was Erickson's ability to join with and ultimately help so many different kinds of people, often with severe or bizarre difficulties, that ultimately earned him his reputation. As Jay Haley has said, "Erickson was as comfortable with a raving psychotic as he was playing jacks with a little kid."

The following classic case, besides demonstrating again the sheer effort Erickson was willing to put out and the troubles he would go to to learn a particular client's "language," also captures something of the way Erickson was able to mix remarkable discipline and dedication to his work with an infectious sense of whimsy and play. Perhaps it was this ability to combine the two that made it possible for him to work as hard as he did.

A mental patient named George had communicated almost entirely in a meaningless "word salad" since his psychiatric commitment five years earlier. Coming to the hospital in George's sixth year, Erickson had a secretary record and transcribe George's word salad. Erickson studied these transcripts until he could improvise a word salad similar in pattern to George's. He then set about executing what may be the most elaborate "joining maneuver" in the history of psychotherapy. This is Erickson's account:

"The author [Erickson] then began the practice of sitting silently on the bench beside George daily for increasing lengths of time until the span of an hour was reached. Then, at the next sitting, the author, addressing the empty air, identified himself verbally. George made no response.

"The next day the identification was addressed directly to George. He spat out an angry stretch of word salad to which the author replied, in tones of courtesy and responsiveness, with an equal amount of his own carefully contrived word salad. George appeared puzzled, and when the author finished, George uttered another contribution with an inquiring intonation. As if replying, the author verbalized still further word salad.

"After a half-dozen interchanges, George lapsed into silence and the author promptly went about other matters.

"The next morning appropriate greetings were exchanged employing proper names by both. Then George launched into a long word-salad speech to which the author courteously replied in kind. There followed then brief interchanges of long and short utterances of word salad until George fell silent and the author went to other duties.

"This continued for some time. Then George, after returning the morning greeting, made meaningless utterances without pause for four hours. It taxed the author greatly to miss lunch and to make a full reply in kind. George listened attentively and made a two-hour reply to which a weary two-hour response was made. (George was noted to watch the clock throughout the day.)

"The next morning George returned the usual greeting properly but added about two sentences of nonsense to which the author replied with a similar length of nonsense. George replied, 'Talk sense, Doctor.' 'Certainly, I'll be glad to. What is your last name?' 'O'Donovan, and it's about time somebody who knows how to talk asked. Over five years in this lousy joint . . .' (to which was added a sentence or two of word salad). The author replied, 'I'm glad to get your name, George. Five years is a long time . . .' (and about two sentences of word salad were added).

"The rest of the account is as might be expected. A complete history sprinkled with bits of word salad was obtained by inquiries judiciously salted with word salad. His clinical course, never completely free of word salad, which was eventually reduced to occasional unintelligible mumbles, was excellent. Within a year he had left the hospital, was gainfully employed, and at increasingly longer intervals returned to the hospital to report his continued and improving adjustment. Nevertheless, he invariably initiated his report or terminated it with a bit of word salad, always expecting the same from the author. Yet he could, as he frequently did on these visits, comment wryly, 'Nothing like a little nonsense in life, is there, Doctor?' to which he expected and received a sensible expression of agreement to which was added a brief utterance of nonsense.

"After he had been out of the hospital continuously for three years of fully satisfactory adjustment, contact was lost with him except for a cheerful postcard from another city. This bore a brief but satisfactory summary of his adjustments in a distant city. It was signed properly, but following his name was a jumble of syllables. There was no return address. He was ending the relationship on his terms of adequate understanding."

WHETHER DEALING WITH A CLIENT LIKE GEORGE or with the many young therapists who came to study with him in his later years, Erickson always maintained a deep respect for the individuality of the person in front of him. Perhaps this is why so many of his students have become well-known practitioners and teachers in their own right. Erickson seemed to have no need to put his stamp on his students nor did he elicit a need to rebel in the talented people whom he instructed.

What was Erickson's appeal to these students? "You could never predict what Erickson would do," says former student Stephen Lankton, author of a recent book about Erickson's methods called *The Answer Within.* "He was always different, always trying to do something in a slightly novel way. He just constantly seemed to enjoy learning, and he drew people to him that had that same spark."

Describing Erickson's "generative" style of teaching, Lankton recalls how Erickson was able to impart "lessons" that never had a simple moral, but lingered in the mind of the student. "We were watching television together one night," remembers Lankton, "and a commercial came on. Erickson, who was always 'on,' asked me to go over and pick up a large rock that was propping open a door. I must have miscalculated how heavy the rock was going to be because as I picked it up I staggered forward and almost fell. Erickson turned to me and said, 'Remember that next time you decide to suck your thumb.' And that was all he said.

"I've turned that over in my mind so many times since that night. At various times it has seemed like he was saying something about false security; at others, something about my keeping my balance; at others, something about picking up things that I can't handle. Ten years from now, I'll still be thinking about it, and I'm sure it will mean something different."

What fascinates us today about Erickson's work is also its chief frustration. It is difficult to capsulize, to translate into a few concepts or summary principles.

Erickson was notoriously leery of theoretical generalizations. He continuously reminded his students that a categorical approach to the study of people, or any subject, denies the cardinal reality of individual differences and discourages the use of one of the therapist's most essential tools—his powers of observation.

GIVEN THE DIFFICULTY IN DEFINING IT, DOES IT make any sense to talk about an "Ericksonian psychotherapy"? To Erickson, who was so relentlessly innovative throughout his long life, the spectacle of legions of therapists simply imitating his methods would probably have been a clear indication that they had missed the whole point of his work. If the term "Ericksonian psychotherapy" does have any meaning, it may be more as an attitude toward the therapeutic enterprise as a whole than as a particular theory or body of techniques.

For Erickson, doing therapy was a calling in which he was continuously absorbed rather than a task he occasionally performed. Throughout his life, he approached it with a spirit of adventure and a fascination with the variety of human experience. His deeply ingrained optimism, self-command and sense of life's possibilities enabled him to approach the people who sought his help with a courageous avoidance of preconceptions. He worked without bringing prepackaged answers to his encounters with clients. The reward for a lifetime of hard work and dedicated self-exploration was the merging of discipline and spontaneity in his work. His point of reference in therapy was not a set of ideas borrowed from others but the application of his powers of observation and his receptivity to the wisdom of his full life experience to the special circumstances in front of him. Erickson was that rare man free enough to consistently bring forth the best of himself in the service of others.

Ultimately, it is probably Milton Erickson himself who has offered the best advice to those of us who

are determined to become "Ericksonians":

"Don't try to use somebody else's technique . . . Don't try to imitate my voice or my cadence. Just discover your own . . . If I was going to work with you, I'd keep you in mind and I'd try to understand your own behavior and I would be my own natural self. I've experimented with trying to do something the way somebody else would do it. It's a mess." ∎

See references, page 173.

FROM IDEOLOGY TO PRACTICE

AN INTERVIEW WITH THE WOMEN'S PROJECT IN FAMILY THERAPY

DOES SEX-ROLE STEREOTYPING UNDERLIE MANY family therapy interventions? Does family systems thinking ignore the crucial importance of the wider social context in shaping family life? Is it the therapist's job to confront the client's sexism?

These are the kinds of questions Betty Carter, Olga Silverstein, Peggy Papp and Marianne Walters, the four organizers of the Women's Project in Family Therapy, have been asking for the past five years. For many, the challenges the Women's Project's conferences and monographs present to accepted therapeutic practices might be easier to dismiss if they were coming from a disgruntled fringe element within the field. But each of the four women collaborating on the Women's Project has established an international reputation as a clinician, trainer and workshop presenter.

Betty Carter, coeditor of *The Family Life Cycle* and director of the Family Institute of Westchester, is well known for her contributions to Bowen Systems Theory. Both Peggy Papp and Olga Silverstein have received widespread recognition for their applications of the Milan approach in the Brief Therapy

Project at New York's Ackerman Institute. Marianne Walters, currently director of the Family Therapy Practice Center in Washington, D.C., is a leading practitioner and teacher of structural family therapy.

In the interview that follows, Carter, Papp, Silverstein and Walters discuss the development of the Women's Project and their experiences in finding ways to clinically implement their feminist ideology.

Q: *More than anything I know of, the Women's Project has highlighted the connection between feminism and mainstream family therapy. How did it get started?*

WALTERS: During the height of the women's movement in the mid-'70s, I was director of the Family Therapy Training Center at the Philadelphia Child Guidance Clinic. At that time, there were only two or three women at the clinic in a position of executive functioning, and a lot of women on the staff were asking me to set up groups to discuss what it was like to be a woman practicing family therapy. The questions they were asking were things like: Why can't I confront men in therapy? What does it mean when a

BETTY CARTER

PEGGY PAPP

woman challenges a man who is the head of a household? Why do we so often put pressure on the women in families to make the changes? How does the fact that we don't have any power in our own system affect our work as therapists?

CARTER: Then in about 1979, Marianne invited Peggy, Olga and myself to do a workshop with her at the clinic called "Women as Family Therapists." When the four of us got together, I remember feeling that we were doing something a little naughty. We all felt some trepidation about doing it.

PAPP: We were concerned that we would alienate our male colleagues. We were very cautious.

Q: *How come? What was your sense of the attitude in the field toward what you were doing?*

SILVERSTEIN: The underlying mythology in the field then, as it is today, was that everything in the world is complementary. You can't really take any

one side. A system is a system is a system. So what were we doing saying that women in this society have special problems?

WALTERS: We were beginning to question some cherished concepts in the field, particularly that roles and functions in a family can be viewed in a social and political vacuum without reference to the larger context which organizes both gender expectations and family roles and rules. We began to look at the family as a system which can serve to maintain or to challenge the inequities of patriarchy. Our goal was to move the field to a place where it would not be part of the problem but part of its solution.

Q: *When did you first sense that a lot of other therapists were sharing your concern with women and families?*

SILVERSTEIN: We had made some tapes at the first small conference we gave at the Philadelphia Child Guidance Clinic—about 80 people showed up.

OLGA SILVERSTEIN

MARIANNE WALTERS

Marianne decided that we should show those tapes at the Orthopsychiatric meeting. We weren't on the program, so we just put up a little sign in the hotel lobby. We thought 10 people would show; instead, about 500 people came. We were not prepared for that kind of interest. We learned a lot from the women at the Ortho Conference.

WALTERS: It turned out to be a long meeting. And a challenge really went up from the audience: "If you are serious, you need to do something about getting the family field to look at women's issues. We need you to assume leadership." We were impressed with the quality and intensity of the response and felt we had been given a mandate to continue.

Q: *What were the most important issues that got raised at that meeting?*

CARTER: It was women therapists talking about their lack of power in their own agencies. Someone

would say, "How can I do such and such in an agency where . . . ," and then go on to say whatever the politics of the agency were.

WALTERS: There was a lot of discussion about the changing role of women and how to respond to that, both clinically and within their own systems—agency systems, family systems, political systems.

PAPP: Many people were asking, "How can we work systemically and still be aware of the special issues of women?" Again and again people said, "How is it that family therapy, which claims to be so evenhanded, so often ends up blaming the woman for whatever happens to the kids?"

CARTER: Someone at the meeting asked, "What percentage of family therapists do you think are women?" All of us agreed, impressionistically, that probably 70 to 80 percent were. Then she asked, "What percentage of the family therapy leadership is

women?" We all agreed it was strikingly minimal.

Q: *By the time the meeting you're describing occurred, Ortho must have already had its share of workshops and panels on feminism and women's issues. Why do you think you drew such a crowd?*

CARTER: Because we were focused on practice. It was not only a political meeting. We were looking at both ideology *and* practice.

Q: *What was the hardest question that came out of that meeting?*

CARTER: I think it was the question of how you can be a family therapist without becoming a guardian of the patriarchal, conservative values that the traditional family represents. In other words, it was the question of how you can be both a feminist and a family therapist.

Q: *As you got more involved working with each other and concentrating on women's issues, how did your own work change?*

CARTER: I can remember literally walking around in a sweat for two or three days before the first large conference we gave after that Ortho meeting. We had all gotten together and committed ourselves to regularly giving conferences and discussing issues. At this first conference, which was in New York, I was going to present on stepfamilies. Normally, if you ask me about stepfamilies, out comes triangles, family structures, and so on. But before this conference, I began to ask myself what were the particular women's issues in all this? I found that I couldn't put together a smooth presentation. I couldn't just slam together my ideas and clinical examples in a workable package, which was something I was accustomed to being able to do on any given family therapy topic. It was like I was retraining myself to approach some very familiar material in a new way.

PAPP: My experience before that New York conference was rethinking a case I had seen and suddenly looking at it in a different way. I had already edited a tape of a family with a suicidal adolescent in which the mother could easily be described as "intrusive and controlling." In the past, whenever I had shown it as a presentation on adolescence, everyone in the audience would have a negative reaction to the mother, feeling she was overinvolved and the only problem in the family. But when I started preparing for the New York conference, I saw it differently. I realized that this woman's husband had never been there, that she had had total responsibility for this child. She had been the perfect executive's wife, never worked herself, and had waited her whole life for her husband to retire. At that point, they had planned to have this beautiful life together. Instead, he took on a new business when their child was about eight years old, and for the next five years he was away from home almost constantly. What else did she have in her life? They originally came in because their son was suicidal and depressed.

In the therapy, the husband came off looking wonderfully sane and reasonable. When we got the father to take charge of the kid, the boy improved and the mother nearly went to pieces. She was on the verge of having a nervous breakdown, and she was crying because we had taken her job away. She had stepped back and her kid had gotten better. What did that say to her? She had ruined her child and her whole life had been in vain.

Olga and I struggled with that and came out with a wonderful intervention. We went back in the ruin and said, "We all realize that it was because of you and all the loving care that you put into your son all those years that made it possible for him to change now by his father's taking over a little more. The credit goes to you." And that is what we did with it. We would never have done that if we had not become sensitive to the larger problems of being a woman in families.

SILVERSTEIN: The thing that sticks out for me about preparing for that first conference was how personal my presentation was and how difficult it was to do. I have been married to the same man for

42 years. I knew he was going to be at the conference, and I also knew that I was going to say a lot of things that I had not said to him. I had said them to myself and to other women, but I had never really said them to him. My husband is one of the most supportive people I have ever known, and here I was going to talk about my feelings of having been in a one-down position in a marriage which he thought had been perfect. It was a lovely, ideal, benevolent patriarchy, but a patriarchy all the same. It was very difficult to talk about. I cried in the middle of my presentation.

WALTERS: My situation was a bit easier because I was talking about single parents, and I had been a single parent for some time. I had learned at first hand about a woman being in a position of executive functioning and was very familiar with both the personal trade-offs and the intellectual and emotional satisfactions of this position. My concerns at that first presentation had to do with ensuring the strength and continuity of our collegial collaboration and not falling prey to some of the one-upmanship and professional "warfare" I had witnessed in the field. I wanted to prove that we could assume leadership, even take different positions, and still retain respect and consideration for each other. It was very important to me that we continue to nurture our very strong friendship.

Q: *In addition to feeling on the line personally and professionally, I would imagine you felt some concern about alienating people at both ends of the spectrum.*

CARTER: That's right. We were wondering which was going to happen first. Were men going to stand up and say, "Oh, you bunch of bitches," and run us out of town, or were radical feminists going to throw stones and tomatoes and call us Aunt Toms.

Q: *So what kind of reaction did you get?*

CARTER: We heard a lot from the men. I thought there were nearly 500 women at the conference and about 25 men; as soon as the panel opened for questions, about 15 of the men were heard from instantly.

They didn't ask questions; they made speeches.

WALTERS: Most of which were along the lines of, "You've done very well." They felt that they should bestow approval on us.

CARTER: It was very interesting. You only had to think of what woman would get up and make a speech in a room full of 450 men, talking about men's issues. After saying we had been all right, one of the men said, "But the thing that disturbs me about the presentation is that there is a very intellectual approach being taken here. I just wonder if we can do family therapy without heart."

Actually, we were all thunderstruck and rather pleased to hear that. Olga said, "Well, thank you very much, Sir, for putting some balance into the system now. If the women are all going to get terribly intellectual, I guess the men will have to get emotional."

Q: *Here's a quote I'd like you to comment on: "Families are the principal arena for the exploitation of women, and, however deeply rooted in social structure that exploitation may be, it is through family structure that it makes its daily presence felt." Would you agree with this statement?*

SILVERSTEIN: Absolutely. The family is constituted so as to protect the patriarchal structure of society and the one-down position of women. The conventional family puts the male figure in the leadership role. The woman's job is to serve. The better she serves, the better she is. If she doesn't serve, it throws everything out of kilter.

WALTERS: The problem is how subtly all this operates. It is relatively easy to wage the struggle in the workplace over equal pay for equal work. The way economic institutions function is much clearer than in the family. You know what you are confronting. But in the family the process is much more intimate, much more related to a woman's fundamental sense of self. I think that is why radical feminists were pushed to take the position that the family is the most destructive force for women. I don't agree

with that position, but I do think that it is much harder to deal with issues in the family. If a woman wants to speak about the nature of marriage, she needs to address her husband as well as the "world." If you want to speak about the workplace, you can muster up more objectivity. You're not confronting your most intimate emotional relationships.

CARTER: The family is the only group or institution in which power transactions are discussed in terms of loving concern. That's so important, because women are extremely susceptible to being told that they should or shouldn't do things because of how they will affect other people's welfare. So, for women, challenging the makeup of the family is a very tricky thing. You might be willing to risk yourself, but it is understood that if you do not play the role as prescribed, you are injuring your children. And, of course, women don't risk their children. You might risk your own existence, your own place in the world, and you might want to change it, but if you are accused of risking your children's well-being, that's something else. That traditionally has been the real grabber.

SILVERSTEIN: You see this enacted in family therapy session after session. When a woman has gone to work and a kid starts acting out, my students typically come up with the hypothesis that the kid is acting out *because* mother went to work. If mother stayed home and took care of the kids, everything would be okay. We know that idea is nonsense, and yet it is still operating.

Q: *How do you respond to that? What do you tell your students when they produce that hypothesis?*

SILVERSTEIN: It doesn't take long before my students know that is not how we look at a family. You have to look at exactly what preceded the problem and what happens as a consequence of it, what the kid's part in it is and what is the father's part. Where is the grandmother, and what else is happening?

Q: *So you try to widen the perspective.*

WALTERS: I would take a different approach. I would say to a student, "You need to find another place to go. This family can't do anything about their financial needs. This mother must work. Find another way to help." I would focus in on how to restructure family functions so as to support mother's work while meeting relational needs. But it comes from the same concept. Whichever way we are going, our frame of reference is the same, although technically we will do some things differently.

Q: *In a recent review she wrote for the* Networker, *Molly Layton said, "In two years working at the Philadelphia Child Guidance Clinic, I don't believe I ever heard anyone draw a daughter's identification with a mother or a son's fascination with his father, or variations thereon . . . It was as if the units in the family were primarily defined as big units or little units, but not necessarily as male units or female units. Suffice it to say that in matters of gender, structural family therapy is plain rather than fancy." Would you agree that most family therapists seem to take an asexual, diagrammatic view of the family?*

SILVERSTEIN: Absolutely. It matters enormously whether the person occupying a particular position in a family is male or female, but too often that is ignored. If there's one thing that the Women's Project has done, it has been to introduce the notion of gender into family therapy. There is no such thing as a symmetrical family in this society. Women's unhappiness in their one-down position is a cause for great distress in families—and not just for the woman. Her basic discontent and the feeling of incompetence have to be projected on the children and throughout the entire family.

CARTER: Up until very, very recently, marriage has consisted of two people joining together to fulfill the man's dream. In 1980, when Daniel Levinson published *Seasons of a Man's Life,* he wrote that it is the young man's task to find a woman to "share his dreams." If that is not questioned, which it usually is not, it leads to a view of the family as dedicated to fulfilling one person's dream. What is the role of the

woman within that kind of family? It is to support the husband in achieving, to take care of *his* home and *his* children for him. While the life-cycle literature focuses on men's work and career, in regard to women it focuses on when she is single, when she is married, when she is the mother of young children, when she is the mother of teenage children, when she is bereft and is in her empty nest, and when she is widowed. It is always the woman in relation to her husband and children.

Q: *So why do you feel that family therapy has been so insensitive to the kinds of questions you are raising?*

PAPP: Family therapy has been controlled by men. Its male leaders were able to develop their potential while their wives stayed home and raised the children. The women in the field did not really take the time away from their own families to put their whole heart and energy into developing themselves and pursuing their careers.

CARTER: Family therapy was developed by a group of psychiatrists who were concerned with the emotional functioning of the individual. For whatever reasons, they backed up and put the individual in a wider context. That was the first time high-level, high-status people like psychiatrists got involved in examining the family. Up until then it was a low-status *schlep* job for social workers, most of whom happened to be women. But in putting the individual in the context of the family, they forgot to put the family in the context of the culture. That is the next step, and that is what the Women's Project is about.

SILVERSTEIN: Originally women moving into the family field were blind to a lot of its biases. As professional women, we took on the lens of the male viewer because that's what we thought we needed to do to be considered "professional." It took us a while to translate our own experience as women into a way of thinking about our practice.

Q: *Let's talk about the role of the therapist. How would you distinguish what you do from a more problem-oriented approach to therapy?*

WALTERS: I am not so sure I am just problem-focused anymore. I don't feel the only issue in therapy has to do with whether the symptom has cleared up. It is the *process* by which the symptom is alleviated that's equally as important. We need to be aware of our own value systems and how those values are reflected in our interventions. In the end, the issue is always whether or not the therapist has enhanced the competency and self-esteem of *all* the members of the family. In relation to women, I have taken a position that, as with any oppressed group, we need to do compensatory work. For me, that always involves enhancing competence, and particularly where it has been constricted by discriminatory practices.

CARTER: I'll give you an example of what that kind of thinking leads you to do in practice. Recently, I was supervising a marital therapy case. The husband is totally reasonable, together: three-piece suit, attache case, straight from the airport. The woman is all depressed and looks like she should be in the nearest loony bin. The reasonable husband says, "Well, for days she has just been locking herself in the bedroom. She doesn't want to do anything." And the woman therapist turns to her and says, "You mean you don't want to do anything?" She is in total alliance with the reasonable husband about this terrible person and what she hasn't been doing. Then the woman looks up and says, "Well, he's been . . . ," and she starts making complaints about the 900,000 things her husband expects her to do while he has been on his business trip. And she says, "I'm not going to do them anymore." And the therapist says, "Are you saying that you are not going to do anything in your household anymore?" Then I knock on the window. I have the therapist come out and I say, "This couple is a steamroller and a doormat. Why are you jumping up and down on the doormat?"

Q: *All four of you seem to be saying that the entire family field has been inducted into a rather traditional*

view of the family and how it should operate. What's the alternative view that you're offering?

SILVERSTEIN: We are saying that there has to be equal opportunity in the world, and it can't be a question of one person's life being serviced by the other. There should be a space for two adult human beings in the family.

WALTERS: There is another fundamental thing I think we agree on. If you define everything in the family in terms of power issues, you are defining the family according to the worldview of men. But everything is not reducible to the question of who is in charge and who has power. We have to move away from being so fascinated by power issues. We need to help parents develop ways of functioning based on competence rather than gender. Feelings of incompetence cut both ways in families. One of the things we've been discovering is how incompetent many men feel within their own families. The fact that men feel so incompetent also has something to do with the opportunities traditionally denied women outside the family. I mean, a woman who has no sense of herself in the outside world is going to fight to keep whatever competence she has inside the family. Only she knows how to vacuum. So we have to rebalance the sense of competence both in the outside world and within the family.

Q: *Let's get back to the question of practice. All of you are concerned with the application of certain notions about the role of women and the role of men to your clinical work. What do you think you have developed clinically that is of special relevance for family therapists?*

SILVERSTEIN: I have a reputation for short-term paradoxical stuff, and you say, "How does that apply to women's issues?" Take a simple little case. You have a divorced, single mother who is having trouble with her kids, and every time she can't manage her kids, she calls her ex-husband to come to take them. He winds up taking care of things. There are all kinds of ways to handle a case like that. You see therapists who say, "Well, the kids need a male role model; they are lacking a strong hand, and mother is incompetent to handle them." I would be concerned with reinforcing the mother's competency. So I might tell the mother that even though she has left her husband, she still wants to give him all the glory—so that he can feel that he is the competent one in the family. When I say things like that, women know what I mean.

Q: *Do you find that your special interest in women's issues sometimes gets you into clashes with families that don't share your attitude toward the value of patriarchy?*

CARTER: It's not that a family comes in about a problem and we start getting the wife all upset about why is she being a doormat and why isn't she standing up and punching this son of a bitch in the eye. Our therapy has nothing to do with getting the woman to realize that she is "oppressed."

PAPP: Let me give you an example to clarify how I handle that kind of thing. This family came in with an adolescent daughter who wouldn't go to school. The parents disagreed on the way the situation should be handled, but the mother went along with the father because she was afraid to say "no" to him. Meanwhile, she would subtly undermine their joint efforts because her heart wasn't really in it. This had been going on for years. The wife felt dominated and controlled by her husband and resented his authoritarian approach with the daughter, just as she resented it with herself.

Now, in the past I would have seen the problem as the mother's being overly protective and undermining the father's efforts to establish rules. But because of my growing awareness of women's issues, I listened very carefully to the mother and found out where she was coming from. I then put her in charge of getting her daughter to school and asked the father to let mother handle the situation on her own. I put him in charge of his son, who was beginning to have problems.

The mother came in to the next session feeling wonderful. She said, "You don't know what that did

for me when you gave me permission to take charge. I felt I had the power to follow through on my own ideas without interference—something I've never been able to do before." The daughter shaped up immediately, and the father was actually relieved because he was in over his head. He had been so intent on winning the power struggle with his daughter that he frequently got out of control, and that was scary for him. The power struggle could now be fought where it belonged, between the husband and the wife, because I had empowered the wife so she could assert herself rather than undermine her husband.

WALTERS: Social class is also a factor in all this. Recently an urban working-class family was referred to us by protective services. The father had sexually abused his 17-year-old daughter over a period of time. Mother is a waitress; father, an auto mechanic. There are four younger children in the family, one of whom has muscular dystrophy. Mother had pressed charges against the father, who had moved into his mother's home a few blocks away. He was in a sexual abuse group. The daughter was in foster care and in terrible conflict with her mother.

Our work went in two parallel directions. We worked intensively with the agencies involved with this family—social services, court, foster care—to extricate the mother and daughter from a system that seems to victimize the victims. Talk about double binds. Here was a situation in which mother needed to prove she could protect her daughter *and* provide economic security for the family *and* adequately parent her five children *and* work full time *and* take responsibility for legal action against her husband *and* press for child support *and* deal with foster parents *and* resolve her relationship with her daughter. All the burden was on her.

Our work with the agencies involved was very productive. At first, the protective service worker took exception to mother's leaving her 3-year-old with an aunt while she worked. The worker felt this indicated parental neglect. Double-double bind! At any rate, while we worked to change attitudes within the larger systems, in therapy we concentrated on the mother-daughter conflict. We told the mother, "Your daughter is pushing you to take a strong position with her, to be a powerful influence in her life." We worked with both the mother's and daughter's competence in dealing with each other, in small ways: clear expectations, organizing time together, managing disputes, dealing with disappointments. Daughter's endless disapproval of her mother and mother's helplessness with her daughter were confronted without reference to "triangles." Instead, we stayed with how it was just between them and helped them find ways to confirm each other. We didn't focus on how their interaction was organized by husband/father. This is a different approach than many family therapists would take. Our goal was to empower the mother-daughter relationship so they could define it for themselves, despite what had happened. In this situation, paying too much attention to the mother-daughter-father triangle would deflect from this primary purpose.

SILVERSTEIN: What Marianne's case illustrates so beautifully is the woman who projects her discontent and unhappiness on the daughter, who is the only one in the family in a lower-status position than she is. In those kinds of families, you have tremendous mother-daughter conflicts, even though the conflict doesn't really belong on that level.

CARTER: Let me give you a middle-class example of the same kind of thing. It was a typical case of a father, his kids and a stepmother, with a total World War III uproar going on between the stepmother and the stepkids. The stepmother and the first wife hated each other and fought endlessly. And the husband came across as Mr. Sweet Guy, while these two bitches are screaming and shrieking at each other. There is also an uproar between the stepmother and the husband's children, especially the oldest daughter. The trainee who was bringing this family warned

me, "Wait until you see this mother. She is a witch on a broom. She never leaves these kids alone. The husband is very reasonable, and he tries his best."

They come into the room, and I watch the session, and the stepmother starts acting like a total witch. She is screaming and carrying on. I never in my whole life saw anyone who could look and sound as totally unreasonable. The daughter is screaming back at her, and we hear about the ex-wife, the first wife.

So I called out the trainee, who has been arguing with the stepmother, and I said, "Why are you fighting with that poor woman in there who feels responsible for how these children turn out, whose father is always away, who are not living with their natural mother? Why are you struggling with someone who feels totally responsible for children who despise her? You go back in there, and you sympathize with what a position she is in."

Well, the trainee was thunderstruck. But she went in and started a whole train of "God, do you worry about them," at which point the wicked stepmother burst into hysterical tears and said, "Oh, I am so worried about this girl, who is doing this, and I am so worried about him." What was the key? It was that women feel responsible for how children are being raised. In this family, it didn't matter that this stepmother didn't have the authority and wasn't being supported by the children's mother or her own husband. In fact, she was being attacked by both the children's mother and father, but she didn't even realize herself that the attack was unreasonable. She was getting more and more frustrated, but she could not articulate the ridiculous no-win position.

Q: *What's ahead for the Women's Project? What is it that you want to accomplish now?*

PAPP: I think one of the most important things is to write about our work. We want to write a book. That is extremely important, because we can reach a much larger audience in that way.

WALTERS: I think the cutting edge for us is an ever more precise definition of the clinical application of the value system our work is based on. Also, there are a number of topics that have been suggested to us by our audiences—like women and success—which we are struggling to articulate.

SILVERSTEIN: There's also the issue of the two-career couple and how to deal with that clinically. But I think the most important thing for us is to make sure that the changes that have been going on in the real world infiltrate the family therapy field. We are not inventing something. It is not that we are coming in with some kookie value system from nowhere. Family therapy has been reactionary in the sense that it has not integrated into its clinical approaches the changes that are actually going on in the world. I think our goal is more and more to synchronize family therapy with social reality. ■

THE THERAPEUTIC STATE

AN INTERVIEW WITH
THOMAS SZASZ

IT IS 20 MINUTES INTO THE RADIO CALL-IN SHOW, and the show's guest, Hungarian-born psychiatrist Thomas Szasz, has already taken on the American Bar Association, the Supreme Court, John Hinckley's parents, Ronald Reagan, the ACLU, government's right to regulate the sale of drugs, and the idea of health insurance companies reimbursing for "marital psychotherapy" ("'psychotherapy' is just a word to get the government and insurance companies to pay for a form of conversation"). In the early morning torpor of the radio studio, Szasz, a trim, fastidiously dressed man in his early sixties, gives off a hyperalert electricity. When on the attack, he talks in quick bursts, a rhetorical machine gun firing on his target of the moment. Szasz, who self-mockingly describes himself as an "intellectual terrorist," has an instinct for battle. He knows just how to sharpen an argument to make his point impossible to dismiss. Like a relentless street fighter, he never allows himself to go on the defensive.

As incensed as Szasz can become, assailing some social injustice that he thinks has been ignored, or a psychiatric practice he considers preposterous, there is usually an ironic twist to what he's saying. "Did you know that a few years ago the American Psychiatric Association voted on whether homosexuality should or should not be considered a disease?" he remarks to the call-in show's host, his eyebrows raised in an elaborate expression of incredulity. "This is complete nonsense. Do chemists vote on the periodic table of elements? Do physicists vote on the atomic weight of carbon? Voting on whether something should be considered a disease is not science—it's politics. Psychiatry is politics concealed as science."

The calls start coming in. One man opposed to Szasz's description of psychiatric commitment as "locking up innocent people" calls him an anarchist. Another woman, upset at his statement that "mental illness does not exist," tells him he is "self-righteous, angry, insensitive and completely ignorant of physiology and biochemistry." Szasz coolly takes notes, obviously used to arousing the ire of strangers. He can turn off his combativeness when he wants to. He addresses each caller with impeccable professorial courtesy, as if he were debating with them at a

departmental colloquium. The show's host comments on how unusually busy the phone lines are. Szasz seems delighted.

The host asks Szasz about his objections to the concept of mental illness: "Isn't this just a matter of semantics, or would the approach to these problems be different if they were not classified as medical problems?"

"You have just asked the perfect question and also answered it," Szasz says, unexpectedly brightening into a smile of schoolmasterly approval. "It is no more semantics than if you are in a courtroom charged with a murder. Is it semantics whether the jury says innocent or guilty? Everything follows from those words. What we call things really determines how we behave."

O NE OF THE UNIFYING THREADS IN SZASZ'S WORK over the past 30 years is his passionate concern with "what we call things." Like George Orwell before him, Szasz has devoted himself to exposing the ways society's institutions and unchallenged mythologies derive their legitimacy and power from the manipulation of language. As Szasz puts it, "Poetry, politics, and psychiatry all come down to language—to the ancient truth which we forget at our own peril; namely, that it is by controlling words that we control men."

In his first book, *The Myth of Mental Illness,* Szasz took the then heretical position that the entire profession of psychiatry was based not on scientific fact but on a kind of verbal trick. By using the metaphor of physical illness to describe what Szasz calls "problems in living," psychiatry has established itself as both a medical specialty and one of the great shapers of modern thought. "Personal misery and social unrest, aggression and suffering, quite unavoidably exist," Szasz has written. "But they are not diseases. We categorize them as diseases at great peril to our own integrity, responsibility and liberty."

John Stuart Mill, the great 19th-century champion of individual liberty, once observed that in a free society a person's right to swing his arm should end where his neighbor's nose begins. But, according to Szasz, the psychiatric establishment, along with the other helpers of modern society, all too often proceeds as if it could take better care of its neighbor's nose than its neighbor can. And, what is worse, such helpers are frequently given official sanction to overextend their reach through such procedures as involuntary psychiatric commitment, which Szasz views as a power game aimed at controlling social deviance, not as a display of benevolent concern. "Szasz has such a distrust of 'benevolence' that he doesn't want anyone 'benevolently' helping anybody," says Jay Haley, whose own writing challenging psychiatric practices began about the same time as Szasz's.

For almost 25 years, Szasz has probably been psychiatry's foremost—certainly its most fearlessly inflammatory—critic. "I would say that the history of psychiatry is very largely the history of lies," Szasz has said. "When the patients lie, we call them delusions. When the psychiatrists lie, we call them 'psychiatric theories.'" In books like *Law, Liberty and Psychiatry; Ideology and Insanity* and *The Manufacture of Madness,* Szasz has conducted an excoriating cross-examination of psychiatry's practices and assumptions free of the temporizing and caution one would expect of someone who is a member of the very club he is attacking. "I think he's taken an awful beating within the psychiatric world," says Haley. "To do what he has done has been very courageous." Certainly, Szasz has won few friends in the American Psychiatric Association by comparing it to a "labor union": "It's a Jimmy Hoffa model. Who can drive a truck? It doesn't matter how well you drive it. It's who belongs to the club."

Perhaps Szasz has been able to speak his mind so freely because early in his career he decided not to concern himself very much with directly addressing his psychiatric colleagues. Actually, that decision

THOMAS SZASZ

may have been helped along by the fact that for many years he was unable to get his papers published in any of the leading psychiatric journals. Instead, most of his 18 books and more than 300 articles and reviews have been written for the general public. With the possible exception of Harvard's Robert Coles, it is hard to think of a psychiatrist who has been so widely published in the country's journals of literary and political opinion.

TODAY SZASZ IS PROBABLY BEST KNOWN FOR HIS well-publicized stands on civil liberties issues, particularly his vehement opposition to involuntary commitment. Back in the 1950s, when he first began to champion this cause, his was a decidedly minority viewpoint. "I remember very well 25 years ago calling the American Civil Liberties Union to try to get an involuntarily committed patient out

of the hospital," recalls Szasz. "I was told that it was not a civil liberties matter; it was a medical matter." Since that time, Szasz has been as influential as anyone in changing legal attitudes toward psychiatric hospitalization. According to psychiatrist E. Fuller Torrey, a leading exponent of the biological basis of schizophrenia, "Much of what Szasz argued for has been accomplished. He inspired a lot of ACLU types to force reevaluation of commitment laws. Things like deinstitutionalization were greatly helped along by his writing and thinking."

Although known as a civil libertarian, Szasz's primary intellectual commitment is less to the rights of mental patients than to his philosophical conception of the balance between the rights and responsibilities that underlie a free society. It comes as a surprise to some people that Szasz's strenuous opposition to involuntary commitment is matched by his determined efforts to do away with the insanity defense. For Szasz, however, the two positions are closely linked. "In my opinion, these two sets of acts are symmetrical," he has written. "In the one, the psychiatrist acts as an accessory to what, morally speaking, is a crime by the state; in the other, he acts as an accessory to what, morally speaking, is a crime by an individual. Moreover, since killing an innocent person is a graver offense than imprisoning him, the American psychiatrist who helps to acquit a killer as not guilty by reason of insanity should be regarded as having committed a graver 'psychiatric abuse' than his Russian colleague who helps to imprison an innocent person as a schizophrenic." As with his writing on involuntary commitment, Szasz's attacks on the insanity defense, once considered an eccentric viewpoint, now form part of the basis of the widespread questioning of the insanity defense that was publicly dramatized in the intense reactions to the Hinckley trial.

It is tempting to try to find something in Szasz's immigrant background that helps account for his extraordinary devotion to the cause of individual

freedom and social responsibility. Did coming to America from an Eastern European dictatorship in the period just before World War II somehow inspire him to become a guardian of the new freedoms he encountered in his adopted country? "That's a lovely, sentimental fantasy, but nothing more," Szasz deadpans when this is put to him. "By and large, it wasn't any different for a teenager growing up in pre-World War II Hungary than it was growing up in New York City—except that the education in Hungary was better."

Since 1956 Szasz has been a professor in the Department of Psychiatry at the Upstate Medical Center in Syracuse, New York. In the controversy that accompanied publication of *The Myth of Mental Illness*, only Szasz's tenured position kept him from losing his job. But the chairman of the department of psychiatry resigned, and many of Szasz's younger followers on the faculty were forced to leave.

SZASZ'S CAREER ALMOST PRECISELY CORRESPONDS with the development of the family therapy field. Certainly, his early critiques of the medical model in part helped create the intellectual climate in which family therapy first began to flourish. Although Szasz might be considered a philosophic first cousin of family therapy, he has become an increasingly distant relative over the years. Like the early family therapists, Szasz began by questioning the psychiatric diagnostic system and the effectiveness of traditional treatment methods.

But, while family therapists interested themselves in the process of change and perfecting increasingly efficient methods for bringing it about, Szasz chose a very different direction. He has concerned himself much less with change than with warning against the philosophical and ethical abuses committed in the name of "therapy." As he has written, "At best, 'psychotherapies' are nonmedical attempts to influence for ethical or unethical purposes; at worst, they camouflage brutal coercion in the name of medicine."

Szasz's critique of psychotherapy extends beyond any particular school or method. His target seems to be the hyped-up modern belief in the quasimagical, curative power of therapy. It is not that he finds voluntary therapy such a terrible thing. Actually, he believes that it can often be useful—and practices it himself. It's just that, in the final analysis, he finds something misleading and rather shallow about regarding any form of "therapy" as an answer to the eternal dilemmas of life.

"I hold all contemporary psychiatric approaches—all 'mental health' methods—as basically flawed, because they search for solutions along medical-technical lines," Szasz has said. "But solutions for what? For life! But life is not a problem to be solved. Life is something to live—as intelligently, as competently, as well as we can, day in and day out. Life is something we must endure. There is no solution for it."

Many people concede Szasz's contribution to exploring the philosophic assumptions implicit in the practice of therapy. They doubt, however, whether Szasz has much helpful to say about the everyday business of assisting people with problems. "I think he's had a great influence on commitment procedures and not locking people up irresponsibly," says Jay Haley. "I just don't think he knows anything about changing people."

E. Fuller Torrey, whose biological orientation could not be more divergent from Haley's, also questions the practical value of Szasz's work. "I think very highly of Tom's work in most areas of psychiatry. But when it comes to schizophrenia, I don't think he understands the disease and doesn't appear to be very familiar with the many developments which have firmly established schizophrenia as a brain disease. And, insofar as the shift in psychiatry is toward understanding the biological basis of the psychoses, his thinking has become irrelevant and anachronistic."

Part of Szasz's function in the mental health field has always been to get people to disagree with him.

Looking back over his career, it seems extraordinary how he has been able to persevere in his largely one-man crusades and to confer intellectual respectability on viewpoints that were initially dismissed as too far out.

"Szasz's position in psychiatry has changed dramatically over the years," says Richard Vatz, editor of a compilation of Szasz's work. "People no longer refer to him as the 'radical Thomas Szasz.' He is no longer considered an extremist or a heretic."

Despite his disagreements with him, Torrey says of Szasz, "He has probably had more influence on the whole spectrum of American psychiatry in the past 25 years than any single individual."

What does Szasz think? "Let's say I've outlived most of the vituperation."

In the interview that follows, Szasz discusses his views of family therapy, his observations about trends in contemporary psychiatry, and the increasing influence of the various power constituencies that make up what he calls "the therapeutic state."

Q: *Your unhappiness with much of what goes on in the name of "therapy" is very well known. But I don't believe you've ever addressed yourself specifically to family therapy. Do you think family therapists have fallen into the same moral and intellectual traps you've accused other therapists of falling into?*

SZASZ: I must say that family therapy is not my cup of tea. Reading the work of family therapists like Bowen or Haley or Minuchin, one gets the sense that they like meddling in people's lives. They act as if they know how this couple or that family should lead their lives.

Q: *Couldn't you say just as well that they have a theory about how problems develop in families and a method for helping families to deal with them?*

SZASZ: I wouldn't call what they have a "theory." Chemists and physicists have theories. A theory is something you can write down, in an article or a book, and then people can read it and do with it what they like. But informing people of one's theories isn't called "therapy." What family therapists have are not theories but rhetorical skills and value systems. By that I mean that they are more or less adept at making people change their behavior, and they have certain beliefs about what constitutes desirable and undesirable behaviors. So they are like priests who tell people to avoid adultery, or they are like advertisers who tell people to buy Ivory soap. I don't object to that. People do that to each other all the time. What I object to is disguising it as science, calling it "therapy." Family therapists pretend they don't have value systems, that they don't propound rules of good or bad living, that they only help families to become "healthy." That's ridiculous.

I also don't like it that most family therapists assume a paternalistic attitude toward their clients. For example, they seem to believe that they need not share their agendas with their patients, that it is okay to trick them into changing in some "desirable" direction. I don't like depriving or relieving people of the responsibility for their lives—even if they ask for it.

Q: *If, as you say, family therapy is more religion than science, what kind of religion is it?*

SZASZ: There are many denominations of family therapy. The situation in family therapy today seems to be much like the situation was in psychoanalysis, when that form of "therapy" was fashionable. Every prominent psychoanalyst was busy proselytizing, trying to convince people that the correct way to do therapy was his way. Now every prominent family therapist is doing the same thing. They are like so many Protestant preachers, each with his own church—Lutherans, Calvinists, Methodists, Presbyterians, Anglicans, Baptists, you name it; Freudians, Jungians, Adlerians, Rankians, Reichians, Frommians, you name it; ditto with family therapists—except they haven't made it so big yet.

Q: *But you've certainly done your share of proselytizing in the past 25 years. One could even say proselytizing*

is your business. I mean, you regularly give lectures around the country, publish volumes of articles and books. By now, isn't there almost an antiestablishment Thomas Szasz industry?

SZASZ: I don't see it that way. You are right about one thing, however. Namely, that I too try to influence people. Everyone who addresses the human condition does that. That's the name of the game. But while every type of proselytizing is a type of influencing, not every type of influencing is a type of proselytizing. The term "proselytizing" implies that the proselytizer wants to foster a leader-follower type of relationship, that he wants to create a social movement—unless he is proselytizing for an already existing movement, like a missionary for an established church.

Now, let me give you an example of influencing without proselytizing. Voltaire tried to influence people. But did he have an organization, like the Roman Catholic Church? No. Did he have an industry, like organized American psychoanalysis? No. You could say that Luther had an industry, after he survived his confrontation with the papacy. Or that Calvin had an industry. But Voltaire, although he was very influential, did not have an industry.

I don't have an industry either. I am not trying to create a "Szaszian movement." To be sure, some people talk about "Szaszian psychiatry." I can't stop them.

What this all comes down to is whether we want to emphasize the similarities or the differences between the mental health industry and what I do. I would rather emphasize the differences. You can't make any money by being a Szaszian psychiatrist; you can't get any university appointments or grants. What would actually happen if a large number of psychiatrists and psychologists really adopted my ideas? They would reject psychiatric diagnosis and psychodiagnostic testing, they would eschew civil commitment, they would refuse to exculpate criminals as "insane," they would not accept third-party payments for "psychotherapy." So what would be

left of psychiatry? Not much. What would happen if all psychiatric help, all "mental health" help, were paid for directly by the consumer—like a head of lettuce or a martini—as I believe it should be? I dare say, the majority of psychiatrists, psychologists and social workers would be out of business.

Q: *Szaszian psychiatry may not be much of a business, but you do make part of your living as a psychiatrist. Even though you have been extremely critical of most forms of therapy, people come to you with their problems and you, in some way, assist them in handling them. What exactly do you do in your practice, and how do you keep from "meddling"?*

SZASZ: My aim is always the same: I try to help the person who comes to me to be better able to take control of his life. Basically, I follow Freud's own models, Socrates and Shakespeare: "The unexamined life is not worth living" and "To thine own self be true." The client and I are engaged in examining his life, trying to understand it—in particular, trying to understand why he does what he does.

Freud was right in emphasizing that so long as a person does not understand what he gains from a "symptom" (or, rather, seemingly undesirable behavior), he cannot "rationally" change it. As far as being true to oneself goes, I believe there is an important task prior to it that many people never master: namely, fashioning a self about which that self feels good enough to want to be true to it.

Perhaps that's a little too general. I might add that what I do is based on two premises: one is that every person, certainly every person who makes his way to my office, is a moral agent, with the liberties and responsibilities of moral agents; the other is that every person is actually or potentially in conflict with other people in his life, especially with the important people in his life.

It is the client's job to balance his desire for autonomy and independence with his need for intimacy with and dependence on other people and to arrive at the appropriate compromises reconciling these

conflicting needs may require. As a therapist, I define my job as helping the person who comes to see me, who pays me, and to whom I owe confidentiality. If I, *qua* therapist vis-à-vis client, do something that hurts the client's wife or children or employer, that's too bad. What I do in such a role may hurt them, or it may help them. In any case, I see my role as trying to help someone in a potentially adversary relationship to others, like a defense attorney or a lawyer representing one or another party in a divorce action.

Of course, I am free to decide whether or not I want to work with someone. But once I accept a person as a client or patient, my job is to advance his interests, not someone else's. I would like to think this is inherent in the concept of individual therapy—with the emphasis on "individual." But I know it is not necessarily so, because therapists, including psychoanalysts, pay only lip service to being their patient's agent.

Q: *I'd like to get a more concrete idea of how you operate as a therapist. I know you were very critical of how the Hinckley case was handled. Would you have worked with someone like Hinckley had he come to you?*

SZASZ: I am not sure that is a question I can answer. Why should Hinckley—I mean John Hinckley, Jr.—come to me? He was not interested in seeing a psychiatrist; he was interested in seeing Jody Foster.

Q: *But don't you ever see young men like Hinckley?*

SZASZ: Let me explain how I would handle such a situation. Typically, the scenario goes like this: Mr. Hinckley calls, and my secretary answers the phone. He says to her, "I would like to make an appointment for my son with Dr. Szasz. When could he see him?" My secretary says, as she is instructed to say, "Dr. Szasz makes his own appointments. Would you like to speak with him?" He says, "Okay." Then I get on the line, if I am free, or I call back, if I am not free. Then the caller says to me, "Dr. Szasz, I have a son who has some problems. When could you see him?" I say, "Please tell me a little about the

problem. I don't mind taking a few minutes on the phone." The father describes the situation. I then say, "It doesn't sound to me like your son wants to see a psychiatrist." And the father says, "You are right, but he is willing to." And I say, "Okay, if he is willing, I'll be glad to consider it. Please have *him* call me. But please understand that I see only one person in the family. If your son comes, I would like to deal with him and with him alone." I also make it clear, tactfully but forcefully, that I will not discuss his son's "case" with him or with anyone else.

Q: *I would imagine that, given that, the son may typically come to see you once, if at all, and then refuse to go back. Does a parent then sometimes decide to see you?*

SZASZ: More often than not, the son will never call. But one or another of the parents sometimes calls back and comes to see me. And then we—I mean, the "designated patient's" father or mother and I—sometimes go on to a very productive therapy trying to resolve the parent's ambivalence about, and difficulties of coping with, the son or daughter. Here again my emphasis would be on the moral agency—the freedom and responsibility—of the person I am talking to.

Let me illustrate what I mean. I might ask the father—à la the Hinckley case—why he doesn't tell his son what he really thinks of him. Why does he support him? Why doesn't he cut him off financially, personally?

Alternately, I would suggest that we discuss the moral and practical implications of supporting the son. What is the father financing? Actually, in the Hinckley case, as I understand it, Hinckley Sr. was sitting on something like half a million dollars of his son's money—money that had been given to him in a trust fund.

In other words, I would have discussed the options the father had other than "psychiatrizing" his son, that is, trying to define him as crazy and controlling him psychiatrically. I would have asked Mr. Hinckley, Sr., why not give his son the money and

tell him to go to Cannes or Honolulu and live it up? Why not tell him to do what he wants and rejoin the family when they—the parents, the other children—can be proud of him instead of ashamed of him?

Q: *From a family therapist's point of view, you would be at a terrible disadvantage in a case like this. By working only with the father, wouldn't you expect the wife to undercut any decision she was not part of?*

SZASZ: You are missing the point. I am not trying to accomplish anything. I am only showing the person I am talking to—say, the husband and father—what sorts of things he might think of, what sorts of options he has. I see this as essentially a process of sharing information. He tells me things, and I tell him things. It's like telling someone in a restaurant that his choice is not simply between hamburger and fried chicken—that is, between psychiatrizing the "designated patient" or business as usual—but that there are many other interesting items on the menu.

Q: *Is that why you say that therapy is "just talking"?*

SZASZ: Yes, provided it is "just talking" and not something else. We mustn't confuse different agendas; namely, "just talking" and, say, "rehabilitating" an errant son like John Hinckley, Jr., or "just talking" and selling magazines. You see, you and I are talking, too. But in talking with you, I am not trying to increase the circulation of your magazine. You may be trying to do that. That's okay. That's your business. My business is to tell you what I think about the questions you ask. It's another way of publishing my ideas. I don't have any other agenda. If your wife doesn't like the way the interview comes out, that's your problem. I am not being facetious.

This is what makes me think that what I do is quite nonmeddling. Take, for example, the hypothetical discussion with Mr. Hinckley, Sr. We talk and talk, and Mr. Hinckley goes home and does exactly the same things he has been doing all along. He doesn't change a thing. Why should he? Perhaps he prefers hamburgers to all the other things on the menu. I would be saying to him, "You don't like

how your son lives. You like to make money. You like self-discipline. You like to take a shower every morning. So do I, but evidently your son doesn't. What he likes is to spit in your eye. If he can't be successful at anything else, by golly, he can be successful at that."

And he may say, "But he is sick."

And I would say, sarcastically, "Of course. That's what 'real' psychiatrists call 'schizophrenia.'" And he would find a "real" psychiatrist, who would find "real mental illness" in his son's head. Real psychiatrists are always happy to discover fake diseases; that's what makes them real psychiatrists!

My point is that a lot of people would rather psychiatrize their deviant relatives than do something else. They simply prefer that option to any other. The way our society is now constructed, they have a right to do that. And then they must live with the consequences of that choice. C'est la vie.

Q: *So your task as a therapist is not to bring about change directly but to heighten your client's awareness of his or her decisions. How do you do that?*

SZASZ: By informing him of the choices he has and by carefully avoiding paternalizing him. That is how the process becomes demedicalized. I believe the problem the client faces is how to act in a difficult situation, perhaps in a sort of chronic crisis. It is not a "disease" about which the "doctor" knows more than the "patient" and for which there is a "cure." The way I do therapy is by initially increasing the client's existential burden, not by diminishing it; and then doing what I can—again, with information, with sympathy, with tact, with common sense—to help him to go one way or another.

Q: *But certainly it isn't that simple. You give much more than information. You are an extraordinarily powerful, persuasive man. Aren't you always doing much more than you consciously intend?*

SZASZ: Of course. But then I have to undo that.

Q: *How do you do that?*

SZASZ: For example, the other day somebody came

to me and made a throwaway comment, "Maybe I am only coming so that I can tell people that I am in therapy with Thomas Szasz!"

And I said, "That and 50 cents will get you a cup of coffee."

Q: *Do you really feel that comment shifts anything?*

SZASZ: Yes, indeed.

Q: *What evidence do you have that it does?*

SZASZ: Evidence? [Laughs]. How can you have evidence in this business? Evidence is a scientific concept that depends on publicly available observations, on public data. Individual psychotherapy is something quintessentially private. So to find out what kind of therapist I am, how effective I am, whether I make my patients dependent on me, and so forth—to discover these things, you would have to talk to my former patients, assuming you could discover who they are. You see, I take the idea of confidentiality very seriously, not like Freud did, not like the despicable double agents called "training analysts" do.

Q: *But you are a persuasive person. You lecture, you write. Don't you have any followers?*

SZASZ: No, I don't. And I consider that to be one of my greatest accomplishments.

People like Erickson, Haley, Minuchin, all have their followers. They took up where Freud and Adler and Jung left off. I felt all along that psychiatry—the whole mental health business—is just a collection of cults. Leaders, followers, private languages, mysterious theories, secessions, excommunications, the works. The various brands of family therapy are no exception.

Q: *If the field of psychotherapy is really a collection of cults, how do you fit in? Doesn't that very situation make it possible for you to exist?*

SZASZ: Absolutely. It is a dialectical affair; others teach psychiatric religions, and I teach psychiatric agnosticism. That's consistent with the fact that I don't have a special method of therapy. I have a critique of methods of therapy. The kind of talking people do with me actually is not very different from the kind of help people may get elsewhere. Of course, some people come to me because of certain personal qualities I possess; others stay away for the same reason.

And then there is the social situation in which we operate today—that people can't talk confidentially about their personal problems with friends, with clergymen, with members of their own families. Everyone now gets nervous about "problems." So people go to psychiatrists and psychologists and social workers.

Q: *How do you go about assessing your effectiveness in what you do?*

SZASZ: Who cares about my effectiveness?

Q: *It would seem to me that it would be part of the ethics of your practice to see that you are truly providing the service that you think you are.*

SZASZ: I think in another five minutes you'll catch on. With all due respect, I consider your question to be absurd. It is like asking the director of a library, "How do you assess the effectiveness of your library?" Since we are talking about my effectiveness as a "psychotherapist," the implication of your question is, "Do you help people, is your 'psychotherapy' good for them?" This is like asking the library director, "Do you help the people who come to your library?"; "Does reading the books in your library improve their minds?"; "Does it make them better husbands, fathers, workers, citizens?"

In a free society, such as ours, we recognize that it is not the job of librarians to bring about such results, however desirable they might be. That is what I wanted to clarify with the analogy between what I try to provide for my clients and what libraries provide for theirs.

To be sure, one could talk about the "effectiveness" of a library in terms of the kinds of books it has, how accessible the books are, and so forth. However, assuming that a person can get to a library, that he knows how to read, that the books he wants are there, assuming all that—the library is

bound to be "effective." How could it not be? People take out books, they read them, they return them, they come back for more. It's not the librarian's business what the clients take away from that experience. One client may discover a cure for cancer. Another may learn how to make bombs. What the client gets is information. I try to be like a library. I am 100 percent "effective."

Am I joking? Yes and no. I give people conversation, ideas, options, new conflicts for old conflicts, new solutions for old solutions, and so forth—and they do with it what they want. The issue is not whether I "help" but what I do. I inform, I amuse, I distract, I relieve boredom, I impart significance. And, of course, I am candid, I am decent, I am reliable. There is always an important element of support in psychotherapy.

Q: *But how do you know when you are being helpful and when you are not, in your own terms?*

SZASZ: I am not talking about helpfulness. You are. You are asking the wrong question. My mode of therapy is a market model. Asking me how I know if I am helpful is like asking a library director how he knows he is helpful. Or, to take a more directly commercial analogy, it is like asking a furrier how he knows he is helpful. His answer would be, "Well, people come to my store. They seem to like the fur coats I sell them. They pay for the coats. Sometimes they send me their friends. They never complain about the coats, they never bother me, they never sue me, they like me, they like my product. That's all I can tell you." That is my model.

Q: *You are saying you don't care whether your customer wears her fur coat or puts it in the closet.*

SZASZ: That's pretty much the idea. The woman who buys a fur coat doesn't have to wear it. She only has to pay for it. Similarly, my clients don't have to change. They only have to pay me. I am a little bit like a teacher who doesn't care if his students learn. In some ways, of course, I would prefer that they do, but if they don't, or if they learn very slowly,

well, fine. This is one of the reasons why, many years ago, I made a deliberate decision to make my practice a very small part of my life, existentially and economically. I don't care how much money I make in my practice. My life doesn't depend on what my patients do, whether I have a big practice. I sell a luxury product, and some people buy it. They do with it what they want.

It seems to me that this is very different from the way someone like Milton Erickson worked. He seems to have been extremely involved in helping people live their lives "better." He was a missionary. That's fine. I have no objections to that. It's what makes the world go round. I am not saying everybody should be like me.

Q: *Your concern with the destructive influence of the therapist's power reminds me of Gregory Bateson's disenchantment with the family therapy that developed, in part, out of his own research. Do you see any similarity between your position and Bateson's?*

SZASZ: Not much. I knew Bateson. I don't think he understood or wanted to understand psychiatry as a power game. He acted as if knowing enough about double binds could cure schizophrenia, like you cure pneumonia.

Q: *That is not the impression I get. People who knew him pretty well tell me that his position was somewhat like yours. He wasn't interested in curing schizophrenia.*

SZASZ: That may be. But schizophrenia, after all, is only a word. As Charles Sanders Pierce said a long time ago—and as Bateson knew damn well—the meaning of a word lies in its uses, in its consequences. And what are the uses of the word "schizophrenia"? Involuntary mental hospitalization and the insanity defense.

That's why I always concentrated on the fact that psychiatrists use mental illness terms—and schizophrenia is the paradigm—to incriminate innocent people and to excuse guilty ones. Did Bateson ever attack these psychiatric practices? If he did, it has escaped me. No, Bateson was like Sullivan, like

Skinner, like Rogers; they all "worked with" committed "schizophrenics"—instead of helping them regain their freedom. To my knowledge, Bateson never objected to psychiatric coercions and excuses.

Q: *So you feel that he copped out?*

SZASZ: That's putting it mildly. He legitimized psychiatry, the VA, NIMH, the whole psychiatric bureaucracy that supported him. He didn't bite the hand that fed him. He was the "insider critic," the great "systems theorist" who helped to make psychiatry look good, look scientific. How can you spend time in a VA psychiatric hospital and never talk about commitment? It's like studying Jews in Auschwitz and never talking about how they got there.

Q: *Do you think that the direction of psychiatry has changed any from the time when you began attacking it?*

SZASZ: Well, there have been a number of significant developments. Just how they relate to my work is perhaps not for me to say. At this moment, the psychiatrists are beating a hasty retreat to the old, pre-Freudian, organic position. Of course, they are again misrepresenting this as a new, scientific breakthrough. As everyone familiar with psychiatry knows, before 1900, and even during the first half of this century, psychiatrists believed that mental illnesses were brain diseases. That's why psychoanalysis was initially a kind of antipsychiatry. Now psychiatry is becoming remedicalized.

But the psychiatrists are fooling themselves. They think they'll impress their medical colleagues with their gobbledygook about psychopharmacology. The fact is that, just as society has stigmatized mental patients, so physicians have stigmatized psychiatrists. Most doctors regard psychiatrists as idiots or quacks who give drugs without understanding their effects and without examining their patients. Physicians also know, deep in their hearts, that psychiatrists—and I mean psychiatrists in the public sector, in the hospitals—take care of poor people, of homeless people, of people no one wants. They know that deinstitutionalization is a fraud.

Q: *Do you think that psychiatry is disappearing or will disappear?*

SZASZ: No, I don't. What psychiatrists do is too useful—not for the patients but for the nonpatients, for the families of "psychotics," for the courts, for society.

Q: *Is there anything that you see that cheers you in any sense about what is happening in the therapeutic world?*

SZASZ: Yes, the so-called mental patient liberation movements. They are emblematic of a social articulation, of a public recognition of the adversary relationship between the mental hospital patient and the mental hospital staff. When I first pointed this out, I was fiercely attacked for it. That was the real heresy, my insisting that the state hospital psychiatrist is not the committed mental patient's agent. Now this is conventional wisdom.

Today the committed mental patient even has a right to his own lawyer! When I was a young psychiatrist, that would have been absurd. Psychiatrists would have said, "What does the patient need a lawyer for? He is sick." Wanting to sue to get out of a hospital was then considered to be a typical symptom of paranoia. Twenty-five years ago, no lawyer would have dreamt of taking the case of a "schizophrenic" who wanted to get out of the hospital. I know. I tried to interest some to do so.

Sometime around 1960, I tried to get the American Civil Liberties Union (ACLU) interested in the civil rights aspects of involuntary mental hospitalization. You know what they told me? That it was not a civil liberties matter, it was a medical matter. "A doctor wouldn't keep a patient in a hospital who didn't need to be in the hospital"—that's what they told me. The ACLU was in the psychiatrists' pockets. Some of the local ACLU branches have since come around to my point of view, but the national ACLU is still endorsing commitment.

Finally, there seems to be, although it is hard to be sure of this, an increase in violence by mental

patients against psychiatrists. That, too, may be significant.

Q: *Significant in what way?*

SZASZ: Significant in the same way as slave revolts were significant. These acts of violence strip away the veneer of "therapy" from the relationship between the psychiatrist and the so-called psychotic and reveal the antagonism, the mutual coercion, the nastiness beneath it.

There is one more development that heartens me that I want to mention. In the last 20 years or so, no major literary figure has had anything good to say about the institution of psychiatry. These authors are, if you want to put it that way, the "Szaszians." They are showing people that psychiatrists are either in the business of letting people escape from life by offering them a pseudomedical cop-out or in the business of disposing of existential crises by removing the offending party from the scene. Ken Kesey's *One Flew Over the Cuckoo's Nest* was a fine artistic illustration of this.

Q: *Your critique of psychiatry is really a part of something much broader than a critique of just the field of mental health. I read something by you recently in which you talked about modern American society being "the therapeutic state." What do you mean by that?*

SZASZ: Let me try to explain that. In this country, the First Amendment forbids the government from having a state religion. Everyone knows this. But somehow people don't appreciate how beautiful an idea this is and how impossible it is to fully realize it. Before the American and French revolutions, all nations had their own religion. Many countries still have a state religion, for example, Israel, Ireland, Iran.

I contend that the state religion forbidden by the First Amendment has crept back in. That's not surprising. People need religion; they need a sense of meaning, of why they are here on earth, of what is good and bad, and so forth. Given the constitutional prohibition against religion, the American

government could not and cannot formally embrace or ally itself with a religion that's called a religion. The courts could not look to Catholic priests or Jewish rabbis to advise them about matters of child custody, divorce, racial integration, punishing criminals and so forth.

But they can turn to psychiatrists, because they are "medical experts." I think something like this was inevitable. No society we know of has ever existed without a shared system of beliefs and values—in short, without a religion. So in Ireland they have Catholicism, in Israel they have Judaism, in Russia they have Communism, which is a religion, of course. And we have Psychiatry, Mental Health.

Q: *So for you, the churches are therapists' offices. But I thought they were the shopping malls and that consumerism was the prevailing religion in this country.*

SZASZ: I don't think that's true today. I would say that since the end of the Second World War, health in general, not only mental health, has become the new salvation. And medicine—medical research, medical "care"—which encompasses psychiatry, is the new religion. That is precisely why psychiatrists cling so tenaciously to their medical identity and why the supporters of the therapeutic state—senators and clergymen and the media and the American Bar Association—so eagerly authenticate psychiatrists as bona fide doctors.

Q: *So in your view, societies are basically organized by people's unthinking obedience to a core set of metaphors and values. If at some kind of mass level people were to become philosophic, in the sense you are talking about, society as we know it couldn't function. We would question too much of what is going on.*

SZASZ: That would be true if people did it across the board. I think you are now putting your finger on how social change comes about—that is, how "piecemeal social change," to use Karl Popper's apt phrase, as against revolutionary social change, comes about. Take, for example, the American antislavery movement. During the first half of the 19th century,

people didn't think about every aspect of Christianity and the Bible and how they were used to justify slavery. They didn't think about every aspect of the economic ramifications of slavery. Instead, they focused on one issue: Was it okay for white people to take blacks by force and keep them in servitude by force? The opponents of slavery wanted to change that one thing. And they did.

This has also been my approach. Is it okay to incarcerate someone who has committed no crime—because of "mental illness"? Is it okay to acquit, as "not guilty," someone who has committed a crime, which he *wanted* to commit—because of "mental illness"? These questions won't go away, and I am determined not to let psychiatrists pretend they are unimportant.

Q: *So much of your writing has been about the issue of psychiatric commitment. Was that based on your thinking that that was the one area where you could have the most effect?*

SZASZ: Yes. But I wouldn't put it that way. Instead, I would say that was the one area where I thought psychiatry was most clearly in the wrong, where it was therefore most vulnerable, especially in a country such as this. You see, in this country, individual freedom is also a quasireligious idea and value. This is not Russia or China. Here you are not supposed to be imprisoned unless you have been convicted of a felony. There is no preventive detention for possible criminal conduct. But it is okay to imprison a person preventively, as it were, if the prison is called a mental hospital.

People often get confused about how simple and basically conservative my position about all this really is. In the first place, some people think I am opposed to mental hospitals and mental hospitalization. Of course, I think it's stupid to provide homes for the homeless under ostensibly medical auspices. But I have no objection to anything that's truly voluntary. If a person wants to go to a mental hospital and pay for it, why shouldn't he? If someone wants

to operate a mental hospital and can get customers to pay him for it, why shouldn't he?

Secondly, few people see that my opposition to involuntary mental hospitalization and to the insanity defense are two sides of the same coin. In one case, a person is deprived of liberty even though he is innocent of any crime; in the other, he is diverted from punishment even though he is guilty of a crime. It is not very important how often these interventions are used. It is not important whether there are 800,000 people in mental hospitals or 100,000 or whether the insanity defense is used often or rarely. These public psychiatric performances are the symbols of psychiatric expertise, of psychiatric power, of the state's recognition of psychiatry as its foremost ally in governing, in ensuring "domestic tranquility." These psychiatric pronouncements and performances are like celebrating the Mass or Yom Kippur. Psychiatrists and only psychiatrists can tell who is schizophrenic, who is psychotic, who is criminally responsible, who will kill and so forth. It's really quite absurd, unless, of course, one believes in it.

Q: *As I've spoken with various people who have made their mark in this field, I am struck by how early on their thinking is shaped. Essentially, you've been writing about the same thing for 25 years. Are your ideas very different now than when you started? Have you changed your mind about anything?*

SZASZ: Certainly, I have not changed my mind about commitment, about the insanity defense, about the mythologies of psychiatry and psychoanalysis, and all that. But I think I have changed in the style in which I present my ideas. Initially, I addressed myself to the psychiatric community. I gave that up pretty quickly. I have tried to address an increasingly wider audience—social scientists and lawyers, college audiences, the community of intellectuals and the general reading public.

Q: *Do you think of yourself as a writer rather than as a psychiatrist or psychotherapist?*

SZASZ: I like to think of myself as all of those and perhaps mainly as a political philosopher and social critic—in particular, as a critic of the alliance between psychiatry and the state, between medicine and the state; as someone who has tried to lay bare—if I may use a medical metaphor—the anatomy of the therapeutic state.

Q: *From what I can tell, after all this time you continue to pursue the causes you have committed yourself to with a kind of cheerful fatalism about just how much you can accomplish. Don't you ever get discouraged?*

SZASZ: Why should I be discouraged? I thank my lucky star for having had the good fortune to end up in the United States at a relatively early age. This enabled me to learn English well enough to write, and to write well, in what I think is an absolutely incredibly beautiful and powerful language. And then I thank my lucky star for the freedom of the press and the academic freedom and the legal protections we enjoy in this country. All this has enabled me to indulge in that greatest of luxuries—and pleasures—namely, thinking clearly and publishing what one thinks. Evidently, there were enough people out there interested in what I had to say.

Actually, I am not discouraged at all. I never expected to change anything. In fact if I had had more impact, I would have felt my original diagnosis was wrong. ■

STRANGER IN A STRANGE LAND

AN INTERVIEW WITH SALVADOR MINUCHIN

B Y NOW, THOUSANDS OF THERAPISTS HAVE SEEN Salvador Minuchin interview a family. The commanding man with the elegant accent and his own version of English syntax who persuades, seduces, provokes, bullies, bewilders families into changing—as the occasion demands—has become a familiar voice in the heads of family therapists everywhere. Memories of his classic sessions have become the standards against which therapists judge their own best work. Describing Minuchin's style, *The New Yorker*'s Janet Malcolm wrote, "Life is supposed to be disorderly, boring, fragmented, repetitive, in need of drastic editing. Watching a Minuchin session, or a tape of it, is like being at a tightly constructed, well-directed, magnificently acted play."

But Minuchin's unquestionable dramatic flair does not in itself explain the galvanizing effect he has had on family therapy. There has been an intensity, a sense of commitment in his work that goes beyond just a love of drama.

"Minuchin really believes that the patient always comes first," says Cloé Madanes, whom Minuchin hired in 1971 to teach Spanish-speaking therapists at the Philadelphia Child Guidance Clinic. "I learned that very soon after I first came to the clinic. I was supervising a social worker in a first interview with the family of an adolescent girl who had been hearing voices and cutting her wrists with razor blades. I thought I could prevent a hospitalization by putting the parents in charge of the girl and setting up a suicide watch at home. I needed the backing of a psychiatrist to support the decision not to hospitalize and to be on call in case of an emergency during the weekend.

"It was late Friday afternoon and there weren't many people around. I found a psychiatric resident and asked him to support me, but he said that the family had come to the wrong place; they should have gone to the mental hospital. I could tell that he was afraid that there would be a crisis, and it would ruin his weekend.

"I went looking for another psychiatrist and saw that Minuchin was giving a seminar to a large group of people. I had been told that an important goal of the clinic was to prevent the hospitalization of children, and as a foreigner, I took everything seriously.

So I said to Minuchin, 'I'm sorry to interrupt, but I need to keep a girl out of the hospital and there is no one else who can help me.' He said, 'Alright.'

"So he came out and spent an interesting half-hour talking with the girl about her voices and her suicide attempts. He asked her if she used clean blades or dirty ones to cut her wrists, and she said, 'Clean ones, of course; used razor blades can give you an infection.' Then he told her that he could hear whole symphonies in his head and asked her what her voices told her. She explained that they called her dirty names. So he discussed with her at length how she could get the voices to say nice things instead and how she could then enjoy them like he enjoyed his symphonies.

"When Minuchin left the room and the therapist went back in, the girl said, 'That psychiatrist is crazy. He thinks I should hear nice voices and symphonies. I don't think I should hear any voices at all, and I don't like symphonies.' She remained at home, there was no crisis, and she improved steadily.

"When Minuchin finished with the girl, he went back to teach his seminar, but not before bawling out the psychiatric resident who had not wanted to get involved."

Madanes's husband, Jay Haley, who spent 10 years working with Minuchin in Philadelphia, thinks there is another side to his former colleague's clinical skill. "Sal is a very courageous guy," says Haley. "He loves stepping into difficult situations. He has a confidence that he can handle anything that comes up. I remember watching a session in which there was a tremendous battle going on between a black mother and daughter because the daughter had stayed out all night. They were screaming back and forth, and things were getting worse and worse. Finally, the mother reached over and snatched off the daughter's wig. Right then the therapist just stood up, looked at the one-way mirror and said, 'Help!'

"Minuchin immediately got up and went into the room. The first thing he did was tell the daughter, who had been crying, to go and wash her face. Then the mother, maybe frightened that he was taking the girl away from her, accusingly asked him, 'What did you do with my daughter?' Minuchin answered, 'You come with me,' and walked with her down the hall, opened the door to the women's room, and showed her that her daughter was alright. Then he said, 'Now let's go back and talk.'

'He knew he had to show the mother where the daughter was. Just saying something reassuring wouldn't have been enough. Sal's confidence comes out of his faith that he can read what's needed in a situation. He has no doubt that he can walk into a therapy room and straighten things out, no matter what is happening."

THROUGHOUT HIS CAREER, MINUCHIN HAS BEEN guided by a sense of social purpose in a way that has set him apart from the other figures who have shaped family therapy. In his work with delinquents in New York City in the late '50s, in his attempts to make the Philadelphia Child Guidance Clinic into a model community agency and, most recently, in his latest book, *Family Kaleidoscope*, Minuchin has persisted in drawing the attention of the mental health field to the problems of the poor. Carl Whitaker believes that Minuchin's interest in society's outsiders reflects Minuchin's own experiences as an immigrant and cultural outsider. Describing the Argentinian-born Minuchin's first arrival in New York City, Whitaker has written, "Sal Minuchin was a stranger in a strange land. If you will, a psychosocial orphan. . . . What did he do with the stress that evolves living in a strange culture?" But actually, by the time he arrived in America in 1950, Minuchin had already spent a lifetime learning to survive in a hostile culture.

Born to Russian Jewish emigrants, Minuchin grew up in a tightly knit clan in a small Argentinian town. His father had come to Argentina in 1905 as part of an organized wave of Jewish colonization.

SALVADOR MINUCHIN

The world Minuchin grew up in was like a transplanted European *shtetl*. He was a member of a community that saw itself as besieged by antisemitism, one in which the prospect of impending catastrophe was never entirely out of mind. But, however alien much of Argentine culture was for Minuchin, it did regularly instruct him in the rituals of Latin pride and how he was expected to defend his honor when the instant call-to-arms "shitty Russian Jew" was hurled his way, as it often was.

Minuchin grew up with ambivalence about Argentina as his homeland. His allegiance was to Zionism and the socialist political movements that it spawned. As a university student, he was an active member of a Zionist student organization. In 1943 he joined a student protest against the rule of military dictator Juan Peron and was arrested. He spent three months in jail and was expelled from the uni-

versity. Upon his release, he went to Uruguay to continue work on his medical degree, which he later completed back in Argentina.

When Israel's war for independence began in 1948, Minuchin joined the Israeli army and spent 18 months serving as an army doctor. In 1950 he came to the United States intending to study with Bruno Bettelheim at Chicago's Orthogenetic School, at which a childhood friend of Bettelheim's had arranged a psychiatric residency for him. When Minuchin arrived in New York, his plan was to spend a short time there before traveling on to Chicago. Instead, he met future family therapy pioneer Nathan Ackerman, who took Minuchin under his wing.

"I am sure he saw me as a maimed bird," says Minuchin today. "He was clearly someone who was touched by maimed birds." Given the choice between studying with Bettelheim in Chicago and taking a position Ackerman arranged for him with the Jewish Board of Guardians in New York, Minuchin chose New York. "It was absolutely the decision of an immigrant," says Minuchin. "I knew New York. I didn't know Bettelheim or Chicago. So like any immigrant, I stayed at the port of entry. I do not know what my story might have been if I had gone to Chicago."

At the Council Child Development Center, directed by Ackerman, Minuchin met his wife-to-be, Patricia, a clinical psychologist with a Ph.D. from Yale. In 1952 they returned to Israel, where Minuchin took a position as the psychiatric director of Youth Aliyah, a program designed to bring orphaned children to Israel to settle on the kibbutzim. "There were kids from all backgrounds—Europe, Yemen, Morocco, everywhere you could think of," says Pat Minuchin. "Sal didn't have anything like a systems perspective then, but he was looking at the kids' problems in nontraditional ways. He was more interested in their life space and cultural inheritance than in psychiatric diagnosis."

Yet, despite his reservations about traditional psychiatry, Minuchin returned to the United States in 1954 to begin psychoanalytic training at the William Alanson White Institute in New York. Why? "At the time, it seemed like the thing to do if you were an exploratory and searching kind of psychiatrist," says Minuchin. Over the next few years, Minuchin took a variety of jobs while he continued his analytic training.

Eventually he heard about a job working as an intake psychiatrist at a residential school for inner-city delinquents called Wiltwyck. He was hired by the school's medical director, Dick Auerswald, who was struck by Minuchin's ideas about the possibility of working with whole families. "I was interested in studying families at that time, but only as a way of understanding the individual kid," says Auerswald.

"Like everyone else back then, I was thrashing around trying to find something that worked, since everything I had been trained to do—child psychiatry, play therapy, psychoanalysis—had shown itself to be ridiculously ineffective with the tough inner-city kids we were seeing."

As he began to work with black families, Minuchin made an interesting discovery. With this group, it was clearly an advantage to be a stranger in a strange land. "I knew I was not an American white," says Minuchin. "So I was not guilty when I worked with black people. I didn't need to save them. That gave me the freedom of being rather straight."

At Wiltwyck, Minuchin began a close collaboration with Auerswald and Wiltwyck's executive director, Charles King. In 1959 their team, inspired by a Don Jackson article—the only family therapy article they had seen at that point—bought a one-way mirror and began observing families. In the beginning, they developed a three-stage approach. First, two therapists met with the whole family. Then, the parents would meet with one therapist and the children with another. Finally, everyone would reassemble to share information. "After a very short while, we realized that you really didn't need to have all those therapists," says Auerswald. In time, they developed a language for describing family structure and methods for getting families to directly alter their organization. "I suspect we focused so much on structure because the ghetto families we saw had so little of it—at least from our middle-class perspective," says Auerswald today.

In his eight years at Wiltwyck, Minuchin developed the foundation for all his later work with families. To many people, his success in developing a way of working with poor families is still Minuchin's outstanding achievement. Says Peggy Papp, "The thing I most admire about Sal is the way he developed techniques for helping those families when nobody else could." It was the work at Wiltwyck, particularly his description of that project in *Families of the Slums*, that first earned Minuchin widespread recognition. "The field supported us," says Minuchin. "We gave speeches. We became flagbearers."

IN 1965 MINUCHIN LEFT WILTWYCK TO TAKE OVER the directorship of the Philadelphia Child Guidance Clinic. It took him three years to transform a traditional child guidance agency into a model family therapy clinic. Along the way, he began to develop his reputation for being demanding and arrogant.

"A lot of his tough image came from his weekly seminars," says Braulio Montalvo, an important member of the Wiltwyck team who accompanied Minuchin to Philadelphia. "People would present their case, and within five minutes he would assess what you were doing, and if he didn't like it, he would go hard into you. Heads would roll, but the assumption was clear—your head would grow back."

Minuchin invited Jay Haley, then a family researcher in California, to join him and develop the clinic's family orientation. "Sal was very intense as an administrator," says Haley. "He used to come out of his office every so often and shout, 'There are too

many people in the halls. There are too many people in the halls. Why aren't they working?' and then go back in. He kept coming up with new ideas and starting programs. Then he'd hand them over to someone else and start something new. That's the way he works."

Among the programs Minuchin started was the Institute for Family Counseling, a training program for community paraprofessionals in which, along with Haley and Montalvo, he developed the essential techniques of live supervision. Haley's popular text, *Problem-Solving Therapy*, first began to take form as a syllabus for trainees in that project.

Probably Minuchin's most lauded achievement at the clinic was his development of treatment techniques with psychosomatic families, particularly those of anorectics. As with much of Minuchin's work, his approach with anorectics developed out of his willingness to take on an immediate challenge.

Haley remembers Minuchin's first luncheon session with an anorectic and her family this way:

"It was the family of a little 9-year-old girl who was starving to death. They came in to talk with Sal, and she was a model child. Then lunchtime came, and instead of breaking, Minuchin decided to send out for food for everyone. All hell broke loose. As her parents prodded her to eat, the angelic little girl turned into a screaming monster. So Sal had the parents try to feed her. And of course they failed, and then he took over. He insisted that she absolutely had to eat. Finally, the little girl agreed to have a peanut butter cracker from the machine in the lobby. Someone went to get it, and she ate it. It turns out she had seen the machine on her way into the building and had asked then if she could have a cracker. But her father had told her, 'No, it'll spoil your lunch.'"

As word of Minuchin's success with the families of anorectics, and later diabetics, spread, other such cases found their way to him. Projects developed and teams assembled to further explore new areas

opened up by Minuchin's clinical flair and willingness to work with high-risk populations.

In 1974 *Families and Family Therapy* was published and soon became the field's most popular text. It was the perfect book for its time—a clearly written presentation of the ideas about change and families that were just beginning to catch on in agencies around the country. "There was a great leap in Sal's international reputation at that point," says Pat Minuchin. "I think that's when the superstar aura developed. The invitations to speak and train began to come in from all over." *Families and Family Therapy*, which has been translated into 11 languages, remains the best-selling book ever about family therapy, with sales of more than 100,000 in the United States alone.

In 1975 Minuchin stepped down as the director of the Philadelphia Child Guidance Clinic, which had by then grown from a staff of 12 to one of more than 300 with an annual budget of $3,000,000. Characteristically, Minuchin, having developed a project to the point that it was stabilized, decided to move on. "I am good at running a small grocery," he says today, explaining his decision. "I am not good at running a department store."

After resigning as director of the clinic, Minuchin served as the head of its training center until 1981. Since then he has pursued interests beyond the family therapy field—most notably writing several plays and, together with his wife, conducting research into the functioning of normal families. In his latest book, *Family Kaleidoscope*, Minuchin attempts to move the discussion of family systems thinking beyond the professional community to reach a more general readership.

TODAY, MINUCHIN, WHOSE WORK HAS LONG BEEN so central to family therapy, has changed his relationship to the field. He regularly gives workshops around the country and conducts a small training program in New York City, where he now

lives, but he seems more interested in providing a commentary on the field as a whole rather than in presenting his own approach. He now discusses the "deceptive simplicity" of his own previous teaching about family therapy with a curious objectivity. He speaks as one who is no longer at the helm of a field, but as a bemused observer—more philosopher than bullfighter.

But as Minuchin has moved into the position of observer, his work has become central to others in the field in quite a different way. A growing number of people in the field questioning the implicit sexual politics in family therapy practice have accused Minuchin of reinforcing sex stereotypes. "Minuchin sees himself as modeling the male executive functions, forming alliances, most typically with the father, and through competition, rule-setting and direction, demanding that the father resume control of the family and exert leadership as Minuchin leads and controls the session," writes feminist Rachel Hare-Mustin.

In a July/August 1984 *Networker* article, Deborah Luepnitz offered an even more pointed criticism of Minuchin's model of family functioning. "A great deal of conservative ideology is couched in serene scientific prose," writes Luepnitz. "One wonders if Minuchin believes, as did Lidz and Parsons, that husbands must perform the 'instrumental' role and wives the 'expressive' role, that children will suffer if this is not the case."

Jay Haley believes that such objections to Minuchin's work miss an important point. "I don't think I ever saw a mother who felt offended by him at the end of a session—no matter how hard a time he gave them early on," says Haley. "A feminist observer might object, but not the woman herself. That's a crucial difference.

"There's also another issue that's been overlooked. Sal did a tremendous amount of work with poor and black families in which mothers got the welfare check and the man was out of work. A lot of his focus was to get the man more integrated into the family. These men had no power, and the therapists tended to support them. Sometimes I think that if the government had given welfare to men, Minuchin's therapy might have developed very differently."

What, then, are we to conclude about Minuchin's contribution to family therapy? How has his work shaped the development of the field? "More than anyone, Minuchin established the legitimacy of family therapy within psychiatry," observes Phil Guerin of Westchester's Center for Family Learning. "Without Minuchin, family therapy might have stayed at the Batesonian level of intellectuality or the Ericksonian level of mystery," says Cloé Madanes.

"Sal has provided theoretical and organizational leadership in so many areas," says Braulio Montalvo. But, perhaps addressing the aspect of Minuchin's work clinicians respond to most immediately, he says, "I think the part that I always related to most was the way he could look at a family problem and quickly see three or four angles that wouldn't suggest themselves to the conventional group."

"Maybe the most important thing about Sal's work is the way it serves as an example to other therapists," says Marianne Walters, whom Minuchin hired to work with him at the Institute for Family Counseling in Philadelphia in the early 1970s. "Many people get so focused on the air of authority he conveys in therapy. But his special gift is how he is able to be both in charge *and* vulnerable. He wants so much for what happens in a session to matter. When he needs to, he can take the risk of not distancing himself. It is the special way he shares his vulnerability with families—not just his command of technique—that, I think, is the mystery of his therapy."

In the interview that follows, Minuchin discusses the role of therapy in the power structure of modern society and surveys the intellectual fiefdoms that shape thinking within the family field. He also responds to recent criticisms of his work and explains

what he means by "the failure of family therapy."

Q: *There seems to be far more of a mystique surrounding the leaders in family therapy than the prominent teachers of the other therapies. In fact, people like Thomas Szasz have criticized family therapy for being dominated by a group of "gurus" and their followers. Do you see yourself as a guru?*

MINUCHIN: The literal translation of the word "guru" is teacher. From that viewpoint, I am a guru. But I don't have followers or disciples. If you look around, you will see that the people I trained are doing very different things than I do. They have moved on. Most of them are not part of my life, and I am not part of theirs. I think Virginia Satir has disciples, but she is an exception. The Milan group has students, not disciples. The same is true of Jay Haley. Certainly Carl Whitaker doesn't have any disciples.

Q: *So why is the word "guru" used so often to describe the leaders in family therapy?*

MINUCHIN: I think family therapy is a field with many people who do not shy away from the pleasure of playing to audiences and being charismatic. This is a field with a lot of very narcissistic people who enjoy that game. But from playing to audiences to gathering disciples is a very big jump.

Q: *A couple of years ago, R. D. Laing said that he didn't write about family therapy techniques because he was afraid of the uses to which they might be put. He saw the practice of family therapy within public agencies as a means of extending the power of the state over people. You have written a great deal about therapy techniques. What do you think of Laing's concern?*

MINUCHIN: I think Laing is right and, of course, wrong also. Today power is no longer exerted in the autocratic manner that it was in the time of the kings. There is a delegation of power to institutions, mental health institutions among them. So we are part of systems of control and stability. Places like hospitals and departments of welfare maintain the status quo. That is just the way things are. Laing is

correct to see it with despair. But one can also see it as an opportunity to produce change. The question for me as a systems tinkerer is, can we find ways to transform these institutions? Are we up to the task?

Q: *I know you read Thomas Szasz's comments about you in an interview the* Networker *(July/August 1984) ran. Szasz criticized family therapists as "meddlers" who try to tell people how to live their lives. What do you think?*

MINUCHIN: There is no doubt we are meddlers, and so is Thomas Szasz. At any point in which we do therapy, we are meddling with people's lives. But in one sense, Szasz is right. When we changed our concepts and moved from the insight-oriented therapy of "what is" to the construction of alternative realities, we clearly began to meddle more.

Q: *And who gives us the right to meddle like that?*

MINUCHIN: The contract. We establish a contract with people.

Q: *Which is almost entirely unstated.*

MINUCHIN: No. There is payment; therefore it is stated. It is a perfectly legal contract. People come to us and say, "We are in trouble." The therapist says, "I am an expert in meddling in people's lives." And they say, "Okay, will you help us out?" And the therapist says, "Yes. And I will charge you for that." And they say, "Fine." So there is a very explicit contract. We are paid to expand the reality of people who are stuck.

Q: *You keep referring to some sort of clear contract between therapist and client, but it's usually a very tangled contract, to say the least. Doesn't the therapist almost always have to resist the initial contract the family offers?*

MINUCHIN: Of course. People come in and say, "Change him so that I can be a better parent," or "Change her so that my life is better." And I say, "Okay, let's talk about that." And we develop an alternative way of looking. This new agreement will be woven out of the family experience and will be expressed in the language of the family. But it will be framed by my epistemology, and it will contain

hope and the seed of change.

Q: *We've been talking a lot about contracts, but I've heard you say that therapy has nothing to do with ethics. What does that mean?*

MINUCHIN: Well, I was referring to techniques of therapy. For instance, to unbalance a couple, I may say to one member, "You are right," and to the other, "You are wrong." And I know I am distorting reality by my punctuation. Nevertheless, I do it because using this distorted reality may produce the intensity necessary for expansion. But a person who is versed in ethics would say to me, "You are unfair." And I would have to agree.

Q: *So the technique of therapy doesn't have much to do with ethics. Does it have anything to do with science?*

MINUCHIN: We are a soft science—like anthropology or sociology—but a science nevertheless. We have made observations of families in different circumstances. We know quite a bit about the predictable patterns that evolve in the life cycle.

But I think changing people is an art. It involves a dialogue between two idiosyncratic organisms—the family and the therapist. This dialogue is always meandering, and it is always full of trial and error. After all these years, there are few family problems that I have not seen a hundred times already. But my dialogue with each family will have to be idiosyncratic. I must take my generic interventions and tailor them within this new encounter. That is the art of therapy.

Q: *You say that there aren't many gurus in family therapy, but you seem to think there are quite a few castle proprietors. Let me read your description of how family therapy has become institutionalized:*

"The old-timers knew that their private truths were only partial, and when they met around a cup of coffee, they gossiped about the beginnings and shared their uncertainties and hopes. But lo and behold, their institutions grew and they needed large buildings to accommodate all their students. Slowly, before anyone realized it, the buildings became castles, with turrets and draw-bridges, and even watchmen in the towers. The castles were very expensive and they had to justify their existence. Therefore, they demanded ownership of the total truth."

Recently you've become a kind of tour guide to these castles. In your presentations you seem to speak as much about other people's work as your own. So can we shift now to talking about some of the major castles in the field? What about your friend Carl Whitaker?

MINUCHIN: The basis of Carl's work is the existential concept that life is absurd. He says that people who believe in their particular reality are crazy. From that premise, he enters into dialogue with them. Whitaker's point of view is one that most people accept when they get older.

Ask Whitaker questions like, "Does life have a direction?" or "Does it have a goal?" and he will smile. He has developed a therapy in which he teases people to be in contact with their absurdity. He is a Don Quixote who challenges you to see that you are charging your own windmills. What he does with families is what he did when he was an individual therapist. But the difference is that he looks at the larger system now. And he shows its members the foolishness of believing that each one of them controls his own foolishness. I happen to agree with Whitaker's premise. I do it differently, but essentially, like him, I am a challenger of people's reality.

Q: *I've heard you say recently that you don't think Virginia Satir is a family therapist any longer. What do you mean by that?*

MINUCHIN: I think she has changed. It happens to many therapists that, as they grow older, they become less interested in changing individuals. They become philosophers or mystics. It happened to Eric Fromm and Wilhelm Reich. They move away from practice and toward an involvement with larger issues. This is where Virginia has gone. She has taken her concern with breakages of intimacy and gone on to consider how they occur on the larger stage of the world. So she has gone to all kinds of

places trying to help enemies get together—Arabs and Israelis, northern and southern Irish, and so on. She thinks that if she can help them tap into their positive affect, something will happen. She has always been concerned with issues of intimacy. Like a surgeon, she goes to areas of disconnectedness and tries to create different ways of contacting. But I think humans are complex organisms. Besides the positive affects—intimacy, cooperation, love, the need to be close and belong—there is also the wish to separate. There is anger and competitiveness and jockeying for power. I think her therapy, focused primarily on repairing the breakages of intimacy, is a very partial view.

Q: *In contrast to Satir's very expansive view of therapy, there's a group of approaches that you've dubbed the "minimalist schools." What are they?*

MINUCHIN: The most minimalist school is, of course, the Mental Research Institute in Palo Alto. The people from the other castles fish with big nets, but the people at MRI cast for one type of fish only; the rest they will throw away. They address themselves solely to the way in which people's solutions maintain their problems. Their goal seems to be to find the smallest intervention to produce the smallest effect. When I spoke with Paul Watzlawick recently, he impressed me, as always, with his erudition, but then he described himself as "a mechanic, not an artist" and said that "every family is unique." To which I replied that I see myself as an artist and have seen hundreds of families formally replicate each other. As you can see, there was not much common ground for a dialogue.

The other school that is concerned with keeping their meddling to the minimum, following Bateson, is the Milan group. In sheer numbers, they are probably the most important family therapy school in the world today.

Q: *Really?*

MINUCHIN: Oh, yes. The Milan approach is very big in Europe. It fits a European bias toward non-

intervention that, I think, is the result of their experience with Hitler and Nazi Germany. In Europe there is a great concern and respect for people's individual boundaries. The Milan school, with its approach of "don't change," with their hands-off, once-a-month type of intervention, fits this particular mood.

Q: *So you're saying it's a kind of counterfascist type of therapy.*

MINUCHIN: I think the positive connotation would be that it is a democratic, respectful therapy. And it is also appealing for other reasons. It has developed a very detailed method. There is one way of doing it. There is one way of interviewing—circular interviewing. There is one way of framing—that is positive connotation. There is a lot of hypothesizing, but there is one hypothesis that includes everything. It is very neat, and this gives the illusion of certainty—that there is one method.

The danger is that this very disciplined method becomes a prison. Some of the people who use this method seem to believe that only positive connotation is appropriate at any point: abuse, family violence—whatever. That is a trap, and here is where the castles begin to develop rigidities that handicap the development of a more scientific inquiry and, instead, encourage playing with words.

Q: *I've heard you do this kind of survey of the field several times now. You never discuss Murray Bowen's castle.*

MINUCHIN: Bowen is an early settler who introduced many significant ideas to the field: triangles and triangling, disruptive visits to your family, control of the emotional system, coaching. He also introduced genograms. And, of course, there is his focus on differentiation. Murray is one of the family therapists who focus more on the individual as a bio-psycho-social entity. And while I think his focus on the animal in us is useful, all his emphasis on differentiation is a throwback to rugged individualism. I think that it takes the invisible connections between

people and cuts them. People are always interdependent. Usually, the main issue in families is how we can be both a whole and a part. I like Arthur Koestler's term "holon" that connotes interdependence much more than Murray's Scale of Differentiation. I think in this, Murray and I are talking different languages.

Q: *How about Jay Haley? Here's somebody you worked with for 10 years at the Philadelphia Child Guidance Clinic. For a while, the two of you either shared the same castle or operated two separate castles under the same roof, depending on how you look at it. How do you distinguish your work from Haley's?*

MINUCHIN: My thinking was very influenced by my training as a child psychiatrist and my wife Pat's background in child development. When I began to think about families, I looked at them developmentally. That is what a lot of the structural approach was about—the description of families as complex systems and the transitions that families and their subsystems make through time. From that perspective, I developed a methodology of change.

Jay's point of view deals more with the immediate problem of change. When we were working at the clinic, it was not "structural" or "strategic" therapy. We were doing family therapy. We worked and developed things together. So opening up family conflict, a technique which I developed with the parents and children in the families of anorectics, reappears in Jay's work with psychotic adolescents. But we do define symptoms differently. For Jay, the symptom is a metaphor for family problems, and its removal produces systemic changes. For me, the symptom is the way family members position themselves around the symptom bearer; therefore, I challenge the family structure.

Jay and I worked together for 10 years. I learned a lot from him. I was also a student of Braulio Montalvo and of Carl Whitaker; I hear their voices as well. The terms "structural" and "strategic" appeared later. They were created to sell our products,

just as "Pierre Cardin" brands the buttock of all his jeans. But I am not a manufacturer anymore. I am not interested in finding new and more creative techniques for changing people. I am not trying to improve a product. Now I only take students who have trained with other people. I am a blender. I think it is time that we begin to see what encourages growth and what maintains homeostasis in the field.

Q: *These days you seem to have appointed yourself to be family therapy's ombudsman as well as its leading tour guide. You have begun to talk about "the future of family therapy." How has family therapy failed?*

MINUCHIN: Today we have hundreds of family therapy institutes around the world, which have trained thousands of people. At the same time, the institutions that serve people have remained unchanged.

Q: *So, unlike Thomas Szasz, you think family therapists haven't meddled enough?*

MINUCHIN: No, I think we have meddled only in a very narrow way. You see, the failure of family therapy has to do with its success. Today family therapy is taught in the universities. Many mental health agencies and hospitals have departments of family therapy. The psychiatric field has incorporated family therapy as a modality of treatment—without, of course, changing the diagnostic categories of individual patients. So, while it seemed we were succeeding, we were in fact co-opted. This is the way society works. It co-opted a movement that was challenging basic ways of thinking about human problems by making the movement official. Today there are even questions about family therapy on the child psychiatry boards. Now that's establishment.

Q: *Okay, but can you give me specific examples of the things that are happening that tell you that family therapy has not had the impact you might have wished?*

MINUCHIN: Of course. The other day there was an article on page 1 of the *New York Times* reporting that almost one in every five adult Americans has a mental disorder; the rates are about equal for men

and women. Apparently, the National Institute of Mental Health gave Dr. Darrel A. Regier a grant of around $20 million to test the mental status of 10,000 American adults. They then proceeded to examine them totally out of context. The editor of the *Archives of General Psychiatry* called this study "a landmark in the development of American contributions to the psychiatric knowledge base." I think it's a $20 million landmark of the failure of systems thinking.

Judith Wallerstein and Joan Kelly's research on children of divorce is another example of failure to change paradigms in the field. They describe the children mourning the breaking of the family, without seeing that the children's confusion and anxiety must be related not only to the loss of one family organization but also to the reforging of a new one. The structure of the juvenile courts, mental hospitals, departments of welfare, foster homes, and so on, has remained invulnerable to the puny challenges of systems epistemology.

The feminist movement has opened the ugly Pandora's box of wife abuse. But the solution it has moved to is saving the victims by dismembering the family. Many women's shelters prohibit entrance not only to the spouse of the victim but also to male therapists. On the news the other day, I saw that police in Seattle have started a program of the compulsory jailing of spouses involved in physical conflict as a more productive way of avoiding domestic violence. Whenever there is an indication that someone has been hurt, there must be an arrest. But the police are finding that they cannot so easily discriminate who is the victimizer.

Q: *Is the picture entirely gloomy?*

MINUCHIN: No, there are some interesting attempts to use family systems ideas in new ways. Don Block's new journal, *Family Systems Medicine*, is strategically trying to join arms with family medicine. Don is convinced that family therapists cannot change psychiatric thinking, so the best way to

change the medical paradigm is to forge an alliance between family therapists and family medical practitioners.

Certainly, divorce mediation is an area where family therapy influenced lawyers to think in new ways. Then there are the hospices, which have incorporated the idea that death is a family process.

Right now Pat and I are doing some work in the "Co-op" Hospital, a part of New York University Hospital, which is hospitalizing patients along with one family caregiver who then provides much of the nursing care. It is an interesting innovation in family care that family therapists should examine closely. The field is certainly not static. There are many explorations pointing toward important beginnings: Carlos Sluzki, among others, has attempted to synthesize techniques of different schools of family therapy; the attempts of a number of family therapists, including the Milan and Bowen schools, to understand and influence larger systems; the increasing interest in understanding normal families—all these are welcome indicators of change.

Q: *Isn't part of the problem of family therapy having greater influence that we haven't really been able to generate much data that says what we do is really effective? Where are the outcome studies that make the case for family therapy?*

MINUCHIN: The dissemination of information about developments in fields like family therapy follows tracks that are extremely complicated. I don't think that large societal changes are based on data. Data do not change ideologies.

Let me give you an example. When I was active in doing research, I thought differently. During the psychosomatic study that we did at the Philadelphia Child Guidance Clinic, I was absolutely convinced that people would be swayed by the empirical evidence. After all, we were reporting an 86 percent success rate. I was sure our work would transform the therapeutic approach to anorexia.

I know now that I was under the rationalistic

illusion that knowledge produces change. How did people respond to our findings? By defending their own paradigms. In response to new knowledge, there is always the question of how to maintain oneself doing the things one was trained in. It is a defensive position. Changing paradigms requires breaking the old schemas. And we have not been able to do that.

But let me tell you an Italian success story. About 10 years ago, the Italians passed a law saying that no psychotics could be hospitalized in a psychiatric hospital; all new admissions must be to regular hospitals. There was to be no more money given to build psychiatric hospitals.

That led to a crisis similar to what has happened here with the deinstitutionalization of patients from mental hospitals. How did the Italians handle that crisis? A large group of radical therapists from the '60s responded to the demands of families with psychotic members by training in family therapy. The mental health needs of the community were filled by a community-oriented family therapy. Maurizio Andolfi and Luigi Cancrini developed a type of training that contributed to the crystallization of what is probably the most powerful family therapy movement in the world. Of course, they were lucky in being supported by two of the most important institutions in Italy—the Communist party and the Catholic church. It would be important to think about the political institutions in this country that might facilitate a systemic viewpoint.

Q: *You have increasingly become a target of criticism for feminists within the family therapy field. They believe that your therapeutic tactics implicitly tend to place the blame for family problems on mothers and that the emphasis in your writing on the problems of "enmeshment" perpetuates a cultural stereotype of the engulfing mother. How do you respond to these criticisms?*

MINUCHIN: When people are exploring a new area, they often develop their ideas by polarizing. It seems to me that many of the creative women in

family therapy—like the group in the Women's Project—have selected me as part of a polarity as a way of developing and expanding their own point of view. I don't think they're right about my thinking, but if making me a foil is useful for them, it's okay.

Why have I become a target? I suppose part of it is my style as a therapist. I am intrusive, my interventions are challenging and intense, I am sometimes pushy, and I tend to encourage conflict in a manner that has been described as South American machismo. This is the most visible part of my style, but it's a very partial description. If you watch my sessions, you can just as well pick up tenderness, empathy, humor, a great respect for people's possibilities, an encouragement of growth and competence, optimism about new possibilities, an acceptance of limitations and frailty, a sense of the absurd, and so on. Since many of the people who criticize me are also my friends, who know my complexity as a therapist, it must be something else.

Perhaps they are focusing on an intervention I frequently make when working with families in which there is close proximity between mother and children, with a peripheral husband/father. This is a family organization frequently encountered in our culture. In this circumstance, I tend to use the father to separate the mother from the children. It is an intervention I find useful because it expands the father's function, shrinks the woman's concentration on the maternal, and creates new possibilities for her to function as a more complex, adult woman, and it introduces perturbation in the parental field. It is an operation which is only the beginning of a therapeutic dialogue. It will shift many times in the process, and it doesn't represent either a coalition of males or a political statement. But feminists have singled out this type of intervention as a skewed way of entering that supports male cultural stereotypes, because one could also enter by supporting the mother's challenge to the husband's disengagement. This is the approach the Women's Project supports, and I

think it's a useful expansion of the clinical repertory. But it isn't the only way.

If they're saying, "Viewing the mother as over-involved and the father as the potential separator is a skewed perspective reinforced by the masculine culture," they are right. If they are saying, "Minuchin uses that intervention frequently," they are also right. But if they're saying I am a knee-jerk chauvinist who doesn't understand the social context in which families live, they are wrong.

Q: *Not all the criticism of the emphasis on the concept of enmeshment in your work comes from women. In his* Networker *review of "Terms of Endearment," Frank Pittman writes, "Aurora and Emma are 'enmeshed,' a state anathema to most family therapists, many of whom don't seem to trust anything that goes on between mothers and children past the age of 12. . . . Contrary to our theories and warnings, most parents and children remain comfortably enmeshed and happy with it for a lifetime." Has the term "enmeshment" become such a bugaboo that it's outlived its usefulness?*

MINUCHIN: I think this term is more poetic than scientific. It describes a skewed version of something that always occurs. I use the word "enmeshment" to describe miscarriages of intimacy, as a way of saying, "Here are organisms that tend to sacrifice individuation to loyalty." Bernice Rosman operationalized it for the psychosomatic project, and it proved to be a useful tool in that research. I think Frank is right that it did become abused as a more general clinical term. But I don't have to defend that distortion.

Q: *As you look at the way family therapy is practiced today, what are the things that most disturb you?*

MINUCHIN: Many family therapists today are versed in techniques but don't understand families. Sometimes I see marvelous interventions that are incorrect because they are not related to a basic understanding of the family in a social context but only to the therapist's repertory of interventions. When I first began to teach family therapy, I did it with a deceptive simplicity. Today I talk a lot more about the complexities.

Q: *And you put much more emphasis on the experience—or lack of experience—of the therapist. You seem to like provoking your younger audiences by saying things like "therapists who don't have children themselves should not see families with children." I don't have children. Does that mean I shouldn't be a family therapist?*

MINUCHIN: No, but when you do family therapy with families with children, you will have to be aware that you have an experiential deficit. You will tend to think that parents should do better than they do. Being a parent is the ultimate training in humility; you cannot be a parent without failing. That knowledge of failure becomes part of your sinews. And when you work with families, you may sympathize with the children, but you will not blame parents for being merely human. Now, this doesn't mean you can't overcome your experiential deficit. It means you have to compensate in other ways. I say more and more these days that people must recognize that not everyone can work well with every family.

Q: *How do you apply that to yourself? Are your difficulties as a therapist related to your own experiential deficits?*

MINUCHIN: Of course. With my style, I tend to have difficulty joining with people who are slow or detached. I need a certain level of vitality to work with people; if it's not there, I may push them to a rhythm that they don't have. In terms of my own development, there was a period in which I was good at working with adolescents and enjoyed it very much. Maybe at this point it would bore me. As I grow older, I am finding there are new groups with whom I work well. I am good at working with people who are seriously ill or have been through catastrophe, because I am familiar with that. I empathize, and I can respond. I do not overempathize. I do not shy away from death.

When I was younger, I had more of a sense of

commitment, and I would accept difficult cases. Today I am more easily distracted. I have less to give. What I am saying to other people applies to myself as well; it is very important to know at what points you are a good convincer, and with whom.

Q: *I once heard you say that you had reached a "plateau of competence" in work with families and were looking for new challenges. How did you go about that?*

MINUCHIN: In 1981 my wife, Pat, and I took a sabbatical year in England. We approached it in a very playful way, as an exploration of incompetence. We decided to go into areas in which we did not know very much. Pat decided to study the oboe, an instrument she had never played before, and I decided to write plays. I'd always thought that my way of doing therapy had the elements of playwriting. But I discovered very early that it was too late to enter a new field with different rules, techniques and skills. I would meet with young people in theatrical workshops and envy the way they could conceive the stage. It was a different way of viewing and experiencing—a new language to me. I enjoyed writing plays, maybe more than anything that I have ever done. There was a great sense of excitement. Probably, I will do it some other time again. But I did not confirm my fantasy that I was really a closet playwright—that I could just open the door and all this wonderful stuff would come out. It just didn't work.

Q: *But you have written a new book about families and family therapy,* Family Kaleidoscope, *that seems very different from what you have done up to this point. What's your goal with this book?*

MINUCHIN: My fantasy right now—one I share with people like Jay Haley and Helm Sterling in Germany—is that we can write to reach a wider audience. I know more about family therapy than Janet Malcolm does; could I reach the audiences that she reaches—the people who read *The New Yorker* and run the world? If I could reach an audience of policymakers, could I communicate certain important issues in such a way that they would question some of the premises that they hold as truth? This is why I wrote *Family Kaleidoscope.*

Since it is a book for the general public, it also gave me the freedom to use a poetic style that I suppressed when I was writing for other therapists.

Q: *The time might be right. Family rhetoric has become part of the official rhetoric of both political parties. Have you sent a copy to Governor Cuomo?*

MINUCHIN: I live in New York City, so I think I will start with Mayor Koch. My fantasy is that one of his advisers will say, "Here is a guy that is talking about child abuse differently. Should we be inviting Minuchin to be a member of the Mayor's Commission for Child Abuse?" Today what happens is that when these people come to us, they don't want consultation at the level of policy-making. They want us to train people to do family therapy. And this shows exactly where family therapy is today. They think we are good at making small changes, but they cannot see that we have a theoretical tool they could use.

Q: *So with the book just out, you are waiting to see what happens.*

MINUCHIN: Yes, and if I am "discovered," I will be sure to tell the readers of the *Networker*. ■

A FROG'S-EYE VIEW OF THE WORLD

AN INTERVIEW WITH HUMBERTO MATURANA

BY THE TIME WE BEGIN SCHOOL, ACCORDING TO Chilean biologist Humberto Maturana, it is already too late. In the very process of learning to talk, we swallow our species' party line. As we divide the world into subjects and objects—into categories of things that act and those that are acted upon—we insidiously indoctrinate ourselves. Unthinkingly, we come to believe that the structure of our language actually mirrors the structure of the world. In doing that, Maturana insists, our whole culture has taken a dizzying series of philosophical wrong turns. What's worse, we have even come to confuse our wayward state with something we have learned to call "knowledge" and "truth."

Over the past several years, some family therapists have tried to apply Maturana's ideas about language and the ways living systems organize themselves to understanding how families operate and what takes place in therapy. Maturana's name has begun to pop up repeatedly in journal articles and on the program of family therapy conferences. In between chores like filling out reports and grumbling about their caseloads, Maturana enthusiasts

have made agencies around the country unlikely staging grounds for rarefied philosophical dialogues about questions like:

—Can one person "control" another?

—Does any model of cause and effect, circular or otherwise, provide a reliable account of how families work?

—Is the therapist's view of the family any more real than that of the family's own members?

To all of these conundrums, Maturana's work, based on the idea that science itself has nothing to do with "objectivity," offers a resounding and unequivocal, "No."

Actually, Maturana is only one among a group of contemporary thinkers—including cyberneticians like Ernst von Glasersfeld, Heinz von Foerster and biologist Francisco Varela, among others—whose work, like that of Gregory Bateson before them, poses a challenge to the basic tenets of the Western scientific tradition. Explaining the basis of this challenge, Lynn Hoffman, author of *The Foundations of Family Therapy*, says, "Among many scientists, the whole concept of objectivity has been superseded by

the constructivist view—the idea that an observer community decides what reality is." In his book *The Invented Reality*, an introduction to constructivist thinking, Paul Watzlawick has written, "Any so-called reality is—in the most immediate and concrete sense—the construction of those who believe they have discovered and investigated it. In other words, that which is supposedly found is an invention whose inventor is unaware of his act of invention."

Biologist Maturana's contribution has been to try to bring these relativistic notions, long familiar to physicists, into the mainstream of the life sciences. "Scientific observation is bound to the biology of the observer," says Maturana. "Science is not a way of knowing a world that exists apart from us, but a particular way of living together."

Even those who profess themselves enamored of Maturana's ideas admit that his writing is very heavy going. For Maturana, words—with their power to confer objective status on perceptions—are the adversary, creating a mine field that must be navigated with the utmost circumspection. Accordingly, his language is agonizingly abstract and circuitous, filled with seemingly endless redundancies, constantly circling back to reiterate underlying assumptions, as in this excerpt from *The Biology of Language: The Epistemology of Reality*: "The organization of a system defines it as a composite unity and determines its properties as such a unity by specifying a domain in which it can interact (and, hence, be observed) as an unanalyzable whole endowed with constitutive properties. . . . In contrast, the structure of a system determines the space in which it exists as a composite unity that can be perturbed through the interactions of its components, but the structure does not determine its properties as a unity."

Maturana talks very much the way he writes, but in person he conveys a sense of intellectual excitement that doesn't survive the transcription of his ideas to the printed page. While he lectures, Maturana, who has the soulful eyes of a scraggly-bearded Charlie Chaplin, is in constant motion, as if tracking the internal logic that often escapes his listeners. What comes across is his absolute conviction that what he is saying is momentous—that no one has ever so carefully thought through the issues he is addressing.

He believes that he has created a "metatheory" that, among other things, provides a way of unifying all the disparate theoretical schools of family therapy. Maturana contends his theory offers a general way of understanding the essential principles underlying the functioning of systems as diverse as an amoeba, a pack of wolves and the board of directors of IBM.

Some family therapists, while willing to concede that Maturana's views as a biologist are provocative and interesting, are less certain that he has very much to say to them. Comments one senior family therapist, "Maturana's work is tremendously over-inclusive. He is in search of a global, universal truth. The small, piddling lives of people do not seem to interest him. When he talks as a biologist, he is on safe ground. But I do not think that he has very much to say that is relevant to family therapy." For others, however, like systems theorist Paul Dell, whose own writing is largely responsible for drawing family therapists' attention to Maturana's work, Maturana's ideas have far-reaching implications for the family field. As Dell, director of the Eastern Virginia Family Therapy Institute, has written, "[Maturana's] breakthrough in understanding living systems . . . is comparable in magnitude to Einstein's theory of relativity."

MATURANA HIMSELF IS CAREFUL TO IDENTIFY HIS work not as philosophy or cybernetics but as biology. He attributes the direction his work has taken to a famous experiment he collaborated on in the late 1950s while on a postgraduate fellowship at Massachusetts Institute of Technology (MIT). The experiment's report, "What the Frog's

HUMBERTO MATURANA

Eye Tells the Frog's Brain," cowritten with Jerome Lettvin and the pioneering cybernetician Warren McCullough, has since become assigned reading in countless introductory psychology courses. But at the time it first appeared, Maturana claims, "it transformed neurophysiology."

In the process of studying the frog's retina, the MIT team discovered that the frog's eye consisted of whole sets of specialized cells. Among these were some asymmetrical edge receptors that could respond to flies moving across the frog's field of vision from left to right but not from right to left. It was as if the various structures in the frog's eye each had a "mind of its own." Perception was not a matter of a picture of the world somehow coming in and recording itself in the frog's brain. The frog had no access to the reality of the world but only to reality as filtered through its sensory apparatus.

The MIT experiment offered neurophysiologists a new kind of metaphor for understanding how perception takes place. "It put a gigantic question mark on the distinction we draw between perception and illusion," Maturana says today. Instead of perception being understood on the model of a photographic camera conveying information to a receptor, a shift was made to see the organism as an informationally closed system that never "takes in" information from outside in any direct way. Rather, what it perceives is always determined by the nature of its own structure. According to Maturana, the MIT experiment challenged biologists to regard the organism as something like an airline pilot making an instrument landing in bad weather, who lines up readings on his own panel and behaves accordingly. There is no direct reference to what is "outside." It is as if the world gives us a vague bump on the head, and we compute from that.

"After this experiment, neurophysiologists could no longer talk about frogs striking at flies," says Robert Shaw, director of the Family Institute of Berkeley. "Instead, when a certain retinal organization takes place, the frog strikes. To translate that to the realm of human beings would be like saying people at a party don't react to each other but to the next set of configurations in their nervous system. That's quite a shift for most of us."

After the publication of "What the Frog's Eye Tells the Frog's Brain," Maturana found himself suddenly elevated from the lowly status of a fledgling Ph.D. to something as close as one can get to celebrity status in the academic world of neurophysiology. Although barely 30 years old, he was offered full professorships at several medical schools. But instead of staying in this country, he chose to return to his native Chile to teach at the University of Santiago—even though he knew it would be impossible to obtain the kind of equipment he would need there to continue to be in the forefront of neurophysiological research.

ANDREA MALONEY SHARA

Nevertheless, once back in Chile, Maturana began doing research on color vision. He was intrigued by the phenomena of visual illusions—that, for example, when white and red light shine on an object, people will see green—even though, spectroscopically, green is not *out there*. In his research, Maturana began to look at color vision as the name for an operation of our nervous system rather than a form of information taken in from the environment. This research crystallized his thinking about regarding living systems as closed entities.

"Maturana is not saying that living systems are unresponsive," says Jorge Colapinto, a supervisor at the Philadelphia Child Guidance Clinic. "It's that we don't process stimuli from the environment the way we thought. The organism functions primarily to keep its organization intact." Since that time, in a series of books and academic papers, Maturana has been meticulous in developing this position and building a general theory of living systems that has moved far beyond the neurophysiology lab.

What are the implications of Maturana's thinking for family therapists? "When you talk to people about Maturana, you tend to get one of two reactions," says Robert Shaw. "People say either 'I don't understand' or, if they are already thinking in the way Maturana is, they say, 'There's nothing new here.' Personally, I find his work fascinating. His thinking completely breaks out of the subject/object split that we live in."

Maturana critic Jorge Colapinto is more skeptical. "Family therapy has always been split between people who are active interventionists and those who think the therapist should not act as an agent of change. Maturana's point of view has been used to provide support for people opposed to the active interventionists. They take him to be saying, 'Human systems are what they are. They do not respond to outside attempts to influence them, only to their own internal perturbations.' With this interpretation, Maturana has become part of a turning

away in the field from fighting in the trenches and dealing with the social environment. The focus today is on changing cognitive concepts rather than on people interacting with the world."

For Lynn Hoffman, however, Maturana's viewpoint is basic to understanding the process of "helping." "He reminds us that we're really all E.T.s to each other, that we can't just assume we know each other's structure," says Hoffman. "The scientists in Spielberg's film simply assumed that E.T. was built the same way they were. So they hooked him up to their machines and, in their efforts to help, almost destroyed him. I wonder if that's what we do sometimes with families."

BEYOND WHATEVER PROFESSIONAL IMPLICATIONS it may or may not have, the world Maturana presents to us is a disturbing one. Each person is unalterably imprisoned within the bubble of his or her perceptions. And, while we may fantasize about getting "outside" ourselves, Maturana insists that any "outside" we might get to would be just as "inside" as the place from where we began.

"I don't know if you can live in the kind of world Maturana shows us in which we're all observers, engaged in 'structural coupling,' commenting on some unknowable ground *out there*," says Shaw. "We all live in the tension between the solitary, isolated point of view Maturana depicts and our life in the culture to which we assign 'reality.' As for me, although I am very impressed with his work, I wouldn't want to continually conceive life the way Maturana does. But maybe I'm too Jewish. I like to be embroiled."

In the interview that follows, conducted in the fall of 1984 at the annual meeting of the American Society for Cybernetics, Maturana responds to some of the criticism directed at his work and discusses the implications of his theory for family therapy.

Q: *You are a biologist, and your presentations are*

concerned with things like the color vision of pigeons and what happens in the retinas of frogs. But some people are claiming that you have some very important things to say to family therapists. Why should family therapists be interested in your work?

MATURANA: This I don't know. That is their responsibility, not mine. But if you ask me what *I* think about the interest of family therapists in my work, I would say that some are finding that I provide a theoretical and epistemological framework within which much of their practice can be explained or validated.

Q: *How can adopting your view help family therapists?*

MATURANA: Systems theory first enabled us to recognize that all the different views presented by the different members of a family had some validity, but systems theory implied that these were different views of the same system. What I am saying is different. I am *not* saying that the different descriptions that the members of a family make are different views of the *same* system. I am saying that there is no one way which the system is, that there is no absolute, objective family. I am saying that for each member there is a different family and that each of these is absolutely valid.

Q: *How is understanding that helpful to the practitioner?*

MATURANA: By accepting this, the therapist refuses to take sides with anyone. The therapist realizes that each family member is acting in sincerity with the system that he brings forth in his or her description. Furthermore, understanding this gives the therapist freedom to allow the system to transform, to disintegrate, to become something else, without the belief that what happens is his doing or that he must help the family to become what it should be.

Q: *From my understanding of the history of family therapy, what you're saying doesn't sound like a new perspective.*

MATURANA: I do not pretend that this is a new

perspective for family therapy. Actually, I have no responsibility for what happens in family therapy. But I do have a theory of knowledge which shows that the different families that the different members of a family live in are not different views of the same family but legitimate families in their own right.

Q: *Nevertheless, there is a message when you present that something very new and startling is being said. But when I hear you, I hear ideas I have read about in Gregory Bateson and Thomas Kuhn, among others.*

MATURANA: So you don't hear me.

Q: *So maybe I don't hear you. Where is the you that is distinguished from these other voices?*

MATURANA: First of all, Bateson and I do not superimpose. There is some intersection, but we do not superimpose. If you read Immanuel Kant and read me, you will find that Kant and I intersect but do not superimpose, and so on and so forth. What I am saying does not arise from taking some from Kant, some from Bateson, some from this, some from that. It is something that arises as a whole, which has certain elements which resemble certain other people's work because they handled similar questions.

Q: *Taken as a whole, then, how would you define what is distinctive about your point of view?*

MATURANA: I take the problem of objectivity seriously. If you read Bateson, you discover that sometimes he rejects the notion of objectivity and sometimes he operates within it. What do I do? I say I am going to put objectivity in parentheses. So I am taking a clear stand from the very beginning. I do not shift back and forth. If you find that I have a language of objects, this is so because language entails the generation of objects. This I cannot avoid. Nobody can avoid it because object generation is constitutive to language. But the point is that I am always consistent and never use the notion of objectivity in order to support my arguments. This is a central point in what I do and say. Indeed, I know

that if I confuse the situation, whatever I say after the confusion is not valid. Now that is new. Not in the sense that people have not done something like that before, but in the sense that I explicitly acknowledge the biological impossibility of making any statement about an objective reality.

The other thing that is completely new is that I take both the observer and language at the same time as instrument and as problem. To my knowledge, you don't find anywhere, either in philosophy or in biology, a theory that says that we are already in language when we human beings attempt as observers to explain language as a biological phenomenon. Furthermore, nobody has seriously claimed, as I do, that it is only in language that we are observers. This is why I say everything said is said by an observer. At the same time, this is why language and being in language as observers are *both* the instrument for the analysis and the phenomena that have to be explained.

I am interested in what happened with us in our history as living systems that we became languaging animals. We are in language, we live through language and we *do* language as we live. How does this occur and how did it come to be? That is what has to be explained.

But, you know, I do not understand your difficulty with what I am saying. [Laughs.] I think there is some idea or notion you are holding on to, or that you are defending, that is getting in the way. I would like to understand what is your difficulty. Do you want to know what is novel or is unique about what I am saying?

Q: *Yes, definitely.*

MATURANA: Okay, what is novel in what I am saying is that I start by accepting that we cannot experientially distinguish between perception and illusion. I recognize that cognition cannot be something which allows us to say things that are independent from us. Now, of course, as a philosophical position about the problem of reality and objectivity this sounds familiar and not new. What is new is that I am speaking as a biologist, not as a philosopher. As a biologist, I am saying that cognition never yields knowledge *about* things. Instead, knowledge is the manner of being.

What do I mean by this? If you ask yourself how you assess knowledge, you will discover that everybody assesses knowledge only in one way, by observing whether the person whose knowledge one wants to assess can perform adequate action in a domain specified by the questions that one makes. If you want to know whether someone knows how to play the piano, what do you do? You say, "There is a piano. Please play."

Now, if you accept what the person does as adequate piano playing, you say that the person "knows." If I come to you and say, "I am a biologist," then you ask me to perform biology which, by the way, is what you are doing now. So what is my performance? My performance is to act as a biologist in front of you. If, after seeing me or listening to me, you say that my performance is adequate in the domain of what you consider biology to be, you say, "Yes, he knows biology."

This is the manner in which we assess knowledge. So I say knowledge is that which we bring forth by the manner we assess it. Knowledge is adequate action in a domain specified by a questioner. Nobody has looked at knowledge in this manner because knowledge has always been considered a something about something that is independent of the knower. This is why people say knowledge must be knowledge about something. I am saying, "Knowledge is *never* about something. Knowledge is being in some manner." So you understand the difference, or not?

Q: *I think so. Knowledge is not my finding out about Humberto Maturana, at this point. You are saying I am measuring your performance against a standard of evaluation that is internal to me.*

MATURANA: Yes, but I want you to listen to the

conceptual shift involved in what I say. If I say I am a musician in the standard way, I mean that I know about music, that I can say things about such a thing that is *there,* independent of me, which is music, because I conceive knowledge as knowing *about* something. In our usual view of knowledge there must be a content to it, something that knowledge somehow embraces and reveals. What I am saying, however, is something completely different. I am saying that knowledge is never about something. I am saying that knowledge is adequate action in a domain of existence, that knowledge is a manner of being, that knowledge has no content because knowledge *is* being.

Q: *It reminds me of old, philosophic quarrels about the mind/body distinction. Traditional Western philosophy saw mind and body as being in separate domains. Many contemporary philosophers no longer make that distinction. You are saying knowledge and the objective world are not separate domains.*

MATURANA: There is no objective world. So there are certain questions that do not arise.

Q: *Right now I am the interviewer, you are the interviewee, and I am trying to learn about you. I am trying to gain knowledge about you and how you think, and what the implications of your work are. So how do you define what I am trying to do with you in your terms?*

MATURANA: We are in a conversation, and to be in a conversation means to be in a situation of recurrent interaction until we enter into a domain of complete coordination of conduct, and then we separate. In that process, our ongoing structural changes will follow a congruent course as drifts contingent to our interactions. And if, in these courses of structural change, you change in a manner such that we remain in congruent behaviors but you stop asking me questions in relation to this subject, then I shall say that you understood what I said. And you certainly would say the same. I would think, "He understood what I said, because I do not hear more questions."

Q: *So you would replace the notion that I am gaining knowledge with the idea that my structure is transformed in some way.*

MATURANA: Mine, too.

Q: *Good, glad to know that. I think I understand the alternative view that you are offering me. But what is the advantage of adopting your view?*

MATURANA: None. It is not the problem of advantage.

Q: *But what does that open up for me? What possibilities does your view create?*

MATURANA: I don't know, you will find out. Maybe nothing. The possibilities that are opened to you by an adequate understanding of the phenomenon of language depend on you, not on me or what I say.

Q: *Do you feel that people understand what you are trying to explain?*

MATURANA: I am a biologist, and all the members of the audiences are expert biologists. I connect with them in the experiential biological domain. Even though they do not completely understand, they realize that whatever I am saying has to do with them. This is why they don't dismiss it. They don't leave. Last night I spoke for an hour and a half, and most people stayed.

Q: *What does that say to you?*

MATURANA: That tells me that what I am saying has to do with *them,* because if this were not the case they would have left.

Q: *Some did leave. Those people concluded it was not for them?*

MATURANA: Yes. Those people found out either that it has nothing to do with them or that it has so much to do with them that they cannot tolerate it because it would require from them an epistemological shift they are unwilling to make. So yesterday some people left. But I would say the least left because what I was saying had nothing to do with them. Actually, I would be daring to say no one left because what I said had nothing to do with them.

Those that left either left because they had other pressing errands or because what I was saying was so strongly challenging that they could not stand it.

Q: *I think some people left because the room was hot.*

MATURANA: This may be the other pressing errand—to get some more air or whatever to do so means for them.

Q: *As you have contact with people who have listened to you, what are the biggest misunderstandings they have of your work?*

MATURANA: If you will allow me to say, I don't think there is an element of misunderstanding. There is a fundamental refusal to accept the consequences of what I am saying.

Q: *You think people get it. They understand.*

MATURANA: They get the fundamental thing. The fundamental thing is the epistemological shift, and they do not like this. Nobody likes it. Not even I the first time I discovered that I had to make that shift.

Q: *I know you work with some family therapists in Chile. What are the kinds of questions that they ask you?*

MATURANA: A while ago, Carlos Sluzki was visiting Carmen Luz Mendez and Fernando Condon, friends of mine who operate an institute of family therapy in Santiago and with whom I collaborate. As we were talking, I said that one of the first things I would want to find out from a "family" that comes to therapy is what its members sincerely want to conserve, because that would tell me what indeed, if anything, defines them as components of a family. They all thought that was interesting because it entailed a shift of attention from change to conservation which, for them at least, was novel.

Now, why was I interested in what the members of a family want to conserve? I wasn't interested in that, because if I know what the people wish to conserve, I know their domain of possible change, and I can interact with them accordingly. You see, if one is a member of a system, one is a member of a cognitive domain, and one is always terrified of leaving that domain because all others seem like an illusion.

So when a "family" consults, you have here a group of people who find themselves unhappy as they generate with their behaviors the particular family that they claim they are, and they are unable to behave differently because this is the only way they presently can be as they come together. Or, in other words, the members of a family become so as they generate the family through their behavior, and if they stop behaving as they do, the family disintegrates and they lose what they conserve by being members of that family. What the members of a family risk with the disintegration of the family is the loss of identity, the loss of the risk-free flow of existence in a particular domain

Q: *Let's shift a little bit to you as a human being embodying a way of thinking in your own personal life. In your daily life, what has been the hardest obstacle for you in being consistent with the set of beliefs you have been describing?*

MATURANA: When one puts objectivity in parentheses, all views, all verses in the multiverse are equally valid. Understanding this, you lose the passion for changing the other. One of the results is that you look apathetic to people. Now, those who do not live with objectivity in parentheses have a passion for changing the other. So they have this passion and you do not. For example, at the university where I work, people may say, "Humberto is not really interested in anything," because I don't have the passion in the same sense that the person that has objectivity without parentheses. And I think this is the main difficulty. To other people, you may seem too tolerant. However, if the others also put objectivity in parentheses, you discover that disagreements can only be solved by entering a domain of coinspiration, in which things are done together because the participants want to do them. With objectivity in parentheses, it is easy to do things together because one is not denying the other in the process of doing them.

Q: *What are the social implications of your view?*

Your kind of philosophy would seem to discourage any kind of political organizing or attempt to convert people to a cause.

MATURANA: Yes, but at the same time, it encourages more tolerance, less ideological constraint and more cooperation for a consensual cause. It makes people realize that different ideologies are just different verses. Of course, if you get into one set of beliefs, then everything else is an illusion. If I have objectivity without parentheses and I hold a particular ideology, what I have is a specification of what is valid and what is not valid. Everything else is wrong. Everything else is mistaken. I will always demand that all the others agree with me. Understanding will always imply a concession to the other, and I shall not be responsible for the sources of validity of what I say, because what I say is the truth.

However, if you put objectivity in parentheses, other views become legitimate verses in a multiverse. It is not that one is mistaken and the other is not, one has the truth and the other does not. Different ideologies become different ways of being, different ways of looking and listening, in which each person is responsible for the way of being which he becomes. Everything that I do becomes my responsibility. Thus, if I claim that I do not like another person and I take action against him, I do so under my responsibility. But when I take the parentheses out of objectivity and I take action against somebody else, the truth that I claim to possess takes responsibility, not I.

Q: *Is there a spiritual implication in all this for you?*

MATURANA: I do not have any religious view. There are many coincidences in what I say with Eastern philosophy, yet I have not come to this through those views. Nor do I bring these in support of what I am saying. I think that the coincidence is legitimate, because I am dealing with some of the same questions considered in Eastern philosophy. But I don't believe in a transcendent existence. Rather, I think that human life is a continuous transcendency, because all takes place in human life as we operate in language, in coexistence, not in the solitude of the brain or the body.

Q: *So you regard language itself as a form of transcendency.*

MATURANA: Exactly. To be in language, to be human, is a continuous transcendency. ■

TAKE IT OR LEAVE IT

AN INTERVIEW WITH CARL WHITAKER

CARL WHITAKER IS BEING CRAZY AGAIN. AT A week-long summer workshop, he has set aside one morning to be interviewed "as a patient" along with a 24-year-old man, once diagnosed as schizophrenic, whose family Whitaker saw in therapy for five years. With hands clasped tightly in his lap, Eric, Whitaker's rail-thin former patient, addresses the floor as he is questioned by a therapist chosen from the workshop audience. Asked about his struggle to support himself and separate from his family, Eric explains that to him "adaptation is a horrible word" and insists that his inability to hold a job is a result of his refusal to accept his various employers' shady ethics.

Whitaker, who has earlier described schizophrenia as a "disease of pathological integrity," announces to the therapist that "Eric is the me that I wished had happened." Turning to the young man, Whitaker says, "I want to talk to you about the sacrifice you are making in fighting so intently for your own growth." He begins to muse about his own isolated adolescence and his belief that he was a schizophrenic throughout high school. "But I became a

trickster and social robot in order to make my way in society," says Whitaker. "I am very admiring of you for having the kind of guts I didn't have."

The young man, who has been sitting on the edge of his chair as if expecting some gigantic foot to descend suddenly and squash him, begins to fidget, offering a modest protest to his distinguished admirer's praise. "Please don't . . .," he begins, groping for the right word. "Idolize you?" says Whitaker. The young man nods his head warily, still mesmerized by the carpet.

It is the kind of odd encounter Carl Whitaker has become renowned for over the past 40 years. As Lynn Hoffman put it in her book *Foundations of Family Therapy*, Whitaker "specializes in pushing the unthinkable to the edge of the unimaginable." During his long career, he has outraged and fascinated the world of therapy with his belief that what he calls "craziness," the inner world of fantasy and unsocialized impulse, is a source of creativity and selfhood to be resolutely defended against civilization's abnormal normality. Guided by an unrelenting confidence in his own craziness, Whitaker has

challenged all the rules and conventions of therapy. At various stages of his career, he has bottle-fed his patients, arm-wrestled with them, refused to allow them to talk, even fallen asleep on them. All this in the interests of righting a balance he believes society has upset, allowing people to acknowledge the unacceptable twists of their inner life, to find some way to hold on to their craziness without "getting their throat cut."

Whitaker's colleagues have not always shared his confidence in his own intuition. As one senior family therapist says, "I don't think there is anything curative in having an encounter with a crazy man." But Atlanta psychiatrist Thomas Malone, who spent 20 years in close collaboration with Whitaker, believes that such criticism is inevitable. "Carl is about as right brain as you can get," says Malone. "In a goal-oriented, left-brain culture, he is an oddity. But you can't make judgments about Whitaker from the context of the left brain. That would be like a grammarian doing an analysis of James Joyce."

AFTER NEARLY AN HOUR OF A RAMBLING INTER-view with Eric, Whitaker and his therapist helper bid him good-bye and return to the 80 people who have been watching on closed-circuit TV. No one seems quite sure what to make of what happened, but one after another they offer mostly approving, if contradictory, interpretations of what went on. Sitting impassively on a small platform, his great lantern jaw resting on his hand, Whitaker listens intently and nods agreement to what people have to say, occasionally offering an association to embellish someone's observation. A woman asks him how it was to share his patient with the recruited therapist. Whitaker smiles and says, "There was some real jealousy there. I felt like the mother whose child has abandoned her to be with father."

Then a beefy man, slumped in his chair, raises his hand. "I have to believe I'm not the only one who saw this," he begins with a nervous edge in his voice. "I saw incompetence, competition, ego issues flying all over the place." He launches into a full-blown tirade about the "shoddiness" of the interview and a lack of professionalism in Whitaker's relationship with the therapist who assisted him. The audience is not prepared for anything like this, and it is as if someone has suddenly sucked all the oxygen out of the room. Finally, the man, his indignation spent, trails off into ". . . I wish I could be more constructive."

"You certainly don't have to apologize," says Whitaker pensively, impassive as ever. "I don't buy what you're saying, but you have your opinion and I have mine." And that's it. When the audience tries to push him to say more, Whitaker calmly reiterates that he enjoyed the session, thinks a great deal of Eric, and then asks if there are any more questions.

With Carl Whitaker, it's take it or leave it—and it really seems perfectly okay with him if you leave it. He doesn't have any interest these days in justifying himself or in persuading anyone of anything. It's not that he is squeamish about conflict. Rather, he seems to have found a way of handling himself that embodies his unswerving belief in the futility of control and persuasion. "Trying to make someone else live life in a certain way doesn't work," he told the workshop on the first day. In Whitaker's hands, the acceptance of an absurdly out-of-control world has become a tool, the "weapon of my own impotence." Thoroughly convinced that "life lives us, rather than the other way around," Whitaker is fabled for his imperturbability in the most bizarre situations.

Milton Miller, chairman of the Department of Psychiatry while Whitaker was on the faculty at the University of Wisconsin, tells this story about a rather chilling Whitaker consultation: "There was a time when an irate paranoid man said, 'Whitaker, I'll get you. And you'll never know when it's coming. Someday when you turn the corner, your fat belly will run into a shiv. Or you'll open your car door and a bomb will go off, or you'll be standing at

CARL WHITAKER

should be encouraged by "bottle feeding, physical rocking of patients, and other aids which stimulate in both therapist and patient the requisite affect for infantile satisfaction of the patient. It reproduces in therapy aspects of the mother-child relationship. More recently the authors have found that if aggression is utilized at this point of therapy, it most appropriately takes the form of spanking."

In a famous four-part review of *Roots* titled "Irrational Psychotherapy: An Appeal to Unreason" published in *The American Journal of Psychotherapy,* psychoanalysts Alexander Wolf and Manny Schwartz offered one of the most blistering condemnations of a book and its authors ever to appear in a professional journal. Describing *Roots* as a "piece of acting out," Wolf and Schwartz wrote that "Whitaker and Malone reject history, culture and civilization . . . investing pathology with moral value and elevating irrationality to transcendental supremacy."

TODAY THE 73-YEAR-OLD WHITAKER IS STILL someone whose work elicits extreme reactions, but he has become such a beloved grandfatherly figure that it is a bit jarring to hear about his once being denounced as a dangerous character. What has changed over the past 30 years? The most obvious change is that the dominance of psychoanalysis has given way to such a proliferation of therapeutic schools that the ideas expressed in *Roots* hardly register as scandalous anymore. Heretics have taken over the field of psychotherapy to such an extent that today traditionalists like Schwartz and Wolf would be hard-pressed to keep track of all the dangerous ideas circulating in the therapeutic circles. Actually, considered in the context of the writings of someone like R. D. Laing, to whom he was a precursor, Whitaker sounds rather old-fashioned.

But cultural and therapeutic fashions aren't the only things that have changed in 30 years. The qualities that were once seen as iconoclastic and threatening in the young Whitaker are viewed differently

a urinal peeing and a steel club will hit your head. What do you say to that, Whitaker?' and Carl said, 'You helped me. Up till now, all I had to worry about at the urinal was getting my shoe wet or meeting the wrong kind of people. You've given me something else to think about.'"

Handling himself under fire is something Whitaker has gotten a lot of practice in over the years, and not only in his dealings with patients. From the mid-1940s, when he and his colleagues first began to develop their idea that therapy was "a nonverbal, shared fantasy experience," Whitaker's work has raised many eyebrows in the professional community. When he and Thomas Malone published *Roots of Psychotherapy* in 1953, all kinds of questions were asked about Whitaker's methods, his ethics, even his sanity. Many therapists took great exception to Whitaker and Malone's belief that patients' regression

now. Thirty years ago, the field listened to what Whitaker had to say and reacted with confusion and alarm. Today Whitaker still confuses people, but the outrageous things he says no longer disturb them so much. After all these years of workshops, live clinical interviews, telling stories about himself and his family, sharing his off-the-wall associations, Whitaker has revealed himself in a way that few people in the public eye ever do. It is hard to distrust someone who behaves as if he has no secrets. Thirty years ago, the question was, "What kind of man would do this kind of therapy?" Today people are more likely to ask, "What kind of therapy does a man like Carl Whitaker do?"

Still, Whitaker's respected position within the field of family therapy is a curiosity. In some ways, his approaches and assumptions fit the world of family therapy today no better than they did the tradition-bound field of psychoanalysis 30 years ago. In a field that has concentrated on developing problem-focused treatment approaches, Whitaker's ideas are utterly outside the mainstream. He insists that he has no interest whatsoever in working on symptoms. He will often go through a first interview getting only the barest information about a family's presenting problems and refusing to respond to their crisis. "I want it to be very clear that I'm not in a panic about their life," explains Whitaker. "I don't care if they change or not." The idea that therapy should have goals or culminate in any clearly definable outcome is utterly foreign to him. One of his workshop slogans is "Process, Not Progress," reflecting his almost religious conviction that if a therapy session is satisfying and alive for the therapist, the clients automatically benefit.

While proponents of other models of therapy have emphasized their ability to work with difficult families and turn around impossible situations, Whitaker has stressed instead the therapist's limited ability to bring about change. Rather than emphasizing the impact that a therapist can have on a family, he tends to focus on the damage the family can do to a therapist: "Most therapists have the idea that when the family shows up, you should give them your left breast. If they bite that, give them the right one. I think *that's* crazy."

Psychoanalytic terminology has long been anathema to most family therapists, but Whitaker's workshop presentations are filled with references to oedipal crises, mother-child symbiosis, transference and, most taboo of all, the "unconscious." In his work, the outer world of the family—its structure, its sequences, its socioeconomic context—is irrelevant to the shared fantasy life where he believes the action is. Says Whitaker's longtime colleague, Thomas Malone, "Carl and Freud would have been good buddies."

There is something elusive about Carl Whitaker that makes it difficult to describe his particular professional niche. Like an avant-garde artist dedicated to alienating his audience, his strategy for remaining creatively alive has been based on disappointing people's expectations. "Carl has a great ability for being noncongruent with whatever group he's in," says Whitaker's former student and frequent cotherapist David Keith. "He's like someone playing a musical instrument who refuses to be captured by the rhythm and the tempo of the rest of the ensemble."

The oddity of Whitaker's work as a clinician is that his dissonance doesn't seem calculated to showcase him personally. What he does often sounds flamboyant in the retelling but does not come across that way at the time. "At his best, Whitaker somehow disappears and finds a way to get all the phoniness out of the family," says Braulio Montalvo, who once produced a videotape of a Whitaker session. "His work doesn't have an immediate, dramatic effect. He takes small jabs at the family's system of thought, challenging the absurdity at the heart of the problem. He goes for the things people don't want to talk about and, in doing that, works on the family rules which restrain the individual."

Consider Milton Miller's description of Whitaker at work back in the mid-1960s: "I remember so well the first Carl Whitaker family interview that I observed. That was some 17 years ago. Carl had come as a visiting professor to Wisconsin, largely on an invitation from Carl Rogers, who was on the Wisconsin faculty at that time. The 'patient,' a young, icy paranoid boy of 18, was burning holes in his arms with a cigarette while his sophisticated professional parents, early examples of the *Ordinary People*, talked in pleasantries about the cool summers of Martha's Vineyard. Whitaker, his shoes off, naive, rambling, incomprehensible, exchanged stories about fishing with night crawlers, then took hold of the dad's hands, rubbed them, later on reached out and put his paw on the boy's shoulder and told him, 'That's the craziest way of getting warm I ever saw. Put the cigarette away.' In the moment of uncertainty as to what would happen next, Whitaker was firmly massaging the boy's shoulders as they began to quiver and pulsate with his sudden sobs. And when Whitaker also began to cry, even the most intellectual of the professors in the audience covered their faces while coughing in order to remove an unprofessional tear.

"Whitaker gave us all something. He laid it on the line with the patient, the family, and the 20 doctor/professors who were watching. In the presence of a crowd of hanging judges, Whitaker bared his neck."

WHITAKER LIKES TAKING RISKS. THE MORE anxiety he can stir up in the family, the better he likes it. "In the final analysis, the most important family factor which relates to change or failure to change is desperation," he has written. "When family members are desperate, they change; when they are not desperate, they remain the same." But as to what happens when the family's anxiety peaks, Whitaker insists that the therapist must, above all, avoid the trap of helpfulness: "The family must write their own destiny. In the same sense that the individual has a right to suicide, the family has the right to self-destruct. The therapist may not and does not have the power to mold their system to his will. He's their coach, but he's not playing on the team."

If there's any aspect of Whitaker's work that draws criticism these days, it's his belief that the therapist's job is to stir up things in the family without having an equal responsibility for resolving them. Some challenge his assumption that families can always handle the kind of stress Whitaker's approach can generate. But Whitaker believes that it is the therapist's job to frustrate the family's wish for a premature resolution of its difficulties: "I believe that the family has hidden more serious problems by pointing a finger at the kid who is stealing cars." In an interview several years ago, Whitaker said, "I am not interested in curing the family's car-stealing kid. So rather than focusing on the kid, I would head for the accumulated anxiety in the family. I might accuse the father of planning to cheat on his income taxes and mother of trying to steal the daughter's boyfriend and daughter of trying to make believe she is just screwing around. . . . So I would be trying to accumulate anxiety in all of them."

Whitaker's preference for these kinds of therapeutic tactics has led one family therapist to remark, "Carl can be provocative in a way that can be destructive." But Whitaker's defenders see it differently. His former student Augustus Napier says, "Early on in therapy, Carl is very challenging. He is like the tough, strong parent of an adolescent. If you look carefully at what he does, you'll find the family sends out its strongest member to do battle with him. At his most provocative, Carl is usually doing battle with the family tyrant."

"It's always safest in a human encounter if nothing happens," says Milton Miller. "But with Whitaker, there are few nonevents. People may love him or hate him, but something happens. He's unwilling

to pretend to go through the motions. It is as if he lives by the principle that the perfunctory kiss is the worst perversion."

WHITAKER HAS BEEN THE MOST AUTOBIOGRAPH-ical of family therapy's innovators. Skeptical about scientific proof, committed to his view that "the only you I know is me," he has used his account of his own family experience to illustrate and, in some way, even validate his thinking about families. Born in 1912 on a dairy farm in Raymonds-ville, New York, Whitaker grew up in an isolated rural community where, with the exception of the Sunday church outings, his family comprised his entire social existence. "I had no social world until I was 13," says Whitaker today. "My brother, my dog, my father and his parents, and my mother and her stepmother all lived together in this huge house. In essence, the whole world was the intimacy of the family."

Life in the Whitaker household was dominated by the need to run the farm and take care of their farm animals, but his family's concern with providing nur-turance didn't stop there. "One summer we had a kid from Brooklyn stay with us," recalls Whitaker. "Then there was a woman whose husband had died of can-cer who lived with us for six months while she put herself back together. Another time there was some asthmatic woman, whom I never identified, who weighed 275 pounds and who kept us up all night."

Whitaker's mother was determined that he receive a better education than the local schools could provide. When he was 13, the entire family left the farm and moved to Syracuse so that he could attend high school. Plunged into this brand-new environment, Whitaker keenly felt his isolation, a shy country bumpkin in a strange world of slick city kids. "I think I was schizophrenic all through high school," says Whitaker. "There just wasn't anyone around to catch me. Then I spent the next 10 to 15 years learning how to adapt to the social structure

after living the first 15 in fantasy only."

His introduction to the curative power of therapy, he explains today, was through his relationship with two "cotherapists," classmates from high school whom he met for lunch several times a week while they all attended Syracuse University. "One boy was the smartest, and the other was the most popular boy from high school," says Whitaker. "They knew a lot about adaptation. Together they socialized me."

At the beginning of his senior year at Syracuse, Whitaker began medical school with an assist from a helpful dean. During his med-school summer vaca-tions, he worked as a counselor at a YMCA camp (where Rollo May was also a counselor). During one such vacation, he met his wife-to-be, Muriel, whom he married in 1937, the year after he finished medi-cal school.

He became interested in psychiatry while on a postgraduate fellowship that gave him his first opportunity to work with schizophrenics. "I fell in love with them immediately," says Whitaker. "Something appealed to my morbid curiosity. Their willingness to expose their insides gave me the courage to make contact with the isolation in me."

In 1940 Whitaker accepted a fellowship in child psychiatry in Louisville. For a year he spent eight hours a day, five days a week, seeing one child after another in play therapy. Like his friend Salvador Minuchin, Whitaker's experience working with chil-dren and, later, delinquents, first sensitized him to the nonverbal and nonintellectual dimensions of therapy.

During World War II, Whitaker was hired by the army as part of the mental health team at Oak Ridge, Tennessee, where the atomic bomb project was under way. Looking back over this period, Whitaker says, "I was doing pretty conventional stuff. The play therapy was out of Otto Rank and David Levy, and with adults it was the sort of pas-sive, supportive therapy that was commonly done back then."

THE TURNING POINT IN WHITAKER'S CAREER came in 1946, when he was named chairman of the Department of Psychiatry at Emory University. At last in a position of authority, he felt a freedom to follow his own clinical instincts. He set about hiring colleagues who would support his iconoclastic inclinations and with whom he felt he could develop close professional relationships. Among these were Thomas Malone and John Warkentin, two young psychiatrists whom Whitaker worked with closely for the next 20 years.

At Emory, Whitaker and his colleagues developed a psychiatry rotation the likes of which no other medical school has ever seen. Each student was required to have 200 hours of psychotherapy, including two years of compulsory participation in group therapy. "We did all kinds of crazy things in those groups," remembers Whitaker. "I remember Tom Malone saying to his eight students in one class, 'We're beginning two years of group therapy. For the first 10 Mondays from 9 o'clock to 10 o'clock, no one will say a word. We will just sit.' And carried it out. Can you imagine?"

As part of their training, the students in these groups were expected to act together as therapists with a single patient. "The patients would come from the medical clinic, where they had some problem like ulcers or asthma," says Whitaker. "Everybody would interview at the same time, and amazing things would happen. The students would get worried about this woman who was sick with asthma and would say, in one way or another, 'How can we help?' And she would say, 'Oh my God, it's terrible. Every time I get in a fight with my husband, I get this asthma attack,' and then they would ask more questions. 'Does your husband ever fight with the children?' etc. The teacher would participate but was careful not to steal the patient away from the group. So these kids had the experience of trying to be useful, and amazingly enough, like Alcoholics Anonymous, they would be. It was training in the role of caring. I would tell the students about a med-school classmate of mine who went out into practice without an internship, determined to be helpful to the world. He died a year later of a coronary. Then I explained that the point of the group was to help them learn how to live longer."

The close working relationships within Whitaker's faculty group led to constant discussion of cases and often to actual cotherapy. Working with a cotherapist gave Whitaker the chance to cultivate his own spontaneity and lay aside the constraining mantle of therapeutic responsibility. Whitaker's freewheeling clinical style began to take shape.

During this time, Whitaker and his group first came to national attention for their view that schizophrenic symptoms were an attempt to solve interpersonal problems, a view that was later to stir up so much controversy in Whitaker and Malone's *Roots of Psychotherapy*. The work with schizophrenics propelled Whitaker even further into his exploration of the clinical possibilities of cotherapy. "Most of us are so frightened of our own craziness that we're terrified the schizophrenic will swallow us up," says Whitaker. "But working together with Malone, I could let myself go knowing that he was there to pull me back if I went too far out."

In 1956 Whitaker and his group were dismissed from Emory. In part, the medical school's move was prompted by adverse reaction to the ideas and clinical methods described in *Roots*, as well as increasing criticisms of Whitaker's administration of the psychiatric training program. "Carl was a lousy administrator," says Thomas Malone. "He had the strange habit of dealing with personal relationships personally."

Whitaker and his colleagues decided to go into private practice together and continue their close collaboration. "We set up what was called a writing group. For nearly eight years, without any financial support for it, four of us met every Thursday morning," recalls Whitaker. "Without an agenda, we would just sit around the table from 9 o'clock to 12

o'clock, and if someone found something exciting, then that person would start to write about it, and the other people would critique it, edit it, and it would become an idea."

During this time, Whitaker's work with schizophrenics began to get him increasingly interested in working with families, although through the '50s he had very little contact with other family therapy innovators. In 1959, largely at the recommendation of Albert Scheflen, he was chosen along with Nathan Ackerman, Don Jackson and Murray Bowen to do a family interview as part of the famous Hillside film series. From there he became more and more involved in the family therapy movement.

By the mid-'60s, Whitaker's growing interest in families had taken him in a different direction from his long-term Atlanta colleagues. Says Whitaker, "The group had gradually been individuating, and frankly, I was getting bored with private practice." So in 1965 he accepted a position in the Department of Psychiatry at the University of Wisconsin and made the decision to commit himself entirely to family therapy. Pushed by students to formulate his ideas more clearly, Whitaker began to reflect more on his treatment methods.

Always a risk taker, his willingness to do live family interviews drew him invitations from places around the country where people were becoming interested in the idea of seeing whole families together. In the wave of interest in family therapy that characterized the late '60s and '70s, Whitaker began to receive widespread recognition. Says Whitaker, "A funny thing began to happen. Not only was I invited to a lot of places, but then I would be invited back."

Whitaker's fame was further enhanced in 1978 by the publication of Augustus Napier's *The Family Crucible*, an account of a family Whitaker treated, which has sold more than 100,000 copies.

In 1982, Whitaker retired from the University of Wisconsin. With the exception of two extended stays at the Philadelphia Child Guidance Clinic, his professional activities since then have been confined to giving workshops around the world. These days more and more of his time is spent at his five-acre home, bordering on a lake in a semirural community about a half hour outside of Milwaukee.

DESCRIBING CARL WHITAKER, FRANK PITTMAN once wrote, "A master therapist is likely to be better at doing therapy than at explaining it. When any of us explain what we do as therapy, we may notice only those things we work at doing and may overlook those things that come naturally." Many people find that much of what Whitaker says about his therapy is less compelling than what he actually does. He has always had a weakness for the global assertion, the loose, quasimystical explanation. In light of what we've learned in the past 40 years, for example, it's hard to accept as more than a poetic conceit Whitaker's notion of the schizophrenic as a kind of holy fool protesting society's sterile conformity. Similarly, there is also a fuzziness in Whitaker's view that whatever takes place in a family—like an individual's absence at a session—is an expression of something he calls "The Great System."

This is how the failure of a teenage son to appear at a session is described in *The Family Crucible*: "With its own unconscious wisdom, the family elected Don to stay home and test the therapists. Did we really mean everybody? Would we weaken and capitulate if they didn't bring Don?"

When Whitaker talks about a family, he sounds as if he is describing a mystical, supraindividual organism. Whatever happens within the family is accounted for as the family's "decision" that this is how things should be. His view of the family's unconscious processes suffers from the same vagueness and insupportable self-validation that led to the widespread dissatisfaction with psychoanalysis.

Carl Whitaker's contribution has not been in the realm of coherent theory building. Instead, what he

offers is a way of working with people that fascinates even those who have little use for his explanations of his approach. For Whitaker, the success of therapy pivots on the peculiar double bind he presents to families. He offers them the seemingly impossible directive "Be Spontaneous" and then, by refusing to give overt direction and insisting that change is irrelevant to him, gives a family an opportunity to be just that. A strange battle ensues in which Whitaker's task becomes finding ways to maintain his own creative edge in the midst of the family's effort to organize him.

"Carl fights with every family he sees," says Gus Napier. "The fight is to see whether they can incorporate him, reduce him to their pattern. And it's always a very personal fight—he will not play professional games to keep them coming."

In the fuzzy, disorienting world he creates around himself in therapy, the family is forced to take initiative if they are to maintain a relationship with him. Salvador Minuchin has described Whitaker's style as "passive-dependency raised to a clinical art form." When people start being good boys and girls trying to figure out what he wants them to do, Whitaker retreats. He distrusts any change that is compelled. His clients must change for themselves.

How many families are willing to struggle through the kind of peculiar ordeal that Whitaker offers? A large segment of his clients through the years have themselves been therapists and more inclined to accept his terms than the general population. But working at the Philadelphia Child Guidance Clinic with inner-city families, Whitaker's clients frequently chose not to repeat their disorienting first experience with him.

Whitaker discourages therapists from imitating his style of working. More than with most well-known therapists, it is difficult to separate Whitaker's therapeutic approach from his personality. Certainly, therapists in most agency settings would have great trouble justifying a therapy based on the principle that every therapy session should potentially be considered the last one. And those in private practice interested in building up a steady caseload are well advised not to look to Whitaker as a model.

For those who stick with him, Whitaker unquestionably offers an unusually challenging kind of therapy experience. But what makes them stick? For all his protestations that the outcome of therapy is irrelevant to him and that his primary concern is his own growth, Whitaker communicates a compassion that allows him to get away with his wisecracks and bad-boy antics. "Whitaker always goes inside himself to find what the other person is describing," says Argentinian family therapist Nidea Madanes, who recently invited Whitaker to her homeland for a workshop. "You never feel one down to him. He lets the other person be."

Along with all the attention he devotes to his own frailties and his preoccupation with taking care of himself, there is an emotional stamina that distinguishes Whitaker's therapy. "When most people sit down to do therapy, they have other things on their mind," says Whitaker's longtime friend Milton Miller, "like keeping the patient from suing them or saying bad things about them or falling in love with them. But Whitaker is different. He comes to therapy without the usual fears and preconditions. He is not put off by the prospect of looking foolish. He says, 'I'm game to be here,' and he means it."

Q: *On the face of it, it seems a bit bizarre that someone who is so famous for violating the canons of therapeutic decorum should become such an established mainstream figure in the world of therapy. Do you ever ask yourself how you ever arrived at such a respected position in the family therapy field?*

WHITAKER: I ask myself that all the time, and I haven't the vaguest answer. I feel like that guy they introduce to the audience at these workshops has nothing to do with me. Sometimes I wonder why

people invite "him" back twice. He just says the same thing every time. But I suspect that most of us are so compulsively organized and so indoctrinated with shoulds and oughts that my pseudocraziness frees people to be more crazy and intuitive in their own way.

The other thing is how I really become the patient in front of a workshop audience. In a funny kind of way, my presentations are free-association experiences in which I throw out whatever pops into my head and don't feel any need to be responsible. I don't even go over the notes I keep. People see how energizing that kind of public therapy is for me, and there's something about that that hooks them.

Q: *And part of your appeal is that you say things that many therapists want to hear but aren't sure are true—that taking care of themselves is more important than treating clients and that they should listen more to their own intuition. With great conviction, you insist that if a session is alive and satisfying for the therapist, it must be good for the client.*

WHITAKER: Well, most people have been trained to think that those things aren't true. Instead, we're taught that we have some magic power. We all live in the delusion that we carry over from our mother, that we should go out and fix up the world so she can get into heaven by being sinless.

Q: *The funny thing about this field is that while we've relegated concepts like "transference" to the scrap heap in dealing with our clients, certain prominent people in the field arouse intense feelings that seem suspiciously like transference. Do you have much sense of your place in the fantasy life of the profession?*

WHITAKER: Very limited, really. I get a lot of invitations, a lot of people seem to want to touch down with me, but mostly I don't take it seriously. It is like there are two me's, one that they see and another one that I feel.

Q: *Which is the one you don't take seriously?*

WHITAKER: The savant, the person who supposedly knows answers that other people are struggling for. And the one I feel is the real me is the little country boy who doesn't understand how people can think he is so smart when he still feels stupid.

Q: *So how do you handle it when people deal with you as the savant?*

WHITAKER: I usually go blank, walk off. I suppose I do the same thing Marilyn Monroe did when people made believe that she was a sex symbol and tried to use her. You appreciate it, but it is a social nod and you can't sit around and buy into it because then you become part of other people's delusions.

Q: *People tend either to see what you do as brilliantly creative or else consider it just undisciplined and whimsical. You must sense a lot of that polarity when you present your work. How do you handle that?*

WHITAKER: I think learning to handle it goes back to my days in Atlanta in the '40s and '50s with Tom Malone and John Warkentin. We were together for 20 years, first in the Department of Psychiatry at Emory and then in private practice. When we first began to do this iconoclastic stuff, like publishing *The Roots of Psychotherapy*, there was a great outcry in the profession against us. When we presented at professional meetings around the country, the audience would assault us. People said that we hadn't been analyzed, that we were pathological and should be forbidden to practice. Then we would run back to Atlanta and cuddle up to each other. Nobody could get to us there because it was too far away. It would be almost impossible to create a group like that in the middle of a place like New York or Philadelphia because there's always the invasion from the outside, the paranoia that the other professionals are going to get you. We didn't have that. In a strange way, we became a kind of guruless sect. I certainly wasn't the guru. *We* were the guru.

Q: *The kind of isolation you're describing reminds me a bit of the context in which Milton Erickson developed his work, although he never had such a close-knit group of colleagues. How do you compare what you do with Erickson's approach?*

WHITAKER: It is a fascinating business because, as far as I know, I have never been a hypnotist. Recently, though, some people have told me that I am, only I just won't admit it. That's possible. In any case, I think Erickson was much more of a thinker than I am. It's only in the past five or 10 years that I've been serious about figuring out what I do. Up until then I've been more interested in living it out than explaining it. I assume that Erickson anticipated what he was going to do and then decided to do it. I usually do it and then either congratulate myself or regret what I did.

Q: *In contrast with Erickson, who is so renowned for his resourcefulness in joining with all kinds of clients, you, in effect, force families to pursue you. You set terms at the beginning that eliminate a lot of prospective clients. You will not see individuals under any circumstances and only see families when all the members you consider to be crucial—like grandparents and ex-wives, and even former therapists—agree to show up. You call that the "Battle for Structure." Why is winning that battle so important to you?*

WHITAKER: I try to bring in as many people as I can get because of my assumed impotence, because I need the consultation. The more people you get in, the more chance there is of something happening. The first therapy session is the blind date. I set it up to make sure I'm in charge of the therapy. I will not accept what they offer. If they refuse to bring in the people I need to work with, I refuse to see them. I insist on being elected coach by the whole team, not by one member of the team who's mad at the present coach or mad at the other kids on the team.

Q: *Let's say you win the battle for structure, how do you orient yourself then?*

WHITAKER: Once the family assembles and I've accepted the temporary responsibility for being its foster parent, then the problem is to force the system into unification. I always begin by assuming the family is split, that marriage is the result of two scapegoats coming together. He's sent out by his family to reproduce them, and she's sent out by her family to reproduce them, and the war is over whose family is going to be reproduced. So I force that. And I force it by my conviction that the family members attached to the couple and their kids need to come in.

Usually, the father has to be dragged in if anything is to happen. And my first job is to get him so that he's not going to leave the session with a sense that I don't understand about life and he does. But in getting the father involved, I have to be sure to keep the mother out, because if she starts taking over, then the father can slip out. So I force her to be last: "You just sit right quiet, Mama. You can veto it all, after they all tell me what the family's about." If I do it the way I want to, I deny the individuals and deny the subgroups and force this family into being a whole.

So I'll say to the father, "Tell me about the family you come from."

"What do you mean? That's a crazy question. How can you say that?"

"Well, you know. If I ask you about the Green Bay Packers, you could tell me about the team. You wouldn't have to talk about the coach. I want to know about your team."

Then if the history is going well, and I get enough data about the family, I may move to a diagnostic second step, which is to say to dad, "What goes on when your wife and daughter get in a fight?" Thus I make each individual in the family diagnose the other triangles, dyads, subgroups, like, "What happens when all the women get together against you, Dad?"

Q: *You get the people talking about all the three generations in the family first, and then you'll break it down and talk about subgroups?*

WHITAKER: Yes. And I try to be careful not to ask anybody about themselves. That's hard for me to get away from because I did it for so many years, but I think if I can block that, then the family begins

to see itself differently. In that first session, I try to get all of the historical data that I can. I try to link up with those people who I respond to affectively, especially the younger children. Then I end the hour. That's the control thing again. "Enough of this fun, I've got to go to work." And I try never to make another appointment.

So I'll say, "Why don't you guys think about all of this? Dad didn't sound like it was all such a hot experience for him, so if you decide to come back, why don't you have him call?"

"Well, don't you want us to come?"

"I don't care if you come, that's your world. But I'm glad to work at it. It's the way I earn my living. So think about it." Then, if they come back again. . . .

Q: *Are there a lot that never come back after the first interviews?*

WHITAKER: Those that don't return are my favorites. Because if I make it incisive enough, powerful enough, confrontive enough, on the way home Dad says, "Hey, look, enough of this—$75 to talk to that screwball! Sue, you're not going to use the car for a month, and you're never going to date that crazy boy again. If you have any more trouble at school, we're going to have a *big* fight. I don't know what it's going to be, but you better be careful." The family is now organized. They've been empowered, which is my real objective. Even if they never come back, I think of it as successful.

If they come back, the agenda is completely different. They have paranoid feelings, I have paranoid feelings. They have fantasy expectations, I have fantasy expectations. They've done a lot of living in the interim and I am available to be useful at whatever they have the courage to start. I'm very cautious never to take control of where they go. It's their life and how they think about it is their business and none of mine. I will be an assistant in any way I can, but carefully fight their transference tendency to make me into a symbol or the wise man or somebody who knows how they should live. I fight for

my right to be impotent: "I don't know what you should do with your daughter."

Q: *It must be so hard for your clients to make sense of you. How do they learn how to use you?*

WHITAKER: Well, here's the kind of thing they're likely to get from me. The husband says, "My problem is that my wife and I are endlessly fighting."

"Well, why don't you win?"

"What do you mean, 'Why don't I win?' We're equal."

"I know, but she's got her mother on her side."

"Oh my God, don't get her mother into this."

"Isn't her mother always in it when she fights with you?"

"Yeah, but I wasn't going to talk about that. I was just talking about our fights."

"Well, what does your mother do when she and her mother attack you?"

"Well, my mother lives in Pocono."

"Well, why don't you go get her to help? Get her on the telephone."

Then the wife says, "Get her on the telephone? This rat is always calling her."

And I say "Now you see why I wanted all of you in here. It's just ridiculous making believe it's just a fight between husband and wife, because that's for the birds. The war is between the two families. And I have great news for you, which may be very frightening—nobody wins. It's just like between the United States and Russia—it will go on forever. So your wife will never stop being her mother's child. But she may grow up so she's a 35-year-old child instead of a 7-year-old."

So I lay out what I believe to be the dynamics of any family and say, "How can I help?"

"You can't help."

"That's what I was worried about. So why don't we stop?"

"I don't want to stop."

"Well, if I can't help, it's ridiculous. You'll come in and waste all your money."

"Well, what are we going to do? I can't stand this fighting anymore."

"Oh, come on, don't kid me. I've seen families who've fought twice as hard as you for 40 years and are still going strong. Have you heard the story about the 85-year-old couple who came in to get a divorce? And the judge said, 'What in the hell do you want a divorce for at 85? You've been married for 45 years.' And he said, 'Well, we made a promise that we wouldn't get a divorce until all our children were dead.'"

So there's the component of teasing them, of transcending where they are, and of breaking their metapanic about what's going on. And the metapanic has to do with "Will he kill me?" "Will she kill me?" "Will he have an affair?"

Q: *What you're saying reminds me of a kind of Jewish humor, of taking some ironic satisfaction in the hopelessness of your predicament.*

WHITAKER: Oh, yes. *The Joys of Yiddish* is probably my favorite book. I don't know of another book I've read cover to cover. There's that wonderful story in it about the guy who comes to the rabbi saying he has had this dream in which God accuses him of not doing right by his son, or some other minor crime, and he says to God, "Well, if you'll forgive me for my crime, I'll forgive you for all the innocent children who died." And the rabbi says, "What a lousy thing you did! If you had pushed a little more you could have saved the whole Jewish race." That kind of humor I think of as psychotherapy, real psychotherapy.

Q: *So if one thing's the lever for you in the process of change, it's mobilizing people's sense of absurdity.*

WHITAKER: But always with the anesthesia of caring. You can't just make jokes off the cuff, because that's just cynical. I want to help the family see over the top of their pain—and mine—to chuckle at how ridiculous it is. It's absurd that I have four suits and there are people down the street who don't have any. Why don't I give the other three away? But at the same time, we have to realize that's how life is.

I think people who come for help are always absurd. She knows that all that she has to do is say, "I got a call from your mother today," and he'll be mad at her. But she does it, and it's absurd for her to do it. She should have said to the mother, "Thanks for calling. I'll have your son call you back at 6:00," or "Oh, it's so good to hear from you. That bagel you sent over last week was just right." But she doesn't.

The dynamic interaction system is built on many, many subliminal stimuli, and when they come to you it's already very absurd, and the question is, can you help them develop enough anxiety about that so they'll break it. Can you empower them to break their system?

Q: *You begin by approaching the family as a kind of homespun philosopher with this absurd sense of humor. But you also provoke and challenge families in ways that get people incredibly uptight.*

WHITAKER: But that's only the beginning. Things don't stay there. And if I do it well enough, we go together. If it gets to the right point, and we've made a therapeutic alliance, this humor that pops into my head is not just mine, in isolation, it's me as part of the alliance. So they go with it.

I'll give you another example of how that works. Assume that there's an affair. They've been married for three or four years—or six weeks nowadays—he comes home and says, "I just read in the paper this morning about this guy down the street who left his wife and disappeared and nobody knows where. Apparently, he's changed his name." They go on with this series of covert messages, the essence of which, as I interpret it, is that they've decided that there's something that has to be done about their sexual life—it's too cold. Somebody's going to go for psychotherapy, and the amateur variety is safer. Then they decide who will have an affair and who will make believe it didn't happen. So he arranges to have the evidence in his pocket, and comes home,

and she finds it. The marriage is in big trouble. Then they come for therapy.

I deal with the absurdity of all this by saying to the wife, "Have you figured out who you'll find to match him? Or you could talk with his mother about it. Ask her if he ever played around with anybody when he was a kid." So you take the set and build the anxiety about it to the place where they have to do something about it. You make it into a public game rather than a private nightmare.

Q: *And it doesn't matter what they say.*

WHITAKER: No. It doesn't matter a bit, because their secret fantasies have been exposed. Here's another good example of this kind of thing—the father comes in with his wife and his daughter, and he's panicked because she's beginning to date. She's using too much lipstick. She shouldn't be using so much eye shadow, blah, blah, blah. After you listen to all this history, you say to them, "You know what? One of the things you could do to solve this would be to make her come in at nine o'clock because nobody's ever gotten pregnant before nine." And all of a sudden the pregnancy, the Oedipus business, the whole pattern of their hidden fantasy, which they do not know, is exposed.

Dad says, "You know, you're ridiculous." I say, "Of course I'm ridiculous, but you guys are kind of ridiculous, too, if you make believe that you can wander behind her and keep one eye open about everything she does after she leaves home until she gets back—which it sounds like you're doing.

"Now you're stuck with it. She can really put you over the barrel. You may be a disgrace in your office and your neighborhood if she gets pregnant. Or even worse, she could get herpes or AIDS. I hope she doesn't get AIDS, because supposedly all those people die, and you'd miss her. You know, she's a very dear member of your family."

So you set up contingencies that are so far left that they regard the stress that they're in as minimal in comparison.

Q: *You move so quickly toward unmentionable subjects in the family, like death, incest, craziness. You stir up an incredible amount of anxiety and discomfort— and then, very purposely, don't resolve any of it. How do you manage to remain so impervious to all of the intensity you stir up?*

WHITAKER: I think what has made it possible for me to work the way I do is that for 40 years, I've always had a partner. I think doing psychotherapy is just too difficult and painful a job to face doing it alone. Right from the beginning, I was always aware of how inadequate my training was and how many doubts I had. So I always felt free to ask for help.

I certainly know what you're saying about the problem of handling the anxiety. It was too much for me for the first 10 to 15 years. When I first took over at Emory at 34, I knew nothing whatever about families, and I was in a state of psychosomatic collapse. Once every few weeks, I would break out in cold sweats and vomiting and go home and crawl in bed and pull the covers over my head and put myself back together. And, of course, endlessly getting support from my wife Muriel and endlessly in and out of psychotherapy. I suppose I've had six years of psychotherapy, and Muriel and I have had therapy together with one or another of the kids— we didn't know enough to get the whole gang together in those days. So I've learned a lot about tolerating anxiety.

And, again, I have to come back to my group of colleagues in Atlanta. Every time we had a new case, we always asked someone else to come in as consultant on the second interview. And usually he would say something like, "You know, there's something wrong with the way you're getting along with this father." We were in a constant process of professional supervision with each other. And not just one or two of us. It was all eight. Whoever happened to have a blank hour was my consultant for the second interview.

Q: *That may be how you tolerate the feelings you stir*

up, but what about the families? Why do you think they put up with you?

WHITAKER: I get away with all this because I really do care. I think that is the anesthesia for all this confrontation. And I care because I've gone through a lot of things. I've been in therapy and had all the kids and all these other experiences. Also, I really believe that all people are the same and I can talk to their guts. So people may find what I say frightening or even terrifying, but not insulting. Something clicks for them, and it's the click that makes the difference. They resonate to what I'm saying, whether they know it or not.

Q: *Are you as provocative in your ongoing therapy with families as you are in these one-shot workshop consultations?*

WHITAKER: When I do ongoing therapy, my first sessions are basically historical. I ask each person to tell me how they see the family, but I do it with much more caring, with much more empathy than in these consultations, because I have ongoing responsibility for their pain. In consultations I don't have to be responsible. The family's therapist is the anesthetist, and, as the consultant, I am the surgeon. I can go in and go right to work. He can stop the bleeding and sew up the wounds afterward.

Q: *So you feel you can be as provocative as you want.*

WHITAKER: Yes, sure. And I have reinforced that by my long-term conviction that people take care of themselves. Therapists aren't all that powerful—that was Freud's delusion system. Since people are more powerful than therapists, families are infinitely more powerful. I don't think there is any possible way you can damage them.

Q: *So after all this time there are no Whitaker casualties? You don't get families where people have left all anxious and things have taken some dreadful turn following a provocative session with you?*

WHITAKER: I suspect there may be, but I have not heard of them. If there were many, I think I would know by now. One family I saw in England a few

years ago wrote an infuriated letter to the therapist, who sent it to me. When I got it, I thought, "Well, I finally had one."

Two months later, he got another letter from them reversing the whole thing, saying that as painful as their session with me was, it was tremendously valuable, and they apologized for the previous letter.

Q: *A lot of the writing in family therapy these days is based on the idea that the therapist doesn't so much discover some underlying truth in the family as make up stories, reframings, that help the family to change—to make up a new reality for themselves. But you come out of a very different tradition. For you, the important thing about families are these unconscious dramas that you keep wisecracking about in your sessions. It's not like you're making them up. You believe they're really there.*

WHITAKER: It's very clear to me that most of my life is organized around an extension of the previous generation. Most of our life is organized around our past history and how it extends to this generation and is then projected through us.

Q: *The more we talk, the more psychoanalytic your assumptions sound to me—only your focus is the family unconscious instead of the individual psyche. You seem to see your task as bringing this unconscious material out in a way that shifts something in the family.*

WHITAKER: It's what I call provoking the family into self-cure. The story that always tickles me about this is a consultation I did for Lyman Wynne some years ago. The patient was a hospitalized psychotic who thought he was Christ. I was going through a standard history interview with this young man and his family and it was dead. It suddenly occurred to me that I was defeated, which seems to be one way to get creative. I said, "You know, I think the problem with you is you weren't baptized right. Now, father could be John the Baptist, and mother could be the Virgin Mary—she looks like she'd make it—and the three sisters-in-law will be Martha and Mary and Mary Magdalen." One of them says, "Oh, I'd

love to be Mary Magdalen," at which point our psychotic gets up and says, "Look, Doc, cut it out. You know I'm not really Christ. You can't really do that."

Now, I think that young man wanted to be Jesus Christ because his family needed him to be. He wanted to be Christ so his mother would stay a virgin. His family didn't really believe he was Christ, but they kept on struggling with it. And I imploded it by taking him seriously, leaving him in the weird position of losing the balance he had with his family. That, to me, is a symbolic experience, that's the kind of empowering the family as an organism that leads to change.

Q: *That sounds like the analytic of the "corrective emotional experience."*

WHITAKER: Of course. It's essentially the same thing. Except that I have given up my fantasy that corrective emotional experiences in the individual can make for successful change in the system.

Q: *So how does having this symbolic experience in the context of family therapy change things?*

WHITAKER: It breaks the balance that's been there. The only way I can think of it that satisfies my experience is to think of it as the system in charge of what is happening with and in the individuals.

Q: *You seem to believe that the family is a kind of mystical, supraindividual organism. So that if the grandfather doesn't show up for a session with you, it's the family that has somehow decided that he won't be there. Everything that happens can then be explained by the family's need to stay the same, or whatever. It's a completely closed system and, like psychoanalysis, you can never disprove it.*

WHITAKER: No. Why would you try to?

Q: *Well, presumably therapy has something to do with science and empirically testing out ideas.*

WHITAKER: I'm deliberately not interested in scientific rigor. I assume that, in the same way that the old general practitioner could walk into a house and say, "It smells like kidney disease," I have that kind of background that I walk into a family session and

smell what's happening. Now, I trust the smell, but I'm also very suspicious of it. And I assume that in my simplistic efforts to solve it I overlook a lot of stuff, and the next generation of therapists is going to have to worry about what is scientifically correct. I'm not really interested. They're going to have to worry about that themselves.

Q: *So you don't worry about would-be Whitakers, whose sniffers aren't very well attuned, doing some imitation of what you do and just getting carried away with their own whimsy?*

WHITAKER: Oh, it's a concern, but I would rather suffer the concern than wait for science to catch up shortly after the third atom bomb or something. I would rather take what I have and go full tilt with it than to be cautious and not get anywhere.

Q: *You don't go along with the idea that it's the therapist's responsibility to treat everyone who comes his way. How do you justify not seeing people?*

WHITAKER: Over the years, I've become more and more convinced that there are a few people whom I can make good contact with and may be useful to, and that there'll be several untreated families left in the world after I die, so why struggle with the ones who society has destroyed and now wants me to fix? I don't intend to be a victim of society's demands. I think therapists are always getting the message from society, "We've destroyed the family, or these people; now you should quickly fix them up." Buying into that is the ultimate absurdity.

Q: *That's an unusual attitude, at least to express publicly, in a field that began by demonstrating its potency with what therapists traditionally considered impossible cases.*

WHITAKER: I think we're delusional in our conviction about our own power, and we've made believe that nothing else happens but success by never discussing our failures. Lord knows, I've had one or two in my time.

Q: *Do you have any sense of the impact you have on this field?*

WHITAKER: Very little, really. I'm very isolated.

Q: *That doesn't seem to bother you very much.*

WHITAKER: Not really. My real life is my real life. My professional life is the way I earn a living. And this doesn't spill over into my real life very much.

Q: *You have a visceral allergy to what you call doing "head trips" in therapy. When you see other people's kind of family therapy, does it seem like "head trip" therapy?*

WHITAKER: You know, in a strange kind of way I don't see it. I don't even know what Salvador Minuchin does. Even though I spent a couple of winters at the Philadelphia Child Guidance Clinic, I don't know what "structural family therapy" is. The only thing I know about it is this business about the separation of the generations and training the parents to be better parents.

Q: *Is it that you're just not curious?*

WHITAKER: I think that's basically it. Part of that is just old age, of course. I'm very aware that I'm more and more fixed in my own orientation. Like I read a fair amount of this stuff on Maturana in the *Networker.* I had this funny feeling of confusion and dissociation. Finally, I said to myself, "Well, he belongs to his club, and I belong to my club. I don't understand his club's language, and I don't expect he'd understand mine."

Q: *Are you ever crazy with your own family?*

WHITAKER: Oh, no. With my family, I'm very laid back, worrying about the sump pump or the roofing, fantasizing about cutting off a piece of the downspout because I want to extend the water drainage from the roof. Worrying about the rigging on the sailboat or the old farmer stuff. Thinking how one of these days I ought to go down and clean up the shop, because the damn thing is a mess, like the farm used to be. I almost never talk about psychotherapy or get preoccupied with the next-door-neighbors' dynamics.

Q: *Could you talk a little about your illness? I'm very happy to see you so energetic, but I understand you were quite sick this spring.*

WHITAKER: It was a crazy business. I had an embolism and as a result was having extra heartbeats, and that put me in the hospital on my back for two weeks with electroencephalograms day and night. It was difficult to get over. I was invalided for a month or two. It was a strange experience, looking at death from a different perspective.

Q: *What do you mean?*

WHITAKER: Well, you know, lying flat on your back like that, you see it differently. It's more real. You really wonder if these tubes they have in your arms and the things all over your chest can keep you going. And what if you should have three or four of these blood clots in a row, which supposedly you won't come out of, etc. So you deal with your aloneness and the fact of your being just one body—if it stops, that's that.

While all this was happening, I was never very panicked, which surprised me a bit. Maybe it was because growing up on a farm, you live with birth and death endlessly. From the time I was very young, it was my job to go out and catch a chicken and cut its head off for Sunday dinner. I saw my dad kill a cow with a sledgehammer, and he took the cow apart for the meat. And in January, we'd slit the pig's throat and watch him bleed to death in the yard, and then put away meat for the winter. That was all part of growing up. And medical school, of course, was one more experience with life and death. So I've been through it in reality and fantasy so many times that I assume that will make a difference in my orientation to my own death. Of course, you don't know.

Q: *What are your major professional activities these days?*

WHITAKER: I don't see ongoing clients anymore. I do give workshops around the country pretty regularly, which I still find a creative experience. And I'm also planning to do more writing, although I've given up the idea of trying to write a book right now. Instead, I think I'll be working on a series of

essays and see what comes of it. But mostly I'm living at home these days and puttering around the house and the dock and the sailboat, and I'm spending a lot of time with my family. This summer, four of my six children came to visit, along with all the grandchildren, of course.

Q: *What projects are you most excited about?*

WHITAKER: It's these family reunions that my wife, Muriel, and I have been leading together over the last few years. We have whole extended families come out here and stay at a hotel nearby. Recently we had 13 people from one family come out. We meet with the families for four or five hours a day over several days. It's an incredible experience in extended family dynamics. What we're finding is that families take more responsibility for things because we're not meeting with them regularly, and what happens seems to generate a much more powerful momentum for them. In some ways, having the extended family live together over that period of time is like a reactivation of the family community of the good old days.

Q: *I understand that besides doing therapy together, Muriel and you have also invented a new game.*

WHITAKER: Well, invented isn't the right word. We've discovered a new kind of muscular free association—playing ping-pong without keeping score. We do it all the time. You should really try it. It just bypasses the whole business of competing that is so much a part of two-person games. After all, keeping score is just a kind of doublethink—just like trying to figure out what techniques work in doing therapy. ■

*B*EHIND THE ONE-WAY KALEIDOSCOPE

AN INTERVIEW WITH CLOÉ MADANES

THERE THEY ARE, IN THE THERAPY ROOM ON THE other side of the huge one-way mirror, Scarlett and Rhett. So what if you don't remember Scarlett in flip-flops, madras bermudas and hair curlers? Who cares if the dashing, thick-maned Rhett of memory has become a glum, shiny-topped man given to twirling and untwirling the few vagrant wisps that still ring his scalp? You've got to realize this is the Family Therapy Institute of Washington, D.C. Here they don't believe self-knowledge fires the engine of change and insist instead that therapy is really just a process of persuasion. Here therapy is about metaphor and boldly sweeping clients along in unexpected directions—and convincing this unlikely couple that they are just like Scarlett and Rhett.

Nevertheless, a visitor might wonder what on earth the institute's clients tell their friends about the things they're asked to do in the name of "therapy." How does the father whose 7-year-old son suffers from chronic headaches describe having to come home from work every day pretending that *he* has a headache? And what does the bulimic woman say about being instructed to go home and, rather than binge and vomit, toss out five dollars' worth of food a day? And just what does the ex-addict with the suspicious wife who compulsively rifles through his pockets think as he stuffs notes in them saying "I love you"?

But questions like these don't excite curiosity around the institute. How clients explain the effect of their therapy isn't much of a concern here. It's just assumed that human beings are adaptable, and if they can get used to spilling out their problems each week in front of a one-way mirror the size of the monolith in 2001, they can get used to anything. Besides, there's an aura about the place, a sense that no matter how ineffective and tradition-bound the rest of the therapeutic world may be, here they produce *results*. With characteristic audacity—some might even say arrogance—they've named the clinic attached to their training institute *The* Clinic. And each year students come from around the world in search of the secrets that will unlock all their hopelessly stuck cases.

Behind the mirror, Cloé Madanes, codirector of the institute, watches with a group of students as

Scarlett and Rhett grudgingly admit to their therapist that, yes, things were a little better that week. "When they first came in, they couldn't say two words to each other without a terrible argument," recalls Madanes. "They got in such a battle in the first session over taking out the garbage that we had to tell them that topics like that were too sordid to discuss in therapy."

Madanes laughs mischievously as she recalls this opening-round victory over the couple's unquestioning dedication to their quarrel. Decreeing garbage disposal off limits as a therapeutic issue has tickled her sense of absurdity. As anyone who has read her books or attended her workshops knows, Madanes is quite at home with the fantastic and the absurd. Her therapy often hinges on seemingly bizarre interventions that sometimes push things to the edge of mockery but then, instead of giving offense, make people smile.

"Soon the therapist discovered that the wife's favorite book was *Gone With the Wind*," remembers Madanes. "So he was asked to tell her that she was just like Scarlett, strong-willed and romantic. And the husband was like Rhett Butler, rough, taciturn, but appealing. So we were starting the therapy by helping the couple to see themselves and each other in the most flattering way. But it's more than that. The wife was diabetic and drinking herself to death. Since they came here, she has stopped drinking."

Where her more sober-minded colleagues might see *sturm und drang*, Madanes sees screwball comedy or, if not that, just a tired soap opera in need of a plot twist. Like a wily director, she's convinced that however impossible a family's drama may seem at first, the production is only a few rewrites and rehearsals away from something quite workable. Her flair for imaginative interventions and her absolute conviction that the problem is always in the play, never in the actors, have earned Madanes a reputation as perhaps family therapy's most daring and ingenious strategist.

STUDENTS AT MADANES'S TRAINING INSTITUTE hang on her words with the absorption of people who don't know what to expect next. Most will admit they've never met anyone remotely like the mercurial Madanes—a woman who manages to be both imperious and childlike, exotic and familiar at the same time. Says one former trainee, "Figuring out Cloé is like trying to analyze a kaleidoscope." Says another, "Being supervised by Cloé, you're always on the edge of your seat. She expects you to do exactly what she tells you. If you work well under pressure, it probably makes you sharper, quicker. But she's so quick, it's hard for her to have the patience for those who plod."

"People often say that they are afraid of me," observes Madanes. "That always surprises me because the part of myself that I identify with most is my shyness." Nevertheless, scarcely a month goes by in which Madanes is not giving a workshop somewhere. Petite and tiny-voiced, she manages to exude the unquestioned authority of a drill sergeant. And what makes the pieces harder to fit together is that, for all her reputation as a master of therapeutic indirection, her conversation typically offers a startlingly frank readout of her mood and personal preoccupations of the moment. Madanes attributes her candor to her Argentinian upbringing. "In Argentina you talk about things that matter," she says. "You seldom make trivial conversation." Her husband, Jay Haley, puts it more simply: "She doesn't like bullshit."

Describing what's distinctive about Madanes's work, Salvador Minuchin says, "Cloé is a true innovator. More than anyone, she has introduced play into family therapy, bringing a sense of lightness and humor to her work that is totally nonthreatening. She has learned from doing therapy with children how to make people follow her ideas without realizing they are *her* ideas." Smiling at Minuchin's comment, Madanes adds, "I don't think it comes from doing therapy with children as much as from my

CLOÉ MADANES

own childishness, really."

Madanes inspires a special curiosity within family therapy these days. Married to Jay Haley, one of family therapy's pioneers, she has carved out her own reputation as someone who has more clever ways to solve the puzzles families present than just about anyone around (in one recent paper she listed 23 treatment strategies she uses). In her two books, *Strategic Family Therapy* and *Behind the One-Way Mirror*, she has tried to persuade her colleagues that spending long days listening to the problems of drug-saturated adolescents and binge vomiters can be fun. With her taste for the fashionable and her unapologetic attitude toward enjoying the good life, she seems out to prove that it can even be rather glamorous. It's a message that family therapy's many toilers in the field have found intriguing.

At their institute and in their workshops over the

past 10 years, Madanes and Haley have trained thousands of clinicians in a style of therapy rooted in the unconventional work of the now legendary hypnotherapist Milton Erickson. During the '40s and '50s, when psychoanalysis was the reigning therapeutic ideology and insight was regarded as the primary vehicle of change, Erickson developed a noninterpretive, action-oriented therapy that regarded clients' awareness of their problems as an impediment to solving them. Instead of focusing on painful past experience, Erickson concerned himself with subtly encouraging his clients to mobilize their personal resources in the present. Rejecting the gloomy, cerebral bent of psychoanalysis, Erickson introduced a distinctly American, can-do spirit into the field of therapy. With his book *Uncommon Therapy*, Jay Haley popularized Erickson's unusual approach to change and turned him into something of a therapeutic icon. Applying many of Erickson's ideas and methods, Haley developed an approach called strategic therapy that today constitutes one of the preeminent schools in the field.

Madanes's professional identity is closely linked with that of her husband, whom she still considers her mentor. In collaboration with him, she was instrumental in developing both the theoretical and technical features of the strategic model. But as much as it is a practical approach, strategic family therapy is also an ideology about change and the proper role of the therapist. Today many therapists still define themselves by whether they see strategic therapists as manipulators purveying gimmicky quick fixes or enlightened pragmatists cutting through the cant and mumbo jumbo of the therapy profession.

At the heart of the strategic therapy that Madanes and her husband teach is the therapist's unswerving commitment to solving a client's presenting complaint. For them, the ball is always in the therapist's court and the goal is unequivocal—to bring about a clearly defined outcome in the briefest time possible.

Like an accountant who doesn't expect his clients to know the tax laws, the strategic therapist doesn't expect his clients to understand what he does. What is important is that the therapist always have a plan and not, as Haley puts it, "just have everybody show up and hope for the best."

THE METHODS AND ASSUMPTIONS OF STRATEGIC therapy are not everyone's cup of tea. Since Haley's earliest writings, some therapists have questioned the ethics of interventions that rely on indirect influence and keep clients in the dark about the therapist's techniques. Others wonder why a therapy that so prides itself on getting results has produced no research validating its claims of great effectiveness. For many, the question remains open about whether the immediate behavior changes that result from strategic interventions actually last.

Recently, many feminists are questioning whether strategic therapy is irreconcilable with feminism. Some of Madanes's work, in particular, has been attacked as degrading to women and reinforcing stereotyped sex roles.

"I don't think a feminist can be a strategic therapist," says Deborah Luepnitz, currently at work on a book-length feminist critique of family therapy. "Feminists have always insisted that people need to understand their conditions rather than be mystified by them. The idea that insight is somehow irrelevant to change is a real disservice to women."

Madanes's repeated emphasis on the underlying benevolence of family relationships has also been challenged as naively ignoring the patriarchal cultural context in which families develop. Says Luepnitz, "Madanes chooses just to focus on benevolent power in families, but I don't think you can understand human behavior by denying what you don't like about it."

In Maryland, where Haley and Madanes trained scores of therapists under a contract to the state mental health system, strategic therapy is a hot political issue. The local chapter of the National Alliance for the Mentally Ill (NAMI), a self-help group for the parents of schizophrenics, has staged what might be called family therapy's first consumers' revolt. They are fighting, quite successfully so far, to block state and county funding for family therapy training and services.

Haley's and Madanes's treatment methods are a special target in this struggle. Says Agnes Hatfield, one of the founders of NAMI and a professor of human development at the University of Maryland, "Haley and Madanes seem rather out of date in totally denying that there is a disease called schizophrenia. Looking at their books, I have been astonished by their unwillingness to review the range of new research in this field. The only people they seem to reference is themselves."

Madanes and Haley invited Hatfield to speak with the trainees at their institute. "The trainees were not impressed with her pessimism about the people she calls 'schizophrenics,'" says Madanes. "I don't think she and the other people at NAMI are as concerned as they should be with the human rights of patients and the abuse of medication and hospitalization."

Not all the criticism of Haley's and Madanes's views on schizophrenia comes from outside the field. Says one family therapist, "They still think it's the '60s and they have to help R. D. Laing save schizophrenics from their families and the mad psychiatrists of the world. They don't understand what it's like to live with a psychotic person."

Regarding Madanes's and Haley's precautions against the use of psychotropic medication, Carol Anderson, of the Western Psychiatric Institute and Clinic and coauthor of *Schizophrenia and the Family*, says, "There's no question about the damaging effect of drugs. But what most patients tell us is that they'd rather put up with the discomfort of the medication and the side effects than with the terror and pain of schizophrenia. I think all the family

treatments of schizophrenia, including what Jay and Cloé do, have promised far more than they can deliver. It's irresponsible to hold out hope for people that only sets them up for disappointment and disillusionment."

"Therapists need to comfort and contain patients through their terror and pain," counters Madanes. "It is unethical *not* to have hope for those who are still living. Giving people irreversible neurological damage from medication is not desirable."

THE HALLMARK OF MADANES'S WORK IS HER ability to find tender affection in the most appalling family mess. In 1986 she wrote, "Love is complex and it sometimes involves hurting oneself or hurting the object of one's love . . . A daughter may make a suicide attempt so that her depressed mother will pull herself together to take care of her daughter and in so doing will come out of her depression. Violence toward others may also have the function of obtaining or of giving love."

Her cases ask us to believe in a benevolent world in which each of us is buffered from life's harshness by almost telepathically sensitive relatives willing to sacrifice themselves if it will only make things a bit easier for their families.

Madanes's main theoretical contribution to family therapy is the idea that most symptoms, and the responses they evoke from other family members, are really metaphors that mirror, at the same time as they disguise, other problems whose direct expression might irreparably injure a family's status quo. So, according to Madanes, something as simple as a child's bed-wetting may metaphorically reflect a father's improper behavior in bed and be seen as an attempt to help the parents by distracting them from their other problems. Accordingly, the best way to understand the bed-wetting is to see how it focuses the mother on the child's problems rather than on her own and involves the father in discussing the boy's bed-wetting rather than his own infidelities.

Where others may need to barely scratch the surface of human relationships to find geysers of deceit and exploitation, Madanes's therapy typically focuses on the discovery of great wellsprings of innocent affection.

Madanes is probably best known in the family therapy field for developing her "pretending" techniques, which are directives instructing symptomatic family members to act as if they had their problem while others pretend along with them. As Madanes explains the techniques, "A therapist can encourage a child to *pretend* to have a symptom. The parent can also be encouraged to help the child when the child is pretending to have the problem. [In this way] the situation will have changed to a game, to make-believe and play . . . when a sequence of interaction is labeled, 'This is pretend,' it is difficult for the participants in the sequence to go back to a framework of, 'This is real.'"

One of the first cases in which Madanes experimented with pretending as an intervention involved a 10-year-old Puerto Rican boy with night terrors. Madanes hypothesized that the boy's fears were a metaphor for his mother's anxiety. "She had lost two husbands, she was poor, she did not speak English, and she was involved with a man in a relationship that had to be kept secret (from welfare investigators) even though he was the father of one of her children."

Madanes devised a play scenario in which the mother would be assaulted by an intruder (played by one of her daughters). The boy's role was to come to his mother's rescue. "The family had difficulty with the dramatization," writes Madanes, "because the mother would attack the make-believe thief before the son could rescue her . . . The message that resulted from this failure to act out the scene correctly was that the mother was a capable person who would defend herself; she did not need the son's protection . . . The son did not have night terrors again."

A DISTINCTIVE FEATURE OF MADANES'S WORK IS the way she taps into children's loving influence in their families, especially in cases in which parents are abusive, neglectful, drug addicted or severely ill. Introducing a provocative variation on family therapists' preoccupation with buttressing the hierarchy and helping parents exert their authority, Madanes developed the strategy of putting children in charge of their parents.

Madanes uses this approach with cases that most therapists might throw up their hands at. One such case involved a mother of four who had repeatedly been brought to the attention of protective services. A former heroin addict, the woman was now heavily involved with her church. Her children, however, had earned a reputation in their neighborhood as unholy terrors. Her 7-year-old twins were encopretic and would stuff their excrement into holes in the walls of their apartment and have contests urinating out the window. They regularly set fires in their home and, on one occasion, to a van in the street. Once they even set fire to a baby in a crib. The mother was suspected of abusing the children. Robert, the most disruptive of the twins, as a baby showed signs of a skull fracture.

The key for Madanes in this case was finding "a framework of love, not of violence or punitiveness." To her, this was not a family wildly out of control, but one in which the children took care of this mother by creating such trouble that outside sources, like protective services, came in to help.

The tape of the first session with this family is one Madanes has frequently shown in her workshops. Recalls one family therapist who has seen it, "I always thought of strategic therapy as rather mechanical and emotionless. Watching that case was absolutely overwhelming. It made me change my mind and see what Madanes does as a way of bringing out the family's potential for love."

The pivotal intervention in the first session occurred after the therapist spent some time sympathizing with the mother over her children's terrible behavior and admiring the mother's willingness to keep her kids in the face of all the problems they caused her. Then, the therapist turned to 7-year-old Robert, the worst troublemaker, and told him to "give his mother a big hug and a kiss." Robert hugged and kissed her for a long time, clinging to her while his 5-year-old brother hovered around and tried to dry the mother's tears. The therapist moved the little one away and asked Robert to wipe the mother's eyes and say to her, 'I'll take care of you. I promise I'll take care of you. I promise, Mama, I promise I'll take care of you.' The child repeated the therapist's words very softly and hugged the mother for several minutes while the mother caressed him.

The therapist said, 'From now on, you are going to be Mama's helper. You are going to be in charge of helping Mama have an easy life. Tell Mama one thing that you are going to do. You are in charge.' The boy said very timidly, 'Clean up.' The therapist said, 'You seal that bargain with a hug and a kiss.' And they did. 'One more thing as the in-charge person,' said the therapist. 'Be good,' said Robert. The therapist said, 'Seal that with a kiss, because from now on you are going to be in charge to see that things go well in your house for your mother. What else?' 'Behave in school,' said Robert. 'Seal it with a kiss,'" said the therapist.

For Madanes, change in this family meant giving Robert a positive way of helping his mother instead of the destructive ways that he had devised. Therapy continued with this family for nine months, but Madanes reports that after this first session all major symptoms in the children disappeared, and there was no further abuse on the part of the mother.

To those who feel that asking children to take charge of their parents in this way puts too much of a burden on them, Madanes responds: "All this is done in age-appropriate and playful ways so that there is no burden to the children, and on the contrary, they are relieved to be able to express their

love and to take care of their parents. The children are not really in charge, the whole organization is in play, more in fantasy than in reality. The parents are moved as they experience their children's love for them and respond in kind, taking responsibility for themselves and for their children."

Madanes's sparse, understated descriptions sometimes do not communicate the sheer emotional power that her reversal of the hierarchy technique can generate. "Everyone cries in the sessions I supervise," says Madanes. "The clients, the students watching, even the therapist in the room—everyone except me. I can't afford to. I have to be thinking about what to do next."

MADANES IS KNOWN FOR THE WAY SHE WEAVES therapeutic webs of illusion in which everything becomes its opposite. Her own childhood, as the eldest daughter of a well-to-do Jewish family in Argentina, had more than its share of sudden twists. When she was eight, for example, her father's department store was confiscated by Evita Perón. Then, at 15, she and her family had to flee Argentina for several years because of their alleged business connections with the Perónists. "Growing up, my life was full of incongruities, and I never expected anyone to be consistent," says Madanes. "If someone loves me, I don't expect them not to hate me. I know that admiration always comes together with disappointment and respect with envy. I believe that change for the better—or for the worse —can be brought about so swiftly in therapy because as a child everything and everyone changed so swiftly around me."

For Madanes, putting children in charge of their parents' happiness is no mere flight of therapeutic fancy. It comes from her protectiveness of her parents as a child. Madanes describes her lawyer father as "extraordinarily intelligent, charming and attractive." "I worshipped him," she says. "I am not only grateful to him for the love and guidance he gave me

but also because ever since I was a child he let me know that he needed me, that I could help him. He had many ups and downs in life, and at times when he was sad or despondent, he looked for my company and let me cheer him up, comfort him, and talk him out of his sadness. That was a great gift that he gave me, the possibility of helping him."

Madanes credits her father with being the inspiration for many of her playful therapy techniques. "I remember being three or four years old, running around in the apartment making trouble on my tricycle, and my father saying, 'Now, Cloé, the bad one will go away' (and I would hide behind the curtain) 'and Diana the good one will come out.' [Diana is her middle name.] I would come out looking like an angel, and he would say, 'Oh, Diana, it's so good to see you. Come and sit next to me. Where have you been?' And so on. I loved the idea of being two people, and in this way he could get me to behave in seconds. It did not make me schizophrenic, it just made me sensitive at an early age to the complexities of human nature.

"My father was always a tease. I remember as a teenager when I would reproach him angrily about something at the dinner table, he would take a knife, hand it to me with the blade pointing to himself, and say, 'Stab me. It would hurt me less than your words.' I would have to laugh at my own anger, which seemed as absurd as his drama."

After getting a degree in psychology in Argentina in 1965, Madanes went to the Mental Research Institute (MRI) in Palo Alto to pursue her interest in research. There she became interested in family therapy and the work of Milton Erickson. Returning to Argentina in 1968, she was one of a few in her country familiar with the latest developments in family therapy. Although most of her experience was as a researcher, she suddenly found herself in demand as a therapist and supervisor.

In 1971 she returned to the United States with her husband, an economist at the World Bank, and

her two daughters. With the help of Salvador Minuchin, she got a job at the Philadelphia Child Guidance Clinic training Puerto Rican paraprofessionals and other staff to be family therapists. For the next five years, she developed her skills as a supervisor.

It was also during this time that, after the breakup of her first marriage, she developed her personal and professional relationship with Jay Haley, whom she had avoided when both were on the staff at MRI in the mid-'60s. "At that time, I was very serious about psychoanalysis," remembers Madanes. "I had taken great offense at Jay's article 'The Art of Psychoanalysis' and refused to meet him," says Madanes, laughing.

Madanes and Haley were married in 1975, and together they founded their own training institute in Washington, D.C. But Madanes found that collaborating with someone who had received such acclaim in the field created problems. "It was very difficult because of our age difference and our difference in status," says Madanes. "It was very important for me to achieve some stature in the field and make some contribution so that I would feel comfortable in teaching next to him. When we started the institute, I was secretary, receptionist and bookkeeper. Jay was handyman and video technician. We took turns doing live supervision. I made sure that all the students got Jay to supervise them. I didn't want anyone to feel that they were stuck with me."

With the publication of *Strategic Family Therapy* and *Behind the One-Way Mirror* three years later, Madanes made her contribution with an approach linked with, but distinct from, her husband's. "They think alike but act very differently," says Salvador Minuchin. "Jay's interventions are much more formal; Cloé's, more spontaneous." Haley agrees: "I might have started being the authority. But that's changed."

After years of following Haley's approach to training and restricting herself to live supervision,

Madanes recently returned to doing therapy. Despite her reputation as the developer of ingenious clinical techniques, Madanes's style as a therapist is surprisingly direct.

MADANES SEES TECHNIQUE AS A WAY OF MOVING people when the therapist isn't able to do so through ordinary conversation. "If I am doing the therapy myself, I will move parents by talking about the love that their children have for them," observes Madanes. "But when I am working with students who aren't yet able to move people through conversation, then I might prescribe a ritual like putting the children in charge. It's just a metaphor that dramatically symbolizes the children's love for their parents."

What's striking about talking with the families who have been the focus of some of Madanes's elaborate interventions is their utter lack of curiosity about the whys of what went on and their relief that someone else took responsibility for straightening out their problems.

"There was no monkey business," says the mother of a 12-year-old girl who had masturbated compulsively at home and school since she was five. In an intricate case in which, among other things, the girl was required to spend three 20-minute stints a day on a rocking horse, and, later on, the father was punished for his daughter's misbehavior, the girl's problem was resolved. "We were told what we had to do. Everything was spelled out. It took the burden off our shoulders," says the mother. Asked if the therapy seemed unusual, she replied, "Oh, it was pretty much what we expected."

In the case of another family, the "Cobbs," Madanes went to great lengths to get the three teenage children to take charge of seeing that their parents had fun and spent more time with each other. Special care was taken to avoid directly addressing the family's presenting problem, Mr. Cobb's drug addiction.

Looking back on treatment several years later, Mrs. Cobb reported that her husband had been cured of his addiction. And what did she think had been helpful in bringing that about? The unusual directives from the nameless person behind the one-way mirror? The way her children were organized to plan out activities for her and her husband? Not according to Mrs. Cobb: "I think the most important thing was how the therapy taught us all to share, to be more open and honest with each other."

Well, if Madanes can transform her clients into Scarletts and Rhetts, why can't they turn her into Carl Rogers? Besides, it's just the kind of twist that should make Cloé Madanes feel right at home.

Q: *Your books present a very impressive, utterly unambiguous catalog of clinical successes. Is the question of what "success" means in any given case really so unambiguous for you?*

MADANES: I don't think I report such a series of unambiguous successes. There are different ways to think about success in therapy. Sometimes it's simply to solve the presenting problem. Sometimes the problems are complex and ambiguous. I do a therapy of total common sense. Often I wish that I had as much common sense about my own life as I do about patients.

Q: *Can you give me an example in which someone else might see ambiguity and you see something simple and commonsensical?*

MADANES: I just saw a case in which the father, a successful professional, was concerned that his 12-year-old son had a serious problem. The boy was afraid that other children in school were talking behind his back and plotting against him. The father felt his son was in real danger of decompensating. The parents were divorced, but both agreed to come to the first session along with their son and 15-year-old daughter.

As soon as they came into the therapy room, the parents made several comments about privacy and confidentiality that were metaphorical of secrets in the family. So I decided to speak to each person individually. I spoke first to the father, who told me that the reason he divorced his wife was that he is gay and that he had decided to live a homosexual life. He said that he knew that this had traumatized his children terribly, and he thought that now he was paying the price and his son had this problem. I asked him if he thought his son worried about AIDS. He said, "I think so, even though I've explained to him that I've always been and will be with one man, that I've been tested and I don't have AIDS."

Next I saw the wife, and she confirmed what the husband said and talked about the trauma of discovering her husband was gay and the pain of divorce. The mother came from a family of physicians. She spoke very intelligently, and when I commented on that, she told me how bright her son was and how he was enrolled in all gifted classes in school.

Q: *What happened when it was the paranoid boy's turn to speak to you?*

MADANES: For a child to really confide in you, he has to like you, and this was a very difficult boy to approach at first. He was playing paranoid, and so I had to begin by saying things like, "I'll look at the floor, I won't look at you." And, "I know that you can't stand me, but just allow me to ask you a couple of questions." And, "It really makes me nervous to talk to a kid that doesn't want to talk to me." I put myself down until he began to be nice to me.

Then I said to him, "I hear that you are worried about your dad," and I asked if it could be that he worried about the father's situation, his being gay, his friends. He said, "Well, he talked to me about everything, and it's alright." And then I asked, "Do you like your father's friend when you visit his house?"

"Yes, but what I don't like is that, because I am a better student, my father spends more time helping my sister with her homework than me."

"Oh, you have a lot of homework?"

"A lot."

"I hear you are in all gifted classes. Do you enjoy them, or would you like to do other things instead of studying so hard?"

"I'd like to spend more time playing basketball."

Then I said, "Do you think that if you could get out of the gifted classes, you would have more peace of mind and you wouldn't be worried about these kids plotting against you?"

And he said, "I think so."

"All right. If I arrange that for you, will you stop with this stuff about the kids?"

"Yes," he said. "Do you think you can?"

"Of course I can," I answered.

So I got the parents back in and said, "I know you think your son should be preparing now to go to medical school, but if he stays in the gifted classes through high school, there will be no medical school. There will be nothing. He'll be burned out by the time he goes to college. All the pressure of school is weighing too heavily on his mind. When he leads the life of a normal boy, and he has time to play, he'll be just fine. So I want you both to go to the school and say that you don't care how or why, but your son is going to be out of all those gifted classes tomorrow."

Then the father said, "But there's more to it than that. We came to therapy because we have a lot of issues to deal with." I told him, "Look, do me a favor. Just go to the school and do what I've asked you. Call me in a month, and then, if you think that there is still a problem, I will continue to see you. But I really don't want your son to think of himself as a patient in therapy at this point in his life. I don't think it's good for him." And he accepted that. I also encouraged the parents to communicate more freely, to forgive each other, and asked the father to help the boy with homework. About the father's homosexuality, all I did was say to the children in front of the parents that they were fortunate because

they were exposed to different life-styles, different kinds of relationships and different types of love that were all enriching in their lives and that would make them better and more interesting people.

Q: *Let me stop you there for a moment. What was it that made you feel so convinced that getting the boy out of the advanced classes should be your focus?*

MADANES: I wasn't tempted by the family's sexual drama. I thought the father was very nice and communicated very well with his children. I thought he had handled that issue with them. For me to come and do it differently would have undermined him and done exactly the opposite of what I was intending to do. I went the simplest road. It was clear to me that the kid wanted to get out of the gifted classes—he had too much work. His problem was not his father's homosexuality.

Q: *So what happened with the case?*

MADANES: A month later the father called me and said, "You knew exactly what you were doing. There hasn't been any problem since we saw you. My son is happy; I'm happy. We've all come to terms with what's happened in the family." To me, this is success. The boy is over his presenting problem, the parents had the satisfaction of going to the school and solving the problem themselves, and they all felt good about each other.

Q: *I understand that recently you've become very interested in the connection between spiritual disciplines and therapy.*

MADANES: I was always interested in Zen Buddhism, but I find that it can very easily be misused in our culture as an excuse to withdraw. You sit and meditate and look for your internal peace. The goal is to achieve that state by yourself and maintain a sense of inner calm. In contrast, the Tibetan Buddhists believe that cultivating compassion is the most important thing. It is a spiritual practice based almost entirely on interaction with others. The whole emphasis is on developing your capacity for compassion, tolerance and forgiveness. In that

sense, it's very similar to Christianity, but is very different in that there is no attempt to convert anybody. There is no righteous sense that this is *the* way. There is an incredible tolerance for everybody. In fact, Tibetan Buddhism is the only organized religion that never went to war.

So I became very interested in how you can find solace in difficult times in your life and the idea of developing your tolerance. For example, one of the most interesting ideas in Tibetan Buddhism is that when you have been kindly to somebody and they pay you back in unkind, mean ways, you should take that person as your master. It is very easy to be compassionate and wise and tolerant when you are all alone or when you are with nice people that love you. But to be compassionate and tolerant and forgiving to someone who is paying you back in bad ways, that is true compassion.

Q: *How successful have you been in dealing with those kinds of masters?*

MADANES: It has helped me a lot. You know, when Jay [Haley] says something sarcastic to me now, I say, "Thank you, Master." Actually, the other day someone was telling me that the real way you do it is that you say, "Thank you for your criticism, this gift that you give me to help me develop myself and my tolerance."

Q: *And when you do that yourself, you're not being paradoxical?*

MADANES: Oh, no. I am totally serious. I have a lot of arrogance in me, and in difficult situations I often tend to think, "Why do I have to put up with this person?" Jay and the people who work with me frequently tell me how all of a sudden I dismiss everything they're saying in a way that makes them want to kill me. So now instead of thinking, "I shouldn't be putting up with this," I think, "This is a wonderful opportunity to practice tolerance and forgiveness. I should feel a great deal of empathy toward this person."

Of course, thinking that way not only helps you in your personal life, but it helps you tremendously as a therapist.

Q: *How?*

MADANES: Well, I always was against the idea of people expressing their hostility in therapy, but I didn't have a framework that put that in positive terms. Ever since I've become interested in Tibetan Buddhism, I start sessions with a couple, for example, by saying, "I want you to understand that the framework in which I am conducting this session and that you are joining me here is one of love and compassion and forgiveness and tolerance. I want you to know that whatever happens between you here, whatever is said or not said, it will always be in the context of the love that you have had for each other over the years and that you will continue to have." When you frame it like that, it is very difficult for people then to say, "Well, the problem is he doesn't take out the garbage."

It is remarkable how people respond to being moved to a higher level of being. A sense of kindliness and peace becomes part of the therapy, so that whether they separate or stay together, it is not with anger or resentment. Ultimately, it doesn't matter what decision they make—life is complicated, and who is to say that one decision is better than the other—but the important thing is that when you're at peace with yourself and the other person you can move on in life.

Q: *How has this influenced your ideas about the nature of therapy?*

MADANES: Basically, family therapy is about the love between people. That's all it is. It's not about power, hierarchy or paradoxical inventions. A family is a family because the people in it love each other and take care of each other or have in the past. And when they come to therapy, they either want to recover their previous love or they want to find a new way of relating, but in a loving way. Nobody comes to therapy to develop hatred, hostility or anything like that. I believe that symptoms are always related to the incapacity to channel that love in some way.

Q: *This is not the kind of description of therapy I associate with strategic therapy.*

MADANES: Given the history of therapy, whenever you begin to talk about love and compassion and all that, you sound like any idiot who doesn't know what to do and is just telling people to be nice to each other. And so the issue is how to be intelligent and also be able to explicitly talk about these things.

Q: *Let's return to the question of success in therapy. Maybe I'm missing something, but I don't believe you've ever written about a clinical failure. Why not?*

MADANES: When you write, I think you should have something interesting to say. If I had intelligent thoughts about failures, I would write about them. But usually a failure is a failure because you were stupid.

Q: *So let me borrow a page from your book. If we were to pretend that you had some interesting ideas about why you fail with some cases, what might they be?*

MADANES: Most of our failures are related to the intrusion of other professionals and agents of social control who have power over a family and who we might not be able to influence. But sometimes I don't succeed because I am lacking in identification with one of the characters in the family drama.

I think that we all have problems empathizing with people who represent the weaker aspect of ourselves. So if I have a weak mother in a session or a weak wife that gets mistreated by a man, I have trouble identifying with them because I don't like to see them in myself. To deal intelligently with a client, the important thing isn't distance but the ability to feel that I am her. So if it's painful to feel that I am her, I will have trouble developing the relationship I need. I will then tend to have trouble engaging and motivating her.

Another thing that can get in my way is the fear of rejection. I am very sensitive to how people see me, and I think that sometimes I might fail at identifying with somebody because I am afraid that if I come close to that person, he or she will reject me.

Being distant is not what leads to intelligent therapy. It's the total empathy that makes me intelligent. When I feel that I *am* each member in the family, I know exactly what to do.

By the way, Tibetan Buddhism is very useful in this aspect of being a therapist. It takes very seriously the funny idea of reincarnation. A belief in reincarnation makes you identify with everyone—men, women and children—because you may come back again as a member of the opposite sex or even as an animal. Tibetan meditation, instead of encouraging you to withdraw into yourself, focuses on your empathy with other living things. So a man might meditate on all his mothers and their suffering in all his past lives and try to identify with a woman giving birth and caring for a child. Even though it is difficult to believe in reincarnation, it is not difficult to believe in the importance of the idea that we are all one, all dependent on each other, and that, in a sense, anything that I can feel or think, you can, too—and probably have, at some point in your existence.

Q: *Your whole approach to therapy seems to rely very heavily on the idea that family members are intensely involved in protecting each other and that the symptom of any one member typically serves a function for someone else in the family. In the July/August 1986 issue of the* Networker, *Jeffrey Bogdan compared the practice of seeking out the function of symptoms to the psychoanalytic practice of foraging for unconscious motives. He challenged your idea that family members "plan ahead" to produce symptoms as farfetched and impossible to verify scientifically. What's your response to that kind of criticism?*

MADANES: It may be that the symptom doesn't have a function—it doesn't matter. The issue is, what is the best way for therapists to think that enables them to help people change? Whether it's true that the child actually plans ahead or that the parents plan ahead or that the symptom serves a function for the family, that way of thinking is valuable because it tells you what to do and how to change a situation.

I agree that there is no way of proving that symptoms do serve functions, just like there is no way in psychoanalysis either. Jay always makes a distinction between thinking in terms of research and thinking in terms of what leads to a successful intervention. Looking at why people do things motivates me as a clinician. It arouses my interest in a case and gives me a way of hypothesizing that leads to my being able to offer alternatives to a family.

Q: *It sounds as if the question of whether people really develop symptoms to protect each other doesn't especially interest you.*

MADANES: I don't know if symptoms truly have functions. I tend to think that they do. I also know that human behavior is complex, and if I think of one function of a symptom, then immediately an opposite one comes to mind. But when you are doing the therapy, you have to believe in a particular function. If you don't believe in it, you don't plan the therapy well. So at the moment I'm supervising the case, I'm absolutely sure the child is protecting the parent. I totally believe it. But ask me a few weeks later, and I'll say, "Well, it was a useful hypothesis."

It is important to understand that there cannot be one theory that encompasses every possible human problem. It is naive to think that the same theory can explain why a 12-year-old misbehaves in school, as well as the problems of a heroin or cocaine addict, hallucinations, suicide and communication difficulties in marriage. You can't lump all this together under one theory of family pathology. Sometimes a symptom serves a function in the family; some symptoms are just bad habits, some are the products of attempts to solve a problem, some are the result of trauma and life's tragedies, some are the consequence of oppression and injustice. The art of the therapist is to understand which one it is. Life is full of ordinary and extraordinary problems, and a therapist has to be wise enough to recognize them.

Q: *In treating schizophrenics, you take a very hard and fast position against using medication and seem to regard schizophrenia as entirely an interpersonal phenomenon. What's your understanding of what schizophrenia is?*

MADANES: I don't want to answer that question asked in that way. I really don't know what schizophrenia is. For me, the issue is still about having respect for a patient, not labeling somebody as "schizophrenic" and therefore treating them as if they are inhuman in some way. The issue is about being able to accept that person with a realization that I could be that person and that that person could be me.

Q: *What kind of response do you get about your way of working with schizophrenics and their families from other people in the field?*

MADANES: This spring, at the meeting of American Family Therapy Association (AFTA), I was in a session in which someone said to me, "Why do you want to force the family to take care of the schizophrenic, instead of relieving them by putting the schizophrenic in the hospital?" And I said, "First, I don't want to force any family to do anything. I never do that. Families want to take care of the schizophrenic because they love him. I help them to try to get together without violence, with sympathy and tolerance for each other, to develop good feelings for each other and then, if necessary, to separate in good feeling rather than with expulsion and hatred." The idea that we force families to do anything is a total misconception of strategic therapy.

Some people read Jay's book *Leaving Home* as if it directed parents to expel children from their homes. Nothing is more opposed to what he said or what we want to do. Actually, the purpose of the parents' taking charge is to help them to be benevolent toward each other and toward the patient. We don't put kids out of their house, even though some people have quoted Jay as recommending locking the doors on their children. There are some problems of children violently abusing their parents in which we do draw the line, and we say, "Lock the

door and change the lock," because there comes a point where the parents' lives are in danger. But that is not the usual treatment for these problems at all.

I want to say that I find some of the ideas about how to treat schizophrenics among family therapists absolutely appalling. One woman in the AFTA interest group I was just talking about said that she helped the parents of schizophrenics mourn for their diagnosed children even though the children were still alive. I said, "I only help people mourn when somebody dies. When people live, there is always hope. I am not going to help them mourn for their child being schizophrenic." There is the implication there that the child will never recover, that it's the end. I think that's totally antitherapeutic. I would never do that. I am totally opposed to those points of view. And there is no evidence to support that position. In fact, the research reports a growing percentage of people diagnosed as schizophrenic who spontaneously recover. But even if only one case in a hundred recovered, I think a clinician should consider that the one exception could be his patient and should deal with that patient in the most hopeful way possible.

Q: *What's your view of the psychoeducational approaches that train families to deal with schizophrenia as a kind of handicap?*

MADANES: I disagree with a pessimistic point of view that assumes that schizophrenia is an incurable physical illness, like diabetes, that follows an inevitable course. Also, the psychoeducational approach is so often just an adjunct to a psychiatric intervention of medication. In many cases, medication gives irreversible neurological damage. I think it's better to have schizophrenia, which is reversible, than irreversible neurological damage.

There is a tremendous emphasis in the psychoeducational approach on getting the person "functioning" back at school or at work. I'm not going to give people brain damage through medication so that they can go back to work. I think that's not ethical. I

think there is a lot of confusion about the difference between financial expediency and good medical care. A lot of the medical intervention in schizophrenia has to do with finances. Getting a person to work is partly a financial problem. Many people are on medication instead of an intensive therapy because medication is cheaper, and psychiatrists are not being taught how to do therapy.

Q: *Since you are a female therapist and teacher, the issues of feminism inevitably come up. At an institute on feminism and family therapy at last year's American Association for Marriage and Family Therapists (AAMFT) meeting, your work was the focus of some heated discussion. Michele Bograd took exception to a number of your cases. Here's how she described one of them:*

"A couple presents with marital conflict that has interfered with their readiness to have children. The wife criticizes the husband; he withdraws. She pursues; he is silent. She gets angry and hits him. He retaliates with more damaging physical force. The intervention: when the wife "provokes" the husband, he should reach under her blouse and fondle her breasts instead of hitting her. Conclusion: the physical abuse stopped, and several months later the couple reported the wife was pregnant.

Bograd went on to say, "Is it ethical to use techniques that draw on and so replicate conventional sex roles? . . . We are most disturbed by the prescription that the husband fondle his wife. As women, many of us would experience such physical advances as intrusive and unwanted. On another level of analysis, this intervention tacitly supports [the idea] that men have the right to unquestioned physical access to their partners." How do you respond to this critique?

MADANES: First of all, that summary is a total misrepresentation of the case. The directive was given after a long session in which this very sophisticated and intellectual couple had discussed their families of origin and analyzed all the factors contributing to their violence and their power struggles. After all this, the therapist said he had a simple solution to the problem. Because the violence of the husband

was always triggered by the wife's hitting him—whether they were in the street, at a party, the theater, or wherever—he would put his hand under her skirt and fondle her or put his hand inside her blouse, whichever he could do first.

The wife, who was a very proper woman and a feminist activist, was shocked, while the husband cracked up laughing. Then the wife blushed and laughed, and then they both started laughing and kidding each other about it. Immediately the mood switched from violence to sexiness. When they came in the next time, they reported that she hadn't hit him, so he hadn't fondled her in response. But he made a point of telling the therapist that he had fondled her in other circumstances.

Although the wife was not intimidated by his violence toward her, she was intimidated by a sexual advance from him. The wife was not going to hit the husband as soon as she understood that he really liked the idea of fondling her in return. And she was going to draw the line and not allow that if she didn't want it. I mean, they had good sex in other circumstances, but if she didn't want sex in a context of violence, she was not going to have it. So she took charge of her sexuality and controlled her violence, and that was what the intervention was designed for.

Q: *But don't you think instructing a husband to fondle his wife as a solution to their conflicts sounds a bit sexist?*

MADANES: There's nothing sexist about it. What is sexist is to think always of the woman as the victim of sex. I approve of husbands fondling their wives. I am not saying that the wife should always be available to him. I never said that she couldn't resist him. I just said that if she attacked him physically, instead of hitting her with his fist, he should fondle her. There was no instruction about what she would do in return. I saw with this couple that there was clearly a strong sexual attraction there. So it wasn't like I was violating the wife. The husband was a very handsome guy, and

she was obviously very attracted to him.

My goal was to introduce a humorous intervention in which the husband is supposed to fondle her sexually instead of abusing her. When you have a very dramatic relationship, you have to introduce a dramatic intervention that is commensurate to what they are doing but that changes it into a loving, humorous thing. It's just good clinical work, that's all it is. And it solved the problem of violence in this couple in one session. Once we had stopped the violence, it was possible to deal with other conflicts in the relationship.

I should also add that I am equally humorous and outrageous with men and with women. Of course, the feminists would say it doesn't matter because all women are oppressed, and so to make fun of the woman is always oppressive. I don't believe that. All women are not oppressed. What more of a way to put oneself down than to think that?

Q: *One of the criticisms feminists have directed at family therapists has to do with putting the burden of change disproportionately on the shoulders of women. Virginia Goldner has written, "Insofar as a woman's identity is wrapped up in her ability to nurture, she will do almost anything to 'fix things.'" What's your comment on that?*

MADANES: I'd like to meet those women that are so willing to follow prescriptions. I find it is as difficult to get women to follow directives as it is with men. Imagine how easy therapy would be if all the mothers and all the wives would just do what you tell them to do.

Q: *Summarizing her objections to your cases, again at the AAMFT institute, Michele Bograd also said, "While certain behaviors disadvantageous to the women were modified or eliminated, the basic rules of their relationships remained unchanged and unchallenged . . . Yet if I respect the family's wishes to keep the status quo, I help maintain a primary interpersonal context that perpetuates inequality between husbands and wives, if not that of women as a class." What's your response to that?*

MADANES: That if the couple wants to change something else, they can always bring it up. But I don't set out to change people against their will. My job is not to require people to have the kind of marriage I think they should have. I think it is unethical to impose one's political ideology on clients.

Q: *I know a lot of people who are drawn to the ingenuity of strategic therapy at one time or another in their careers. Many go to your workshops; some come to study at the institute for a year. But it seems to me that of those, relatively few identify themselves as strategic therapists. Is it that practicing strategic therapy and being so conscious of the gamelike quality of family interaction makes therapy less emotionally satisfying for the therapist?*

MADANES: I don't think family interactions are gamelike. You must be thinking of a different school of therapy. I think the problem is the opposite. People claim to be strategic therapists who know little about it. My therapy is very emotional. Everybody cries in the sessions, and the therapists often cry behind the mirror. To see how it is possible to bring out the love that people have for each other is very moving.

Q: *How long would you say it takes to become a strategic therapist?*

MADANES: A therapist can learn a great deal in one year of training, but it takes a minimum of three years to become a strategic therapist. I can think of one person, for example, who took three years of training with us but then, as he became a supervisor, still was using every opportunity to be supervised himself. Still, today, after 10 years of working with us, he says, "Will you do a case with me?"

Q: *How strategic are you in your personal relationships?*

MADANES: Not at all. I am an idiot in my personal life. I am very open. I am very vulnerable. When I am fond of somebody, I could never take enough distance to manipulate the situation at all. I have a very clear dissociation about how I think with patients and with my own family. Actually, I have a lot of problems because now that I have become more prominent, colleagues and friends and students often think that I am being strategic when I am not at all.

Q: *How strategic a parent are you?*

MADANES: I am the kind of parent who tells my children my problems. I ask for their advice. I worship and admire Ingrid and Magali, my daughters. If they get angry at me, I cry. I attempt to set up a punishment and then, for example, Magali says, "How can you do that?" or something like that, and I say, "Alright, I'm sorry."

Q: *Do you put them in charge of your happiness?*

MADANES: Yes, totally. I mean, I try. Jay says to Magali, "How did you get your mother to change completely everything she wanted you to do?" Magali says, "Oh, I cried." I can't stand to see them cry. I'm always like that. Anybody in my family that confronts me a little bit gets away with anything.

Q: *You've written that you try to come up with an intervention uniquely suited to each case you see. But after nearly 20 years of doing family therapy, isn't it hard not to fall back on old formulas? How do you keep your work fresh?*

MADANES: I am always fascinated by people. Therapy is never boring because there is always something to discover, a new puzzle to solve.

Q: *Does the optimism in your books come from your personal life?*

MADANES: Not really. I like to start my days pretending to be Humphrey Bogart in *Casablanca*: all my illusions have already been shattered, so I can face the day without any risk of disappointment. ■

GOOD-BYE PARADOX, HELLO INVARIANT PRESCRIPTION

AN INTERVIEW WITH
MARA SELVINI PALAZZOLI

PARENTS MILDLY CHAGRINED AT THEIR REBEL-lious teenagers, couples vaguely aware of something missing in their marriages, families who think it would be a nice idea to learn how to communicate better—steer clear. Milan's Nuovo Centro per lo Studio della Famiglia is not for you. This is not a center for your run-of-the-mill family problems; it's for the cases most therapists would consider impossible, like the "Santinis."

It's hard to imagine that Mr. and Mrs. Santini, both sourly avoiding each other's gaze right now, ever cared very much for each other. Nevertheless, they have stayed married for more than 30 years, even though most of the time they live in separate residences. Of their five children, two are former heroin addicts and a third, 19-year-old Rodolfo, has had auditory hallucinations for the past year and insists his older sister speaks to him through the TV set. In their first session, 60-year-old Mr. Santini accused 20-year-old Paolo, a handsome university student, of sleeping with the family maid. It was soon revealed, however, that it was actually Mr. Santini who was sleeping with her. Mrs. Santini is now

threatening to get a divorce. After the second session, Paolo called the center to report that his brother Rodolfo had propositioned him and told him, "I want to have your baby."

It is now the middle of the third session, and the family's therapist, Mara Selvini Palazzoli, a small woman with an enormous, electric smile, is discussing the metaphorical significance of the presents that Rodolfo, the identified patient, gave his parents last Christmas—a big, ornamental heart for his mother and a tiny walrus contained in a huge gift box for his father. "To mother, Rodolfo gave a heart, as if he was telling her, 'You have no heart; I will give you one,'" says Palazzoli with great gusto in her sonorous, dramatic voice. "To father, he gave a very, very small animal to make fun of him. He has treated him as a *castrati*, an impotent old man, as if he were saying, 'Papa, you are not giving me a very potent image of you.'"

So far, Palazzoli has kept up an almost constant barrage of what she calls "terrible questions," her method for quickly penetrating to the family's emotional core. She has asked Mrs. Santini why her husband

cheated on her in her own home, inquired of Paolo whether he thinks Rodolfo's homosexual proposition was a message to his mother or to his father, and requested Rodolfo's help in understanding why his father sleeps with maids.

Meanwhile, the Santinis sit almost motionless, as if mesmerized. Despite Palazzoli's provocative questioning, they appear fascinated by what is going on, as fascinated with Palazzoli as she is with them. Whatever terrible things she may be asking, her rapt attention, her expansive gestures and that blazing smile keep saying to the family, "However uncomfortable this may make you, you can trust me. Nothing you can say will throw me off." But there's more than that—a kind of delight she takes in the whole process. It's as if she has never talked with a family as interesting as this one, never explored family relationships quite this baroque and intriguing.

Readers who associate Palazzoli with *Paradox and Counterparadox*, the celebrated book she cowrote with Luigi Boscolo, Gianfranco Cecchin and Giuliana Prata, may, at this point, be wondering what she is up to. That book proposed that client families enter treatment with both a request and a warning, a double-level, paradoxical message that goes something like, "Please change us/Don't you *dare* change us!" To deal with the help-seekers who resist help, Palazzoli and her colleagues argued, therapists must be change agents who argue against change. At the heart of their paradoxical approach was an unswerving commitment to clinical neutrality and "positive connotation," a way of explaining to the family how even the most troublesome symptom was ultimately in the service of family harmony.

But whatever happened to positive connotation and neutrality? And when is she going to advise the Santinis against change? Well, the fact of the matter is that Palazzoli's ideas about treatment have changed dramatically since the days of *Paradox and Counterparadox*. Right now, with the Santinis, she's confronting what she calls the "dirty games," the

maneuvers family members use to hide their coalitions and strategies for controlling each other. It is Palazzoli's controversial contention that schizophrenia always begins as a child's attempt to take sides in the stalemated relationship between his parents. And what is even more controversial, she believes that she has developed an "invariant prescription" that can shake up the whole family game and, in the process, cure schizophrenia. But first that game must be very clearly understood, and that's what she's trying to do with the Santinis.

BY THE LATE AFTERNOON, THE 70-YEAR-OLD Palazzoli has spent nearly three hours interviewing the Santinis, including two lengthy consultations with two members of her current team, Stefano Cirillo and Anna Maria Sorrentino. The team thinks that the pieces of the family puzzle are finally falling into place. The session is moving toward its climax.

Turning to Rodolfo, Palazzoli asks, "If your mother wants to divorce, with whom do you want to live?"

"With Mama," replies Rodolfo, who has stayed at his mother's home since he first began showing psychotic symptoms. It is the first time that his mother, who early in their marriage left the job of childrearing to her husband, has cared for her child.

"Why did you have to go mad to be with your Mama? Couldn't you do the same as a sane person? Wouldn't she have been moved by you if you had not gone mad?" asks Palazzoli.

"No," replies Rodolfo.

Turning to Mr. Santini with a quizzical look, Palazzoli asks, "Can it be, Sir, that by going to bed with the maid, you have put your son on the side of his mother?"

Behind the mirror, Cirillo and Sorrentino are suddenly on their feet. They're afraid that the session has taken a wrong turn. "No, no. He's not siding with the mother," says Cirillo. "Mara's missing the

MARA SELVINI PALAZZOLI

point." He leaves to knock on the door of the treatment room, summoning Palazzoli to come out. Excitedly he tells her what he has seen.

"Rodolfo wants to stay with the mother to subdue her, to go on with the game!" he says.

Palazzoli, who has been sitting with arms folded, looking up at Cirillo like an attentive schoolchild, is now beaming. "That's wonderful!" she announces, arms skyward in a gesture of rejoicing. "Thank you so much." Turning to a visitor, she says, "Now I can say good-bye to Rodolfo because we understand. According to our model, Rodolfo considers his father the loser. He wants to stay with his mother to kiss her, to be tender with her, to show his father that he, Rodolfo, is a true man, a big walrus. When you understand, everything is clear. But to understand without the team is quite impossible."

Returning to the session, Palazzoli lays out the

DENNIS CAUDILL

team's conclusions with great verve. There is nothing paradoxical about her goal of kicking Rodolfo out of his parents' relationship. "Rodolfo wants to grab from his mother the tenderness that his father, a perfect idiot, couldn't obtain. [Turning to Mrs. Santini] If you divorce, Madam, Rodolfo will have you there for 30 years, caressing him endlessly. [Turning to Mr. Santini] And while you lost the game, Mr. Santini, Rodolfo has won it already. He has got his mother, but the price paid is very high: he has to be psychotic. [Turning to Rodolfo] Now you, Rodolfo, are saying 'Good-bye, Father, now I must go to live with my divorced mother, to get all the caresses that you, a sane person, were not able to get from her.' But it is a completely stupid project. [Turning again to Mrs. Santini] If you divorce, Madam, you will end up living with someone who will get you to submit. Rodolfo will push you around for years."

She then tells the parents that she wishes to see only the two of them next time and once again warns Mrs. Santini, "Don't forget about Rodolfo's project: to get you on your knees. To transform you into the warmest mama, he needs to act crazy. It's a Pyrrhic victory. For now this is it. Good-bye."

THE SANTINI FAMILY HAS NOW COMPLETED THE first phase of a treatment that Palazzoli has used with more than a hundred families in the past seven years. What lies ahead is the invariant prescription, a fixed sequence of unusual directives that Palazzoli uses with all the families of schizophrenics and anorectics she treats in her research project. Among other things, the invariant prescription requires parents to disappear without forewarning or contact with their children or anybody else in the extended family. Beginning with a few hours, these mysterious outings can extend to whole weekends away. In one case, Palazzoli and her team had the parents disappear for an entire summer. It's a method family therapist Lynn Hoffman, one of the foremost

explicators of Palazzoli's work, has said "cuts into every family triangle as far as the eye can see."

Palazzoli has reported that extraordinary family transformations take place when clients faithfully follow the entire series of prescriptions. Using this procedure, she claims to have consistently brought about the "complete cure" of schizophrenia and anorexia. Much of her time these days is spent collecting data at her center to support her claim.

Just how to use the invariant prescription remains obscure. So far, only a handful of therapists have traveled to Milan to observe Palazzoli and her team practice their new therapy. Never interested in training, Palazzoli is unconcerned with preparing clinicians to use her new approach. What is known about the invariant prescription has been pieced together from Palazzoli's rare public presentations. Nevertheless, her latest work has already generated considerable discussion and criticism, much of it in reaction to an address Palazzoli gave at the 1985 meeting of the American Association for Marriage and Family Therapy (AAMFT).

At AAMFT, Palazzoli described the results of 19 cases in which she used the invariant prescription. In the 10 cases in which families accepted and diligently followed the prescription, there was a complete alleviation of symptoms in the schizophrenic and anorectic identified patients. Concluded Palazzoli, "The therapeutic power of the invariable prescription, when obeyed, had now been confirmed beyond all doubt."

She also elaborated on her team's concept of the dirty game: "A game was dirty, in our opinion, when the actors resorted to foul means such as subtle cunning, brazen lies, relentless revenge, treachery, manipulations, seductions, ambiguous promises, and ambiguous betrayals . . . Our hypothesis was that the psychotic behavior of the identified patient was directly linked to a dirty game. We were repeatedly able to confirm this hypothesis."

Some in the audience were appalled by Palazzoli's emphasis on dirty games, seeing it as a disrespectful and potentially destructive perspective to take on families. "The whole idea of 'dirty games' is based on a very negative idea about people's motivation," said one attendee. "It carries an enormous connotation of blame and disapproval. I just don't think it's useful for therapists to adopt an I'm going-to-get-you view of human beings."

Others greeted Palazzoli's reports of dramatic results with skepticism and charged that she was making exaggerated and unsupported claims for her work. In a pointed rejoinder to the publication of Palazzoli's address, schizophrenia researcher Carol Anderson wrote: "What . . . is the impact of claims, such as those made [in Palazzoli's address], of astounding results with a new method when the evidence for such claims is not apparent from the work reported? Unsubstantiated claims could be a major disservice to clinicians and families, who may experience their therapy as a personal failure when they cannot achieve these same results. Might this not cause, rather than alleviate, problems, by raising unrealistic hopes and expectations?"

Said another prominent family therapist, "I was totally outraged by her claims. She never even said what her criteria for success were. The idea that there is this magical cure for problems as difficult to treat as schizophrenia and anorexia is ridiculous. It flies in the face of everything we know about human behavior."

Palazzoli, however, has long been more than willing to fly in the face of conventional assumptions about behavior. Throughout her career as a therapist and researcher, a restless search for fresh challenges has alternated with total dedication to the projects that have seized her imagination. She has repeatedly reinvented herself and shifted her perspective to embrace a whole new range of ideas. Palazzoli has been psychotherapy's most operatic researcher, someone whose influence has been felt not simply in the data she has furnished but in her

distinctive tales of therapeutic "miracles," "disasters" and "shocking discoveries."

AFTER WORLD WAR II, ITALIAN PHYSICIANS ENcountered a kind of patient many had never seen before. Parents started bringing in emaciated teenage daughters who refused to eat. The conventional medical opinion of the time maintained that these young women were suffering from Simon's disease, a disorder of the pituitary gland that affected appetite. Palazzoli, who was then a young physician specializing in internal medicine at the University Clinic in Milan, became fascinated with these young patients. If they were suffering from a purely endocrinological problem, why had so few cases of this malady been reported during the war years? Moreover, why did so many of these young girls go to great lengths to fool their parents into thinking that they were eating? And if these girls had a psychological reason for starving themselves, what could it possibly be?

"During the war, there was no food. Once the shops began to be filled with food again, there was an invasion of anorectic patients into the clinics," recalls Palazzoli. "Today we can see clearly that if there is no food, there is no way to use food to make a move in the family game. But then it was a great mystery." Palazzoli became so taken with this mystery that she decided to switch careers and become a psychiatrist. Over the next 17 years, she emerged as one of Italy's most prominent psychoanalysts and the author of a book and many articles about anorexia nervosa.

In the early 1960s, however, Palazzoli became increasingly disenchanted with psychoanalysis. "I needed hundreds and hundreds of sessions to have some effect on my anorectic patients," says Palazzoli. "I decided psychoanalysis was not an adequate treatment for this illness." In 1967, searching around for another approach, she came to the United States and became interested in family therapy. Back in

Italy, she formed a group of psychiatrists to develop a new treatment approach. Says Palazzoli, "I was very arrogant. I did not want to invite family therapists from the United States to train us. I wanted to invent something different." Smiling broadly, she proclaims, "I wanted to be *original*."

For several years, the group floundered, unable to fit together their psychoanalytic orientation and the new family therapy ideas. "We treated families with interpretation, showing them what was going on in the session," says Palazzoli. "We had very disappointing results." In 1971 the group split, with Palazzoli and three young psychiatrists, Luigi Boscolo, Gianfranco Cecchin and Giuliana Prata, staying together. They resolved to discard their psychoanalytic mind-set and develop a therapy founded on systems theory. To avoid being sucked back into conventional psychiatric thinking, they cut themselves off from the professional community and created a kind of intellectual island.

"We laughed a lot and enjoyed each other's company very much, but in a way we were like monks," recalls Cecchin. "We were afraid to be contaminated by nonsystemic ideas. *The Pragmatics of Human Communication* was like our sacred text." The team would meet two days a week to see families together, two members of the team serving as cotherapists with the family while two watched behind a one-way mirror.

As first among equals, Mara Selvini Palazzoli provided the team with clinical leadership. Dealing with the most difficult families, using a method that called for long intervals between sessions and uncompromising neutrality, Palazzoli remained faithful to her clinical theory no matter what the crisis. Once a panicked wife called to request an emergency session with Palazzoli, saying that her exhibitionist husband was threatening to cut off his penis. "Do not accept any alliances," Palazzoli told the team member who took the call. "Tell her, 'This is a surgical problem, not a psychological one.' Let her know that we realize that she and her husband will suffer

very much before their next session."

The team developed an approach that sought to shift the family system without either overtly challenging it or blindly succumbing to it. Each session had an elaborate structure including preliminary hypothesizing, repeated team consultations and a questioning process that continuously tested the team's hypotheses. Sessions climaxed with a closing prescription in which the entire system of interactions around the presenting symptom was positively connoted and the family was typically advised against change. Without being told so, the family was left to ponder the cost of continuing on its present course.

Frequently these closing prescriptions sounded a bit bizarre, as bizarre as the family game they were designed to disrupt. Once, nearing the end of therapy with a family in which the 8-year-old, named Claudio, had been diagnosed as autistic, the team decided the parents were trying to lure them into extending treatment, even though the boy was doing well. The team saw the parents as seeking to evade responsibility for their children, and Palazzoli addressed the following prescription to 8-year-old Claudio and his mischievous 5-year-old sister, Detta: "There is a city, a large city in England that's called London, where there are a lot of theaters . . . There is one theater where for the past 22 years the actors always act in the same play. They know it all by heart, and they play their parts every day, year after year, and they can never change it! The same thing has happened to your mother and father. Ever since they got married, they have been playing the same part. We heard it here today. Daddy played the part of the good and the healthy one, and Mommy played the part of the bad and crazy one. [At this, the father tried to laugh, and the mother remained with her head bowed.] We doctors have tried in every way possible to help them play different parts, where the father isn't always good and healthy and the mother bad and crazy, but we haven't been able

to, not at all. So we have to give up, but we are putting all our hopes in you. We have seen how much you have changed, and because of that, we hope *you* can do something. Who knows that, in time, you won't get some idea of how to help your parents change their parts, since we haven't been able to do anything. We are going to give you a lot of time. We will meet here in a year—to be exact, next year on July 7."

Detta (immediately): But next year I have to go to school!

Claudio (chanting): School days school days, no more baby games now.

Palazzoli: Surely, and you will have a lot to do, and you will learn a lot in school. Let's hope you get some ideas as to how you can help your parents change their parts, since we have not been able to.

Following the session, the team analyzed the impact of the prescription in this way: "The therapists had abdicated the parental role conferred upon them by the couple, declaring themselves incapable of responding to their expectations, metacommunicating upon the conflictuality of these expectations, and leaving the field. In such a way, they declared this task requested of them impossible to fulfill. At the same time, they asked the children *to accomplish this impossible task in their place*. Such a prescription is doubly paradoxical. The therapists not only were prescribing something which had been proven impossible for them to fulfill, but *were prescribing something which the children had always tried hard to do*. The children had reacted to this explicit prescription by refusing the task and leaving the field ('I have to go to school!'). The parents were struck by this turning of the tables. They were the only parents left in sight, there were no other parents than themselves."

The team began to see dramatic shifts in families. "In a few sessions, using the so-called paradoxical prescription, some of our most difficult patients gave up their symptoms, and their families began to change," recalls Palazzoli. "For me, that was very

important because as a psychoanalyst I never had such astonishing success."

WORD OF WHAT THE MILAN TEAM WAS UP TO spread slowly. One of the first American family therapists to become interested in the Milan team's work was Peggy Papp, today one of family therapy's leading trainers. In 1974 she managed to get hold of a manuscript of *Self-Starvation,* a book written by Palazzoli but not yet published in the United States. It described, in part, Palazzoli's break with the analytic method and her team's use of rituals and paradoxical prescriptions in the treatment of anorectics and their families.

"I was taken with their ideas about paradox," recalls Papp. "They had gone beyond reverse psychology and just instructing oppositional people complaining of imaginary headaches to go home and start having headaches. They weren't just prescribing the symptom, but the family's whole reaction to the symptom as well."

That summer Papp arranged to visit Palazzoli and her team in Milan. "I was astounded by their discipline," recalls Papp. "They would meet for an hour before each and every session. Mara would read the minutes from the previous sessions and then the four of them would discuss the case with tremendous enthusiasm. They'd have lengthy conversations during the session and then meet afterwards to analyze what had gone on. It made every therapy session I had seen before seem haphazard and shoddy."

While the team's methods had developed out of long deliberations about Batesonian epistemology, cybernetic loops and the pitfalls of Newtonian thinking, what impressed Papp as she watched them work was their flair for the dramatic. Says Papp, "They turned everything into a theatrical presentation. With all their detailed questioning, they managed to take the hidden subjective life of the family and turn it into a heightened performance. Eventually each family's situation would take on the dimensions of a great opera."

After a week in Milan observing the team craft its unusual prescriptions, Papp returned to the Ackerman Institute both eager to try out new ideas and terrified at adopting the disengaged, neutral Milan stance. "My heart was in my mouth for the first few sessions," she remembers. "I was saying things to families that seemed absurd, crazy. I was deliberately exaggerating one part of the truth, and it was a struggle to maintain my perspective."

The results, however, were exhilarating. Papp grew almost giddy with the effects of her new tool. "Instead of trying too hard to persuade people to change, I was sitting back throwing out messages and watching families react in remarkable ways," recalls Papp. "I soon realized, of course, that paradoxical interventions don't always work. I later modified much that I learned from the team and put it in my own framework. But I discovered something very important about bypassing what I normally considered resistance. In some way, I was leaving the decision to change up to the family. I thought to myself, 'Oh, what a relief to have such a tool.'"

As the Milan approach became known around the world, many therapists were to have experiences that paralleled Papp's. An important impetus to the team's reputation came in 1977, a year before the publication of an English translation of *Paradox and Counterparadox,* at a special by-invitation-only conference sponsored by the Ackerman Institute. The Milan team arrived a week early and taped a number of consultations with the most difficult cases the Ackerman staff could come up with. "Seeing the team work together was electrifying. They absolutely turned my mind around," recalls Lynn Hoffman. "Their method provided a way of exploring the underlying logic of the problem within the family."

Even those who were suspicious of yet another approach that claimed clinical miracles came away impressed. Recalls Betty Carter, director of the

Family Institute of Westchester, "I can only describe myself as sitting there in a state of total skepticism, tapping my foot, with eyebrows raised, thinking, 'Okay, show me, Buster . . . show me your miracle cures.' I looked at their tapes through my theoretical orientation, and I found all kinds of things wrong with them. I felt very critical. But then there was this little thing that told me something important had happened in the families. . . . I tried like hell to dismiss it, because it was foreign to my orientation, but I couldn't."

As the Milan team's popularity and influence grew, their critics raised questions about some of the tenets of their approach. "I think the Milan approach is based on an utter distrust of people," says Frank Pittman, longtime observer of the family therapy scene. "It's an approach that assumes people are more interested in defeating the therapist than changing. That's just fallacious. I don't think I'm that much less obnoxious than other therapists, but when I tell people what to do, they usually do it. And when they don't, it's because I've messed up the relationships so badly that they prefer to do the opposite of what I say."

"In 1979 I went over and spent a week watching the team work together," says Jay Haley, known for his strategic approach to therapy. "I thought they were doing very skillful interviews, but typically they did the same intervention at the end of the session— which was to tell the family to stay the same. It seemed to me they were still thinking like psychoanalysts, trying to stay neutral and relying on the same method in every case rather than taking a strategic approach and changing what they do with each case. I think 80 percent of their popularity came from their model of working together as a team. Most therapists starting out with families don't know what they're doing and like to have company. That way they don't have to take individual responsibility, which is a relief to a lot of therapists."

Perhaps the most telling critiques of the Milan approach had less to do with the original team's work than with the uses it was being put to. In their interest in the technical side of the approach, many therapists ignored the enormous effort the team put into understanding what made a family tick. They failed to realize that much of the credibility of the paradoxical prescription with clients came from the fact that it was grounded in an exhaustive inquiry into the family's process and patterns.

"Some people thought the Milan approach was a way of outwitting the family," says Lynn Hoffman. "Whatever the family did was a maneuver, and therefore the therapist was justified doing a maneuver, right back. What those people missed, I think, was the heart of the approach, which was a way of developing a systemic mind and inquiring into the very basis of the family's life together."

AFTER YEARS OF CLOSE COLLABORATION, THE Milan team finally split up in 1979. Faced with a deluge of requests from therapists eager to learn their method, Cecchin and Boscolo decided to open their own institute and concentrate on training. Palazzoli and Prata, neither of whom needed to rely on their clinical work for income, chose to continue their research collaboration but change its direction. Palazzoli seemed to feel she had gone as far as she could go with the paradoxical approach. She soon absorbed herself in developing an entirely different clinical method, one that she first described to American family therapists at a much anticipated 1982 conference featuring Palazzoli and two other well-known clinical innovators, Salvador Minuchin and Carl Whitaker. Expecting to hear her discuss paradox, the audience instead heard that after a few sessions, she was giving the following prescription to the parents in every family she saw in her research project: "Keep everything about the session absolutely secret at home. Every now and then, start going out in the evenings before dinner. Nobody must be forewarned. Just leave a written

note saying, "We won't be home tonight." If, when you come back, one of your children inquires where you've been, just answer calmly, 'These things concern only the two of us.' Moreover, each of you will keep a notebook carefully hidden and out of the children's reach. In these notebooks each of you, separately, will register the date and describe the verbal and nonverbal behavior of each child or other family member that seems to be connected with the prescription you have followed. We recommend diligence in keeping these records because it's extremely important that nothing be forgotten or omitted. Next time you will again come alone, with your notebooks, and read aloud what has happened in the meantime."

Although Whitaker expressed his delight at Palazzoli's new approach to the "greased pig of schizophrenia," most of the audience at the conference were puzzled by her presentation. Was she saying that she had developed the ultimate intervention, a tool so magical that all other approaches were now irrelevant? Or was she presenting preliminary data of a highly specialized research project? Palazzoli seemed content to drop her bombshell and let others draw their own conclusions. It was left to Salvador Minuchin to warn the audience against adopting Palazzoli's "interesting research methodology as an everyday clinical tool."

Soon after the conference, Palazzoli and Prata ended their partnership, and Palazzoli formed a new team with three younger colleagues, Anna Maria Sorrentino, Stefano Cirillo and her youngest son, Matteo Selvini. The team also enlisted researcher Maurizio Viaro to analyze the team's interview techniques.

The new team soon became interested in the invariant prescription as a research device. Carefully analyzing their sessions and the observations parents were recording in their notebooks, Palazzoli's team began to see the prescription as a means of eliciting family patterns and comparing responses across

families to a controlled clinical stimulus. They concluded that the very blueprint for schizophrenia and anorexia had emerged from their study.

Palazzoli now maintains that a single developmental process takes place in all families of anorectics and schizophrenics. It begins—where else—with a conflictual, stalemated relationship between the parental couple. Eventually a child is drawn into the game, first as an interested observer and later as an active participant. What the child sees is that one parent appears to be more provocative than the other. According to Palazzoli, "He wrongly considers the actively provoking parent to be the winner and the passive one as the loser, and he takes sides with the 'loser.'"

The child then takes on a very ambitious project. He begins to display unusual, troublesome behavior that requires parental attention. But the message of the behavior is covertly directed at the parental "loser." It is a demonstration of how the winner can be defeated, as if the child is saying, "Watch me and see how to dominate."

But then everything goes awry. Instead of understanding the child's message and joining with him, the loser sides with the other parent in disapproving of the child and even punishing him. The child feels misunderstood and utterly abandoned. Instead of becoming depressed, however, the parental "betrayal" challenges him to escalate his behavior. Says Palazzoli, "His competitiveness becomes unlimited. His unusual behavior having failed its purpose, he will now resort to crazy behavior in order to prevail at all costs. He will bring the winner down on his or her knees and show the loser what he, the child, is capable of doing."

Finally, the family system stabilizes around the symptom, and all members devise strategies to turn the situation to their own advantage. It is this grand model of "psychotic family games" that Palazzoli thinks may be the most lasting contribution of her research.

PALAZZOLI'S LATEST WORK COULDN'T BE MORE out of step with the political climate in American family therapy today. It seems oblivious to the impact that groups like the National Alliance for the Mentally Ill, an advocacy organization founded by the parents of schizophrenics, have had in sensitizing therapists to how people outside the profession react to theories that appear to blame client families. In this atmosphere, one could hardly imagine a more inflammatory label than Palazzoli's concept of dirty games. What's more, the field as a whole has become increasingly skeptical of anything that sounds like a miracle cure. As a result, Palazzoli's invariant prescription has been widely dismissed as a preposterous therapeutic gimmick. As one family therapist put it, "Wouldn't it be horrible if the invariant prescription worked as well as Palazzoli says it does? I'd be afraid somebody would use it with me."

Nevertheless, some believe that rather than being out of step with the field, Palazzoli is addressing one of family therapy's glaring needs. "As a field, we are rich in interventions but poor in theory," says Peggy Penn, director of training at the Ackerman Institute. "What is most intriguing about Mara's latest work is her suggestions about the sequential development of coalitions in dysfunctional families. I know some people think she has gone over the edge, but that always happens when some theorist moves away from the identifiable center."

The next few years will tell what impact Palazzoli's current work will have. She believes that the publication of her book about the invariant prescription, due out next year, will clear up her critics' misunderstandings of her research and encourage therapists to try her model. Right now, however, there seem to be few therapists around the world who have adopted the invariant prescription as a clinical tool. Penn thinks that's because "most clinicians regard it as too difficult to apply and don't have a team to support them in trying it."

Whatever the outcome of her current research, Palazzoli has already established herself as one of family therapy's most influential innovators. "Mara has made contributions that have endured and become part of the public domain of the field," says Salvador Minuchin. "Paradox, circular questioning, positive connotation—these are no longer just her ideas. They are things that everybody uses."

"Mara is a discontinuous genius," says Lynn Hoffman. "Periodically she comes out of nowhere with brilliant new ideas that seem out of the context that shapes conventional thinking in the field. That's what makes her so important. She's dramatic and unconventional, and sometimes I don't agree with her. But I think she has done more for the field than almost anybody I know. I would hate to see anybody clip her wings."

In the interview that follows, Palazzoli discusses why she discarded her paradoxical approach and describes the implications of the invariant prescription for understanding problems like schizophrenia and anorexia nervosa.

Q: *It seems to me that many of the theoretical differences among clinicians come from their different ideas about what a therapist should be. What do you think is the most important quality in a therapist?*

PALAZZOLI: If you wish to be a good therapist, it is dangerous to have too much of a desire to help other people. In my opinion, a therapist should be, above everything else, a very intellectually curious person. People who want to help too much can fall into the sentimental trap of love and concern while understanding absolutely nothing. When I was a psychoanalyst treating schizophrenics, I was full of love and concern. I kept falling into my schizophrenic patients' game without realizing it. I was in the game they wanted to play with me, not the therapeutic game I had to play with them.

Q: *Your ideas about the therapeutic game have changed a great deal in recent years. Although people*

still identify you as a master practitioner of therapeutic paradox, your current work has nothing to do with paradox. What led to such a dramatic change in your therapeutic approach?

PALAZZOLI: That is very difficult to explain because it was not always clear to me what direction my clinical work was taking. But I was always compelled by the desire to improve my therapeutic method; I had too many failures using paradoxical methods with psychotic and anorectic families. Paradox gave us a general model of intervention, but we had no guide for understanding the particular game going on in a family. Our only guide was our previous experience and intuition. Often we were so blinded by the inessential characteristics of families that we were not able to see what was essential.

Shortly after we wrote *Paradox and Counterparadox*, two members of my team, Gianfranco Cecchin and Luigi Boscolo, decided to begin a school to teach family therapy. I decided I did not want to be involved in the institutional aspects of training. Training and research are, in my opinion, two different things. If I am concerned with training. I cannot change my ideas and methods every six months! Moreover, training is too time- and energy-consuming to allow me to do the research I wanted to do. For that reason, the team separated—there was no fighting. Cecchin and Boscolo left, and Giuliana Prata decided to stay with me to continue research.

It was when Giuliana and I first began to work as a team of two that my method changed. There was a case for which I had invented a prescription that proved so effective we decided to use it with all families presenting psychotic and anorectic members. This case involved a family of five—father, mother and three girls. The oldest girl was 20. She had become anorectic at 15, displayed psychotic behavior, and was also suicidal. We could not understand what game was going on in the family. The only thing that was clear was that the conflict between

the parents was very strong. But the three girls kept intruding heavily into the conflict of the parents. They clearly held tyrannical control over the parents. I decided to invent a prescription to kick the daughters out of the parents' problems.

So for the fifth session, I decided to invite the parents alone and prescribe a secret to them. I had them swear not to tell their daughters or anyone else about what went on in the sessions, and I directed them to begin to go out on mysterious outings. It was the reverse of what you might do in a family in which the parents do not give freedom to the children. Instead of telling the parents, "Let your children go out," we told the parents to disappear without giving their children an explanation or forewarning. So we prescribed adolescent behavior to the parents. The parents obeyed, and shortly afterwards the anorectic girl began to gain weight.

Q: *When you worked with your original team, you sometimes saw parents apart from their children. How was this intervention different from your previous work?*

PALAZZOLI: In some cases, especially with chronic anorectic patients, when the patient did not improve in three or four sessions, and a heavy conflict between parents was evident, we would tell the anorectic and the other children, "You have done so much to help your parents, but you have not been successful. They are very unhappy and imprisoned by their conflicts. Leave your parents here, and we will try to improve their situation." Sometimes, after we designated the parents as the true patients, the identified patient improved. But even when that happened, we could do nothing for the parents because they would become hostile to us and present themselves as an irreparable couple. And *pour cause*! Because if the child would have been cured, it would have been clear that the symptomatic behavior of the child was their fault.

Q: *They would feel blamed even though you tried to positively connote the symptom?*

PALAZZOLI: Yes. The parents felt blamed because

there was something teasing about positive connotation that the parents didn't really believe. We were saying to them, "You are so good, but you have an anorectic child." I am convinced now that we invented positive connotation, because when I first started treating families, I lost them all. The parents felt blamed and were offended. So we decided to positively connote every family to prevent dropouts. But reading the transcripts of sessions from that time, I can see that in the second, third, fourth session, we were not really so positive.

Q: *So these days you are not so concerned about positive connotation?*

PALAZZOLI: No. After two or three sessions in which we try to clarify the family process in a compassionate and understanding way, we are severe with the children. We kick them out from the treatment, telling them that they are stupid for meddling with the parents' business. [She laughs.]

Q: *Many people don't understand what your new work on the invariant series of prescriptions is all about. What is there about this intervention that makes it effective?*

PALAZZOLI: On an implicit level, this prescription contains a great amount of communication. First, the parents must agree never to tell anyone else what goes on in our sessions together. This is an iron pact. An air of mystery surrounds the therapy, and I involve the parents in a secret with me. For the first time in their lives, they have a secret as a couple with a third person: Nobody can know what they say with the therapist, where they go, why they are doing what they are doing. So I support the parents as the heads of the family. They are only implicitly blamed for the past but clearly held responsible for the future. They are told, "If you obey my prescription, you will save your children." And by having them keep their notebooks on how their children and extended family react when they follow the invariant series of prescriptions, I can study much more closely the game that is going on in the family.

Q: *Doesn't it get boring giving the same prescription to every family?*

PALAZZOLI: We never get bored, because we are always discovering new things. For example, by giving the same prescription to different families, we discovered that we had a new method for learning about schizophrenia. Instead of just asking questions to the family, we compel the family to *do* something. This gave us a way to treat a clinical syndrome by one method. Yet, inevitably, this invariable series of prescriptions produces different reactions in different families and in different members of each family. These differences allow us to compare and learn. One learns through comparisons. In one family the oldest child will get furious because the parents went out without forewarning, while in another family the oldest child is very happy. Through these invariable prescriptions, we could enter into the many intricacies of the psychotic games.

Q: *You seem to think there is one underlying game in all families of schizophrenics. Can you explain that?*

PALAZZOLI: The variety of games between husband and wife are not infinite. Schizophrenia seems to us an extreme version of a game that takes place in many families. Typically, one spouse is more actively provoking than the other—most commonly this is the wife. The husband is usually more passively provoking, at least in Italian culture. But the child observing what is going on between father and mother makes a wrong interpretation. He cannot understand that the passive partner is a very powerful provoker. The child does not understand how provocative the message "I am indifferent to your provocation" can be. The child only sees that the mother provokes the father and that he is not able to counteract. At a certain moment, the child decides to enter into the game between the parents, but in conformity with his wrong interpretation.

To give you an example: I recently saw a family in which the mother, a clever and beautiful blond woman, came from a poor family, and the husband

worked in a big shop owned by his own family. They asked for help because their only son, Paolo, 26, was a chronic schizophrenic. For many years, from childhood to adolescence, Paolo had sided with his mother because she was unhappy and hardly worked in the shop that was ruled by the powerful mother-in-law. Years after, when her mother-in-law had died, this fascinating woman became the queen in the shop. Meanwhile, the husband began to drink heavily. The mother accused the husband of drinking too much and leaving all the responsibilities of the shop on her shoulders.

When Paolo was 16 years old, he began his unusual behavior. Although he was a very brilliant student, he suddenly stopped going to school. It was his first active move in the family game. Where before he had sided with the mother, he went over to siding with the father because, in his opinion, the father had been dethroned and kicked in a pub to drink. In the son's opinion, the mother had too much. She was beautiful, she was triumphant, she was rich; she was the queen in the shop. But what was worse, she had gotten married to the shop. There was no more husband, no more Paolo, only the shop. She was an adulterer with the shop.

Paolo decided his only weapon against his mother was to take away his triumph in school, because that would be *her* triumph. So Paolo stopped going to school, and step by step he began to renounce the qualities in himself which could make his mother proud. By the time he was 19, he was psychotic. It was a very sad story.

At the very beginning of therapy, in the first and second sessions, I had clarified the game, and I told Paolo that he was meddling with the parents' problems. He had decided to show to the father how to deal with his triumphant wife—by failing and therefore humiliating her. Then I invited the parents to come alone for the third session.

Q: *And you advised them to disappear?*

PALAZZOLI: Yes. But there was more. After two sessions with the parents, I was sucked into the couple's game, because I had the same destiny as the shop! The mother fell in love with me—so enthusiastic about therapy, always taking the initiative about the outings, while the husband became more and more passive and withdrawn. It became clear that the couple's game had not been broken up by the clarification. Moreover, my team decided that I too had fallen in love with this woman. I had to criticize her, to demonstrate that she was humiliating her husband, that she wanted to be the queen also in the therapy. I understood it was the right thing to do, but it cost me great suffering. Anyway, I did it. Moreover, I had to face the risk of losing my only ally. I told the husband that I badly needed his help because, like the clients in the shop, I was in danger of falling in love with his wife. This would be a disaster, because to rescue his child I needed him. To this he reacted positively because I was sincere.

Q: *Did his wife get depressed?*

PALAZZOLI: Yes. For a brief period. But she remained motivated for therapy. And, moreover, she later discovered that she was getting a real husband, a man who could make decisions and be very active.

Q: *Do you find you form a different sort of relationship with families using the invariant prescriptions than when you were using your paradoxical method?*

PALAZZOLI: Yes. Using the paradoxical method, it was as if treating families was a sort of contest. We had to strip them of their secrets. After seven years of work with the invariant prescription, I no longer feel that a family is an adversary in a guerrilla war. With this approach, I am very peaceful because I know that I have a better tool. Before, I was so tense, anguished by the fear that I would not be able to understand. At the time of *Paradox and Counterparadox*, each time we began with a new family we felt like explorers in a new continent. We had no model to help us make a hypothesis. We had to invent a new hypothesis for each family. Now I have

a general model of the game which I have to embody in the specific variables of each family. So I know that in an anorectic's family, the child thinks, "My father is such a clever man, so honest and important. My mother is such a mean woman. But he is incapable of defending himself against her. So I have to humiliate my mother because my father cannot handle her."

Q: *But isn't the father also humiliated by the daughter's anorexia?*

PALAZZOLI: No. He is secretly satisfied, because when a daughter is anorectic, in his opinion, it is the mother's fault. When I was a psychoanalyst trying to understand anorexia, I used to wonder, "Why is the struggle about food?" I proposed explanations concerning the oral period, the introjected object, all those complicated psychoanalytic ideas. I wrote a great amount of useless things. But now it is simple—in our country it is the mother who prepares food. The mother is the one in the kitchen, nourishing the children. It is incredible that it has taken me so long to understand this. Now I can work quickly with some families. Recently a family I treated with success five years ago came back to see me. There were two daughters, and the younger one was anorectic. So the family comes back, and now the older daughter is anorectic. Five minutes into the first session I explain to the family that now we know what anorexia is. It is the stupid meddling of the daughter trying to punish the mother and revenge the father, who, in her opinion, is not capable of making himself respected by his wife.

Q: *And then the girl started to eat?*

PALAZZOLI: Yes. But the session was very interesting because, when the family arrived, the scene was exactly like some ancient painting representing Christ between two angels. There they were in front of the mirrors—the father (a very important politician) with a beautiful daughter on each side. Across the room sat the mother, alone. This powerful man appeared to be a weakling in his own family, always being criticized by the wife. The two daughters were convinced that the father was a victim—not a passive provoker of his wife.

Q: *So sometimes just laying out the family game and the strategies of all the players is enough without continuing with the parents and getting them to follow your prescriptions?*

PALAZZOLI: Sometimes. In very recent cases we have had some very quick successes after the first sessions when we clarified the couple game and teased the anorectic patient, calling her a naive meddler. In the last two months we have had three cases in which the family phoned that the anorectic had gained several kilos after only a few sessions, and they decided to stop for the moment because apparently she was cured. But in many cases, explaining the game is not enough.

Q: *So what is the vehicle for change in all this? Understanding?*

PALAZZOLI: Each anorectic and psychotic family plays covert games. An anorectic, for example, would never declare what she is doing, her illicit connivance with her father, and so on. Our actual experiment is: Can a family who plays with covered cards continue to play with uncovered cards?

Q: *Let me see how your intervention works. The first step is to spend two or three sessions gathering information until you are able to explain to the family the game it is playing.*

PALAZZOLI: Yes, but it is very, very important to embody our general model in the specific, essential variables of the particular family. Only then am I credible to them. You cannot approach the explanation as a formula. We had some followers who misunderstood the approach in *Paradox and Counterparadox* and used it in a generic way. They would say to the identified patient, "You are a very good boy because you keep your parents together with your symptoms." This is a generic intervention destitute of results. To be credible to the family, you cannot just say, "Ah, we know what your game is. Your

child is convinced that his passive father is the victim because his mother is a very active provoker." To present it that way is just beating the air.

The general model must be embodied through the very, very intense work of collecting information about the specific ways of a specific family. So the team always has to understand precisely the ordinary behavior of all the family members. What are the strategies of the father and the mother in the couple's game? In what way does the child side with the father or the mother? What are the positions of the other children? I find that once we have presented our understanding to the family, they are often deeply shocked.

Q: *How does change take place in those families once you've described the game?*

PALAZZOLI: Each member is hit by the explanation in a different way. Some may not be able to repeat the maneuver they did before. Others may continue to play their part but find that the other members don't react in the same manner because of the very shocking information they've received about their position in the game. But there are families in which so many strategies are tied to the persistence of the symptom, and where each member of the family has so much at stake in continuing in their strategy, that the family does not change. In those cases, after we have clarified the game, we begin working with the parents with the invariable series of prescriptions.

Q: *And you sometimes ask parents to disappear for weeks without letting anyone know?*

PALAZZOLI: Actually, it is very seldom that we have to do that. Commonly, after the parents were able to leave for weekends, the problem has been solved and the family has changed. But there are chronic cases in which the parents are not able to leave for the weekend to follow the prescription, and we have to stop. Only with a few families was it necessary to have the parents go away for longer. In one case of a chronic schizophrenic, an only child,

he was cured when his parents disappeared for the entire summer.

Q: *Without telling him anything?*

PALAZZOLI: Without telling him, without phoning, nothing. When the parents came back, they found he had a fiancée and was looking for work. It was the first time he realized he had to stay alone and survive.

Q: *Asking parents to disappear without warning is a pretty extreme request. How do people react to that prescription?*

PALAZZOLI: The family senses immediately that disappearing threatens the game. Sometimes we need hours to push the parents to accept so simple a thing as to go out for a few hours in the evening without forewarning and without explanation on return. Why? Because they know that this will disrupt their game. For example, when a father deeply involved with his anorectic daughter goes out with his wife, it's as if he is saying to the daughter, "I was a liar, I prefer your mother." This message breaks up the game. For that reason, we have a great deal of difficulty in persuading people to follow our prescription.

In families with a chronic schizophrenic, we often find that the parents do not accept the prescription. In my opinion, this is one of the most important findings of our research. Imagine parents arriving here after months of waiting for the interview. They have a chronic schizophrenic girl and have been through years of real torture. They tell me, "Dr. Palazzoli, we believe you are the only person who can help us."

After a few sessions, I begin with the prescription and ask the parents to disappear from home for three hours in the evening. I tell them that if they follow the prescription, we have the probability that their daughter will improve. And this deserves a risk. But what do many of these parents say? "We cannot. We would be too anguished."

Let me explain this another way. Imagine a man

who had a ship worth millions of dollars. There is a tempest, and the ship goes down in the ocean. He comes to a magician and says, "They told me that you are a powerful magician and can help me get my ship back."

"Oh, yes, but you have to work. You have to obey my prescription."

"What prescription? We will do anything."

"Go to a little river, take seven little stones, and each morning for a week at five o'clock, go to the seashore, say this prayer and throw a little stone in the sea, and you will see your ship emerge again. "

And what is his answer? "Five o'clock? For so many days! My God, I cannot. It's too early for me."

My conclusion would be that this man does not really want his ship back. The parents are the same. They're desperate, but a very high percentage refuse to follow my very simple prescription. They understand there is a danger, for their game, not for their child. The anxiety for the child is their alibi.

Q: *What percentage refuse?*

PALAZZOLI: In families with chronic anorectic or psychotic children, probably 50 percent. I have not yet made the computation.

Q: *Even after waiting months to arrange an appointment to see you?*

PALAZZOLI: Yes.

Q: *And you'll start off by asking them to stay away for only three hours, and they'll just say, "No, we can't"?*

PALAZZOLI: Yes. This is the fact we have to explain, a very intriguing fact. Moreover, not infrequently we succeed in persuading the parents to try. They agree to go on a mysterious outing, and nothing bad happens. On the contrary, the identified patient begins to improve. But the parents stop, they insist they suffer too much.

Q: *Do you have a limit on the age of the children in the families in which you ask the parents to disappear?*

PALAZZOLI: If the children are very young, we have the parents get a baby-sitter, but one unknown to the extended family. So if the grandparents

phone, they find a person whom they do not know. Often the extended family is very offended, especially the grandmothers, but not the children. If there is an aunt who is a confidant of the mother, she's very offended, but the children are not. They seem to think of it as a happy vacation, except if a child is the confidant of one of the parents. In that case he's very furious.

Q: *Say more about how the children react.*

PALAZZOLI: If the identified patient is not an only child, he's usually very happy because, for the first time, he sees that the other siblings also do not know where the parents are. For the first time, he's on the same level with them. We have seen many, many astonishing things. For example, in one family the identified patient was a catatonic 16-year-old boy. The parents agreed to leave both this boy and his 8-year-old brother alone in the house, but they were terrified. The parents had a fantasy that the psychotic would kill the little brother. They had to take sedatives to follow the prescription. When they came back after being away for a few hours, they found that the 16-year-old had cooked dinner for his brother and put him to bed. It was the first time in his life this boy had the opportunity to be considerate and responsible. From that time on, he was totally different. After that, he was a tender mother to his little brother, and eventually he got a job.

Q: *Have you had any disasters using this method?*

PALAZZOLI: We have never had a disaster. Sometimes a child may break something around the house as a way to tell the parents not to continue to disappear, but these problems are always very minor.

Q: *Why don't the children escalate the power struggle and become more outrageous to keep their parents from leaving so mysteriously?*

PALAZZOLI: When the parents disappear, following our prescription, there is a big change. The reciprocal control between parents and children is suspended. The children begin to feel responsible for themselves, as if they are being treated as adults

for the first time. Children who never cared for themselves cook their own meals. What is more, they clean up afterwards!

Q: *When you first started asking parents to disappear for the weekend, didn't you ever feel frightened about what might happen?*

PALAZZOLI: No, because we are a team. But the parents are very, very anguished. Sometimes we need months to find ways to get them to obey the prescription because they are so anguished.

Q: *What success have therapists outside your group had using this intervention?*

PALAZZOLI: Some years ago, I presented our prescription at a congress in France, and I suggested that the audience try and experiment with it. But nobody was able to have good results because they were so terrified about giving the prescription. If the therapist who's prescribing the prescription is terrified or skeptical, that is communicated to the family, and they will not obey. It is necessary that the therapist knows that there is a risk but also realizes that it is necessary to confront the risk.

Q: *You seem to differ from many people in the field right now in your interest in finding a single grand pattern underlying problems like anorexia and schizophrenia. Philosophically, the major influence in family therapy appears to be the constructivist position and the idea that each family makes up its own distinctive story about itself, that there are no grand patterns that explain everything.*

PALAZZOLI: Yes. I know I am alone in striving to make a general model, and I also know that my model of the family game is my own construction. I know that there are many stories, but I worked for 10 years to construct this story. I work as if my model is true, even though I'm sure that nobody knows what reality is. But if with this road map I can repeatedly be confirmed by the family and arrive at success, maybe we are near *a* true story but not *the* true story. I am dreaming of the time in which other therapists will try to work with our general

scheme of the psychotic process in the families and find it useful.

I am not a philosopher, I am a clinician. I have studied the work of thinkers like Humberto Maturana and Francisco Varela, but I could not find suggestions on how to understand my "schizophrenic" families in their writing. They are biologists, they know everything about cells and their organization. But cells are not strategic, men are. Cells obey the natural laws, while men create covert games with rules, and then they sometimes disobey both their own rules and the natural rules. Why? It depends on the strategy they have in mind. Men need to be powerful. You know why men need to be powerful? To be free to choose, to increase their range of choices, to be responsible.

A man is never completely predictable. A person in a system or in a game is influenced and limited by the game, but at the same time he remains free and responsible, even in the most extremely constraining situation. For example, put a man in prison, nail his hands and feet, and ask yourself, "What will he do now? Will he eat or not?" You cannot predict. He has choices. A cell will always eat because it obeys the natural law. Could you imagine a cell deciding not to eat? But man is different.

Q: *This interest in the choices of the individual sounds different from your preoccupation with the system and its rules in* Paradox and Counterparadox. *Back then it was as if the family had a kind of mystical life above and beyond that of the people within it.*

PALAZZOLI: During the period I was working on paradoxical interventions, I was terrified about falling back into my psychoanalytic orientation. I had tried so hard to grasp the systemic thinking, which was, for me, an important step toward a more complex way of thinking. But, as the time passed, I realized I had fallen out of the frying pan into the fire. I had lost the subjects, the actors in the game. In the absence of living persons, I was personifying the family. The family became a person who asked

for treatment, wished to change, resisted change, etc. But the family is not a person. All the members have their own strategies, their own choices, their own ideas of therapy. "Family" is an abstraction. In our current work, we have rediscovered the individuals in the family without falling back into psychoanalytic theory.

Q: *How do you mean?*

PALAZZOLI: When you direct the parents to disappear, you are compelled to pay attention to the different reactions of everyone in the family. The prescription gives us facts that enable us to determine the different strategies of each member of the family in the game.

Q: *So let's say you find out that the eldest daughter is furious that the parent leaves. What does that tell you?*

PALAZZOLI: If the eldest daughter is furious, that probably means she is the privileged confidant of either the father or the mother. Knowing that, I can begin to put other members of the family in their place. We try to put together the jigsaw puzzle, being sure that each piece is in the right place.

Q: *But are there some jigsaw puzzles that are inherently better than others? In other words, do you have some basic idea of how a healthy family should function?*

PALAZZOLI: Not at all. I don't give the prescription with the idea that we have to help the couple to learn to spend time together and make each other happy. I don't believe in this kind of conventional happiness. In my opinion, it is wrong for therapists to impose their ideas of how families should be.

It is very interesting in Italy now because many young fathers in their twenties are taking maternal roles with their children—changing diapers, taking their children to gardens, etc. In the past that would have been unthinkable. An Italian man would not only have been unhappy but very ashamed to do this. If a therapist had tried to prescribe this maternal role to these fathers in the past, it would have been ridiculous. But now it is happening spontaneously as part of a change in the culture. Families

evolve in their own spontaneous manner. Therapists cannot impose their own ideas of how families should be on them.

Q: *In the United States, some feminist family therapists have been critical of what you do. They feel that your work, like that of many other prominent figures in the field, ignores the wider social context in which women don't have the same freedom as men. How would you respond to that?*

PALAZZOLI: That's a very interesting question. I can answer with my clinical observation. In the families of anorectics, it appears that the mother is a nuisance. She is a very exasperating person, always protesting, always declaring she is the martyr, always nervous, always controlling. She is a typical mother of the patriarchal society, where oppressed women typically become very reactive. But the most prejudicial character in these families is the father, because he is signaling to the daughter, on the analogical level, how boring her mother is— "What a good wife you would be for me. And I have to tolerate this woman for the family's sake." He seduces the daughter and pushes her against the mother.

Q: *But that's not quite my question. I'm really asking about the idea that men have more power and more choices than women in the family. What do you think?*

PALAZZOLI: I find that this position overlooks the importance of the games in the family. There are many, many women who obtain very much by playing the part of the oppressed victim. Last week I saw the family of a very rich man who feels himself powerful in his home, like a dictator. His wife is a humble, quiet woman, so good, so obedient. All the four children are against him. He had forced the whole family to come to family therapy, and everyone was against him and, therefore, against me. So I told the father, "You are so triumphant and feel so important, but your wife has stolen all the children away from you. You have your business, but she has four children. I can do nothing until your wife decides by herself to come to family therapy to

change the relationship between you and her." One could feel sorry for this poor woman and forget that she has four children in love with her. But I felt that this naive man was alone, and I pitied him.

Q: *Last year, Carol Anderson wrote a paper that was strongly critical of some of your work. She especially took issue with the idea that your work can truly be described as research. She argued that sufficient distinctions weren't made between the types of psychosis amongst the children in the families you saw and that, consequently, it really wasn't clear exactly what sort of problems you were treating. What's your response to that?*

PALAZZOLI: In the book we are writing, we will specify according to DSM-III.

Q: *The other point that Anderson raises seems even more fundamental. She says: "Although Palazzoli suggests that her study is based on work with 114 families, she limits her statistical description to the use of the invariable prescription with 19, only 10 of which accepted and followed the prescription. On the basis of this experience, the author concludes that the therapeutic power of the prescription was confirmed beyond all doubt. This would seem to be a gross overstatement when two families refused the prescription and were dismissed, four were partially compliant with poor results, and three claimed to have followed directions but also did poorly. It is particularly offensive that she concludes that these last three families must have lied because they could not have done poorly if they had done as they were told. Using this logic, mustn't we also conclude that some families have lied when they say they have done well?" What's your reaction?*

PALAZZOLI: In that paper, I had referred to a previous "historical" paper I had written in 1981, after we had treated our first 19 families with the new method. The 10 successes we had (a miracle for us, because all the cases were very severe) aroused our hope of being on the right road. Concerning our suspicion that these families must have lied, this reveals our naiveté at that time. We were not yet aware of our mistakes in giving the prescription,

unable as we were to grasp the first signals of a negative attitude in the parents. So we blamed the families when things got worse.

Q: *Do you have other additional data beyond the result of your work with these 19 families?*

PALAZZOLI: I am very cautious. The follow-up is a big problem. We may phone a year after treatment to get news from the family, but we get news only from the person who is on the phone. Maybe another person will give different news. How to evaluate the results of our treatment is a delicate problem, and we are far from a solution.

Q: *Anderson also takes exception to some of your negative ways of characterizing families, especially your concept of "dirty games."*

PALAZZOLI: Carol Anderson was scandalized because I used this term "dirty games," by which I referred to the secret coalitions and connivances in families. I knew it was a moralistic term, but I also know that there are "dirty" games in all systems—in convents, in large organizations, in nations. Why is it only a scandal to talk about dirty games in the family? Do we have to believe that families are only full of love, understanding and honesty? The family is our learning context. In families we learn how to be strategic and maybe how to play the "dirty" games we play in other systems.

Q: *Is the invariant prescription a universal intervention, or should it just be used with the families of psychotics and anorexics?*

PALAZZOLI: I don't know. At my center, we receive mostly severe cases. We do not see problems like school phobias or couples who fight too much.

Q: *What is your evaluation right now of the effectiveness of the invariant prescription as a clinical method?*

PALAZZOLI: The intervention strategies are still in an experimental phase. I still need to see many, many cases. I am very cautious in teaching what I do. I prefer to explain to therapists how I see the process in the family, and then they can find their own way to intervene.

Q: *In your work, you devote so much attention to understanding the strategies people use in their families. What about your own family of origin and your place in it?*

PALAZZOLI: My family of origin was very, very unhappy. I was the youngest of four, and my parents were very busy because they had a great number of businesses to look after. My father owned factories, farms and a chain of supermarkets, but his great passion was racing horses. He had a great number of horses, and he spent a great amount of money on them. He was a very genial man but difficult to tolerate. My mother was the administrator, very religious, very obedient. Because of their bond with my mother, neither my two brothers or my sister was able to rebel against my father. My mother's message to my brothers was, "Stay with me, I am alone." And they both remained working in the family enterprise even though they were unhappy.

I was the youngest, younger than my oldest brother by 11 years. When I was born, my parents sent me to the country to a milk nurse, and I was there for three years. That was the custom at that time, and with my nurse, Rosa, I was very, very happy. It was as if my family had forgotten me. When they remembered they had a fourth child and brought me back to the house, it was a disaster. They had to get my milk nurse to live with us in the house for some time because I refused to stay home without her. I would run away, and they would find me in the street asking people, "Would you take me to my mother in the country?"

Q: *What sort of a child were you?*

PALAZZOLI: I was always trying to be treated like my older brothers. Whenever my mother refused me permission to do something my brothers did, I would demand to know why, and she would say, "Because you are a girl and they are boys." So very early I fell in love with school and studying. It was my own way to be a feminist. I was in love with Latin and Greek. My family was convinced I was

mentally retarded because I had to study so much. In my exams at the end of high school, I was given a page of Greek to translate. I translated it into Latin because it would have been too easy to translate into Italian.

Q: *But you weren't a rebel? You didn't fight with your parents?*

PALAZZOLI: It was difficult to be a rebel in my family because my mother was really in a very difficult position. My father spent so much time and money on his horses, and she was always preoccupied. So for that reason I decided to take a road outside the family and fell in love with school.

Q: *How did your parents react to your success?*

PALAZZOLI: When I was young, they were completely indifferent to my successes in school. At the end of the year, I always received the gold medal, but my parents never came to the ceremony. As a woman, it did not matter how I did in school. Women were expected only to marry, have children, and stay home. But when I went to the university, my mother became very proud and began to be interested in my examinations. She began praying for me to do well. I found that intolerable. Finally, I had to forbid her to be interested in my examinations. I told her, "It is impossible for me to study now that you control my success."

I never fought with my mother. All the fighting was with my father. I was very defiant with him. I told him, "I'm not like my mother. I am different. I will never obey you. Absolutely never." My mother died when I was in medical school, when all my siblings were married. So my father and I were alone in this big villa. And we would have great scenes with each other because he was furious that I would never comply with him. My father was unhappy when I got married because it left him alone only with servants, but he accepted it. He was very generous. When he died, we had many financial difficulties, because he was deeply in debt. For me it was good because I hated to be very rich. Having so

much money means being busy with the administrative things that I don't like.

Q: *So he relieved you of that burden?*

PALAZZOLI: Yes. My father was in love with me and perhaps I with him. In his will he left me the ring he always wore.

Q: *Do you see any connection between your experience in your family of origin and your ability to work in teams as you have over the past 20 years?*

PALAZZOLI: Maybe it is a reaction to my family of origin. With my husband and children I am very tolerant. I was never controlling with my own children. I had too much to do. I was always confident that they would never do anything bad. I think I am that way in the team and with patients. I treat the schizophrenic as competent and responsible. For example, when I begin a session, I never ask the parents about the schizophrenic behavior of the child, but almost immediately I put the question directly to him. For example, if I see in the telephone chart that his sister just got married, I will ask him, "Who in your opinion was more sad when she got married, your father or your mother?" He becomes competent because he's treated as a competent person. He answers perfectly: "It was my mother who was very sad."

Q: *So what is ahead for you now?*

PALAZZOLI: What is most interesting for me is to work here in the center. On Monday, Tuesday and Wednesday, my team and I see families. We cannot afford to have the team together all week. I also think it is better for a team to not always be together. The other days I look at cassettes of our sessions and I write. When I cannot understand the reaction of a family in a session, I can look at the cassette and take a day to think about it. So I study. I read. I look at the trees through my office window. I like so much to work here in silence.

Q: *Here you are, a leader in this with many followers. All of a sudden the leader is saying, "This fascinating work with paradox that you were all so impressed with before—well, it doesn't really matter very much to me anymore. I am much more interested in something that is completely different." Don't people get angry with you?*

PALAZZOLI: Very often people are angry because they put me in competition with myself. "You were so brave before. Why did you change?" "But 10 years ago you said so and so." I am not interested in what I said 10 years ago. But this is typical for me because I have the tendency to despise everything I have already done and to be interested only in what I will do in the future.

Q: *So it doesn't disturb you when people get angry at you and want you to stay loyal to your old beliefs?*

PALAZZOLI: Sometimes. But I cannot help feeling that research is ever on the move, and I want to move with it. ■

See references, page 173.

*L*IKE A FRIENDLY EDITOR

AN INTERVIEW WITH
LYNN HOFFMAN

LYNN HOFFMAN IS NOT ONE FOR CLINICAL RAZZLE dazzle and instant problem solving. There's even a sly note of pride as she describes herself as a "boring" therapist, someone whose style is likely to elicit such comments as, "You must have a lot of patience to work like that." As she readily acknowledges, she is not likely to spellbind many audiences on family therapy's workshop circuit—or, as she puts it, our "dog and pony show."

With a dedication rare in a field known for its indifference to theoretical issues, Hoffman has established a reputation as an illuminator rather than as a clinical innovator, a student of ideas who explicates the abstract concepts and assumptions her more pragmatically minded colleagues take for granted. Through a series of papers examining the enigmas of systems theory and, most notably, in her book, *Foundations of Family Therapy*, she has brooded over the fundamental assumptions of clinical practice and served as an intellectual pathfinder connecting family therapy to developments in the wider scientific community.

Since she left a position at New York's Ackerman Institute and moved to Amherst, Massachusetts, in the early 1980s, however, Hoffman's career has taken another turn. Although she has at one time or another been associated with just about every major family therapy approach, she had not found a method with which she was entirely comfortable—until recently. In what follows, Hoffman discusses how her interest in constructivism has led her to discard many of the ideas about systems and change that she once held dear.

Q: *I'm sure it's no secret to you that a lot of clinicians think of terms like "second-order cybernetics," "the new epistemology," "constructivism," as a kind of esoteric mumbo jumbo that doesn't have anything to do with the real business of helping people. What do you say to people who question whether any of these abstract ideas are relevant to the experience of the ordinary clinician?*

HOFFMAN: My starting point is that even though many therapists have been challenging the idea of labeling people, we've never challenged it in a fundamental enough way. It seems to me that constructivism—or social constructivism, as I would rather

put it—is just a way of saying that whatever we describe is made up by us. Therefore, we must be very careful about assuming an "expert" position and trying to diagnose or influence the people who come to us for help.

But there's even more to it than that. I think the mistake many family therapists made was believing that once they got beyond an analysis of the individual psyche, they had a "real" description of the world. A description of how a family works isn't any more "real" than other kinds of description.

Q: *Why do you think constructivism has attracted family therapists' attention?*

HOFFMAN: I think we're in the midst of a swing away from a behaviorist orientation toward a more cognitive view. Family therapy began with a focus on changing the way people acted rather than on how they thought about things. Now, within the field and within other disciplines as well, there's a movement toward what I would call "story theories." By this I mean an agreement that we organize the world in little packets of meaning—call them stories, call them parables, call them premises, call them themes. It's as if reality consists of the tales people tell themselves to make sense of the world and to navigate within it. In other words, maybe it's not sufficient to try to change somebody's behavior. Maybe we have to get to the narratives they are using to make sense of their lives, the metaphors they live by.

Another impression I have is that the entire systemic view on which family therapy is based is coming into question. In our descriptions of social systems, we are moving away from the timeless circle metaphors that represent this view—such as homeostasis, circularity, autopoiesis—to rivers-in-time metaphors, concerned with narrative, history, flow. The cybernetic analogue for human groups, which is essentially spatial, may be on the way out. For me this has meant that I have had to question some of the ideas I was most identified with.

Q: *Why do you think so much of the discussion of this movement seems obscure and hard to grasp?*

HOFFMAN: Well, once you move from a focus on behavior, to a focus on meaning, you find that it's harder to talk in precise terms. Behavior is readily observable, but ideas are not. You can't see them change. Also, I don't think ideas reside "inside" people the way fortunes reside in fortune cookies. Ideas are more like time flows—they arise in dialogue and are always changing, though sometimes rather slowly. A therapeutic conversation takes advantage of this fact.

Q: *Perhaps you could make this discussion a bit more concrete by describing how embracing a constructivist perspective has changed how you operate as a therapist.*

HOFFMAN: It changed me drastically. I started by asking myself how my work would look if I gave up all ideas of instructing people and stopped trying to take an expert position. And that was like bowling; all my old ideas started to fall down like ninepins. When I was at the Philadelphia Child Guidance Clinic, I found that [Salvador] Minuchin's managerial style of doing therapy didn't fit me at all. I used to say I needed a Therapy of the Feeble. However, I never did anything about it until now.

The way I have begun to work moves away from the stance of trying to change people. It's much more a matter of sitting down with people to help them tell their story—like a ghostwriter, you might say, or a friendly editor. I might suggest some alternate framings, but it's basically their text. And if what I do together with people works, they start to feel better about themselves and the problem either becomes easier to resolve or else it doesn't, but it stops being seen as a problem.

But let me emphasize that what I do in therapy shouldn't be called Constructivist Family Therapy— it's only my own application of these ideas to clinical work. The things I do haven't changed so much as the fact that I've become more personal and less concealed as a therapist. Individual therapists have

LYNN HOFFMAN

always been scandalized by the fact that the therapeutic relationship is the stepchild in family therapy. I'm trying to put the relationship back.

Q: *Could you give a clinical example of how you put your philosophical position about constructivism into practice?*

HOFFMAN: Okay. Let me tell you about a mother and young adult daughter who came in to see me three years after a huge quarrel had estranged them. The family had been this little island of three women—grandmother, mother, and daughter—but after the grandmother died, the mother wanted the daughter to be more available to her. The daughter, who was already living alone, backed off, saying, "I have to live my own life." So they had this big fight and stopped seeing each other. They tried once to see a therapist to settle some things, but quarreled all over again.

HYAM SIEGEL

After several sessions of failing to reconcile them, I asked myself whether I really understood their conflict. So I told these two women that I thought I'd been going in the wrong direction. My trying to push them together could have been the worst thing in the world for them.

The mother had scars up and down her arms from a terrible skin condition that had kept her dependent on her own mother for many years. I said that if they had stayed too close after the grandmother's death, mother and daughter might have healed together like Siamese twins.

I also said that I might not be the right therapist for them because my own grown daughters had become estranged from me. I said that for that reason, I might be trying too hard to push them back together again.

I had been feeling more and more indignant with the mother because she was so angry, but when I said that I felt my own anger fall away. The first thing the mother said to me was, "Then why are we paying you for therapy?" A little later, out of the blue, she turned to her daughter and said, "I want you to know that I don't hold you responsible for my depression after Nana's death." After that mother and daughter had their first positive exchange in three years.

Q: *I'm not sure I see how the case reflects constructivist thinking.*

HOFFMAN: I think because I stepped back and reflected on what "story" of my own could have been influencing me and shared that reflection. In former days, I would have defined the couple as "resisting" me and would probably have thought up some counteracting maneuver. I would not have paid attention to my feelings. I particularly would not have discussed my plight in regard to my own daughters.

Of course, there were some things on the level of technique that you could say were "constructivist." For example, the way the mother and daughter were

constructing "reality" wasn't very helpful so I offered a different way to construct it that they both felt comfortable with. The problem was still there, but I tried to shift its meaning. I also used a word—"healing"—that came from their experience while placing my forearms together to illustrate "stuck together." So I used references to their story as a source of metaphor.

But my stance was very different from former days. When I stopped being an "expert," I also became less distant and less anonymous. I will now share a much more private side of myself, and I will admit error if I think I have been in the wrong. So many models of family therapy have kept therapists standing on a mountaintop or hidden behind a screen. I feel less and less comfortable with that.

Q: *Let's talk about some of the fundamental concepts of family therapy that you are questioning. First of all, you seem to be challenging the idea that the family should be the primary focus of the therapist's work.*

HOFFMAN: Yes. That took a lot of doing because I had been one of the most enthusiastic proponents of the family system concept. Harlene Anderson and Harry Goolishian have experimented with terms like "problem organizing, problem dis-solving [sic] system." I prefer the formulation that instead of the system's creating a problem, the problem creates a system. I say that what I am struggling with in therapy is not a problem but a conversation about a problem. Very often the problem persists but people no longer need to have a conversation about it. That, for me, is the equivalent of a "cure."

Q: *You also seem to be unhappy with the idea that family problems are linked to confusions in the family hierarchy. What's wrong with that idea?*

HOFFMAN: I had always felt vaguely unhappy with the emphasis on hierarchy, but I accepted the idea from organization theory that a functional family has clear boundaries between status lines. I'm not so sure of that now. A family is not a bureaucratic establishment like the Army or the Church. I prefer to think in terms of position and perspective rather than up and down. How does where people stand influence the way they feel and see? In addition, if you construct a dogma as to what is a normal pattern for a family, you implicitly accuse families. That's what consumer groups like the National Alliance for the Mentally Ill are vociferously objecting to. Too many families have felt blamed for the difficulties of their children.

Q: *How would you compare your critique of family therapy with that of feminist family therapists?*

HOFFMAN: I don't hold the position that family therapists should take up the feminist cause and fight for the rights of women. Instead, I prefer to examine how gender-linked ideas bias our clinical thinking. If you start doing that, all sorts of idols go down. One idol that is associated with men's values in our culture is a power stance. In family therapy, there has been this rule that the therapist has to "win the battle for administration" and "take control." It's a top-down power system. First comes the therapist, then the parents and then the children. I don't agree with that at all anymore. If anything, I sit in a family like a big beach and let the waves come and break on my shore. Before, I used to think in terms of families' trying to outmaneuver me. Therapy became like a military operation—either a straightforward campaign we had to win, or an underground guerrilla war. I don't know which made me feel more uncomfortable. Women aren't trained to think like that.

Q: *So this is where your emphasis on therapy as a conversation instead of a game comes in?*

HOFFMAN: Yes. If you use the old metaphor of the therapist as someone who is engaged in a "game" with clients, you continue to see therapy as an adversarial process. I prefer to approach therapy as a special kind of conversation. As an image for the therapy process, the metaphor of the conversation feels more accurate than that of a game. A conversation is egalitarian and not especially goal oriented, people

don't take sides, nobody loses and nobody wins.

Q: *Within that conversation, you seem to believe that intention and conscious purpose should have a very limited role.*

HOFFMAN: Yes, it's the idea that if you too consciously try to get a result, you can come in for a nasty surprise. This is in line with the systems thinking critique of common sense. People who simulate human systems on computers find that common-sense solutions to complex problems have widely inappropriate outcomes, usually in the opposite direction of what was intended. As the group at the MRI say, the solution becomes part of the problem. Family therapy drives away consumers who feel blamed by it. Medication and psychiatric labels make emotional illness worse.

I call these "first-order" views. "Second-order" views are one step removed from the process and allow you to see more clearly your otherwise hidden influence and how your meddling is making the matter worse. A first-order view would compare the therapist to an environmental engineer trying to change the course of a river. A second-order view would compare the therapist to a whitewater canoeist who is navigating upon the river. A constructivist position automatically gives you a second-order view as well as a first-order view. So it's not better, just more inclusive.

A lot of my distrust of too much planning comes from my own experience, too. The more I tried to control therapy from behind the scenes, the more insecure I became because I could never count on things going right. Sometimes they would, sometimes they wouldn't. Part of it was because I was so fixed on making people change. Now that I have given up that goal, I find I am far more effective.

Q: *Isn't there the danger that if we give up our interest in results and our sense of being in charge as clinicians, therapy will become terribly vague and unfocused? It could get hard to tell the difference between therapy and channeling.*

HOFFMAN: Sure. Adopting the constructivist perspective makes it harder to clearly justify what you do or to define a therapeutic outcome. Therapy becomes frankly subjective. But that has an advantage. For a long time, I subscribed to the idea that the therapist should be able to be "neutral," take a "metaposition." This got many colleagues upset because they felt that I was taking a hands-off approach to problems of violence and brutality. A constructivist position gets me out of that controversy because it holds that you can't take a God's Eye View. All you have is an awareness of your own subjectivity. That means that you are always operating from your own value system and/or that of the agency you are working for. I now share these value systems with clients if they have some relevance to the therapy. But always as "my opinion" or "the position taken by the state," not as "the objective truth."

Q: *It sounds as if in the therapy you do, confrontation has no place. Can you ever imagine trying to break through a client's "denial?"*

HOFFMAN: If you say someone is denying reality, you are judging what their reality ought to be. I don't do that. However, many therapy methods depend on getting somebody to see or do what you think they should see or do. Not only do these first-order methods not work very well, not only are they resisted, but now here are some people saying that we don't have absolutes based on objective criteria that will back these methods up. I get around this problem by saying, "This is my idea of reality. It may not be yours, but it is the best I have."

Q: *What about people who say that your way of working has too much of an atmosphere of sweetness and light?*

HOFFMAN: I think they're right. This is a very low-key way of working, almost Rogerian. People remark on how this shows the family "respect." I'm always surprised by that, as if we wouldn't be trying to show the family respect, anyway. And then I remember how miserable my own experience in

family therapy has been, how inadequate I felt, and how hopeless. Most parents have a horror of discovering that they have harmed a child, but much family therapy is based on the premise that they have. This thought gets communicated even when it's tacit. To get around that, I think family therapists have to be much more careful than individual therapists. I notice that since I've been working in this more careful way, people I see are apt to say, "I feel more comfortable with you," and they never said that before.

Q: *I know that you've become especially interested in an approach called the "reflecting team." How did it originate?*

HOFFMAN: It was developed by a Norwegian psychiatrist named Tom Andersen, who had been trained in the Milan approach. One day several years ago, Tom was supervising a trainee from behind a one-way screen. He kept trying to get the trainee to positively connote what was going on in the family, but the trainee kept going in and saying these negative things. Tom realized that the more he put the trainee in the wrong, the more he was in conflict with his own ideas about positive connotation. What he finally did was ask the trainee to ask the family if they would like to listen to the team behind the screen. They agreed and the team began to talk about their ideas while the family and trainee listened. Once the family had heard the team's comments, they were asked to comment back. The upshot was that everyone felt relieved. It took the supervisor out of the position of criticizing the trainee, stopped the trainee from criticizing the family, and gave the family a seat of honor at the table. This is a nice example of the kind of work I call "putting the client on the board of directors."

Q: *What role, if any, does strategy play in the reflecting team approach?*

HOFFMAN: None, that I know of. I myself don't do strategic therapy anymore. I am more and more dedicated to sharing the reasons for what I do with clients. I might come up with a strategic idea, but I will share the rationale for it. And I will talk about my own theory of therapy—how I see problems and what I tend to do about them.

Q: *What about rituals and tasks? Have you given them up as well?*

HOFFMAN: I did when I first began to think this way. Then Gianfranco Cecchin said, "Oh, in a reflecting team you don't give a prescription, you give an 'idea' of a prescription." So I give people the "idea" of a task or ritual. I tell them that whether they use it or not, the information that comes back is what is important. I should add that Tom Andersen's group doesn't use tasks or prescriptions at all. I am still influenced by the models in which I was trained where one offered suggestions and directives. In that sense, I'm not very pure.

Q: *What about losing the privacy of the conversation between therapist and team, or therapist and consultant? Have there been any negatives?*

HOFFMAN: Mostly positives. Obviously, there are some occasions when you can't share your thinking, but much of the time you can. And I am convinced that the practice of exchanging negative comments, clever strategies and laughter behind the screen, the way I used to do in Milan-style therapy, creates an unconscious climate of distance. The reflecting team is useful because it trains people to use a positive description in talking and thinking about clients. It also counteracts the pejorative language of diagnosis and assessment.

Q: *I'm struck with the emphasis you place on benevolence. Why do you make such a point of seeing all motives as so positive?*

HOFFMAN: Well, that has to do with the belief that—in family therapy, at least—people find it hard to change under a negative connotation. I sometimes think that 99 percent of the suffering that comes in the door has to do with how devalued people feel by the labels applied to them or the derogatory opinions they hold about themselves.

Q: *These ideas about constructivism and therapy seem to have taken root in Europe far more firmly than in the United States. How do you understand that?*

HOFFMAN: The Europeans, especially what I call the "social justice" countries of Northern Europe, seem to be enthusiastic about Bateson's ideas and the ideas of some of his colleagues like cyberneticians Heinz von Foerster, Humberto Maturana and Ernst von Glaserfeld. They have also been heavily influenced by the work of the Milan therapists, Luigi Boscolo and Gianfranco Cecchin. I think the Europeans respond to the distrust of technology implicit in this group's thinking and the consequent notion that therapy is an I-Thou matter rather than a matter for social engineers. Perhaps they're also pulled by the emphasis on a collaborative relationship instead of one that makes the therapist the "expert." But I agree that constructivism has not had much impact in the United States. It's not in line with American pragmatism and the can-do spirit. The day when there are no more ads in the *Networker* for the tapes of the "Master Therapists" is the day when I will believe that being a "Master" is not an abiding ideal of American family therapy. ∎

REACHING OUT TO LIFE

AN INTERVIEW WITH VIRGINIA SATIR

BEING LARGER THAN LIFE WAS SOMETHING VIR-
ginia Satir knew about from her earliest days.
She grew up bigger and smarter and more
keenly aware than any of the kids her age in the
Wisconsin farm community where she was raised.
By the time she was three, she had learned to read.
By the time she was 11, she had reached her adult
height of nearly six feet. Even though her schooling
was interrupted by long stretches of illness, she started college after only seven and a half years of formal
education. As she described it, "I never had to worry
about being like everybody else. I always knew I
wasn't."

Growing up a big, awkward, sickly child, Satir
drew from her experience of being an outsider a
finely tuned sensitivity to other people's fears that
they were different or strange. Maybe it was that
sensitivity as much as anything else that accounted
for her ability to connect with something very deep
in the people she helped. Satir had a way of making
people feel that she appreciated, as perhaps no one
had ever before, just what set them apart from anyone else running around the planet and that their

differentness was neither a defect nor a burden, but
a treasure of inestimable value.

From the very beginning of her career, starting
out as a schoolteacher in the late 1930s, Satir was
drawn to people who were haunted by their sense of
being different. At night she would visit the homes
of the students in her class to find out what was getting in their way, what triggered the feelings of low
self-esteem that weighed so heavily on some of
them. In the process, she discovered the power of
the family and its role in constraining a child's development. Later, when she became a social worker
and grew increasingly interested in figuring out the
subtle dynamics of family life, it was the outcasts—
the schizophrenics, the institutionalized, the unwed
mothers, the lost souls of the world—who drew her
deepest sympathies.

By the late '50s, Satir was already receiving
widespread recognition as one of the foremost practitioners of a new approach to change called family
therapy. In 1964, with the publication of *Conjoint
Family Therapy*, her down-to-earth introduction to
the art of this new therapy, she gained a worldwide

reputation. Constantly on the road from that time until the very end of her life, demonstrating her dramatic techniques and deeply empathic way of working, she became a kind of living legend as family therapy's most celebrated recruiter and goodwill ambassador.

As Virginia Satir's reputation spread, she became perhaps the most imitated family therapist of her time. Posters of her favorite sayings decorated the offices of government agency workers around the country. Practitioners everywhere tried to copy the intimate, folksy, comforting style they saw Satir use with such skill and such moving effect. Thinking they were following in her footsteps, they urged their puzzled clients to throw themselves into symbolic postures and hug each other and give voice to feelings many never dreamed they could utter to another living soul.

But while many therapists were able to imitate Satir's mannerisms and the basic elements of her techniques, far fewer were able to get anything like the results she achieved. They didn't realize that what Satir did worked because it fit her so completely. At the core of her approach was her unshakable conviction about people's potential for growth and the respectful role helpers needed to assume in the process of change. These deeply rooted principles formed the basis of how she saw her task as a therapist.

In 1985 I published the following interview with Virginia Satir in *Common Boundary*, a journal concerned with the links between psychotherapy and spirituality. It provides an unusually crystallized discussion of the beliefs that lay at the heart of Satir's views about the art of therapy. In this memorial issue exploring her contribution to psychotherapy, it seems only fair that she be allowed to have her own say in the matter.

Q: *I've had the opportunity to watch you work several times, and what stands out is how you create a thera-peutic world in which ordinary resistance does not seem to exist. How do you understand your ability to get people whom other therapists might consider unbudgeable to make changes in their lives?*

SATIR: Some therapists think people come into therapy not wanting to be changed; I don't think that's true. They don't think they *can* change. Going into some new, unfamiliar place is a scary thing. When I first begin to work with someone, I am not interested in changing them. I am interested in finding their rhythms, being able to join with them, and helping them go into those scary places. Resistance is mainly the fear of going somewhere you have not been.

I had an experience once that taught me a lot about how to lead people into scary places. I was in Europe, staying with some friends. I wanted to descend into a cave but was very frightened. My friend said, "I'll carry the light. If you give me your hand and allow me to lead the way, then maybe we can go down together." Now, look at the decision I had to make. I had to choose to allow him to lead me. That was something I was willing to do because I was interested in getting down there. Unless he had been willing to give me his hand, and unless his hand felt trustworthy, I would not have gone.

When people come to see me, I don't ask them if they want to change. I just assume they do. I don't tell them what's wrong with them or what they ought to do. I just offer them my hand, literally and metaphorically. If I can convey to the person that I am trustworthy, then we can move and go to the scary places.

Q: *Do you ever come across people who, for whatever reason, will not take your hand?*

SATIR: Very seldom. When I am completely harmonious with myself, it is like one light reaching out to another. At the outset, it is not a question of "I will help you." It is a question of life reaching out to life. All life talks to life when it is in a harmonious state. If my ego is involved, or if I need them to get

VIRGINIA SATIR

well, then it is a different story. This is one of the secrets of what I do, if there is a secret.

Q: *So if you are in pretty good shape with yourself, the first step with a client is never a problem.*

SATIR: Let me elaborate. If you and I meet at a revolving door which only has room for one, we have to decide who will go first. In going first, I have to go on the faith that my energies translate in a positive way to the other person and that they follow. Now once we get outside, I say, "Where do you want to go?" I no longer set the direction. I need to find out where they want to go.

Being asked that question shocks many people. They cannot believe that anybody really wants to know the direction in which they want to go. They keep rationalizing, justifying, questioning, and so on. Finally, they decide, "Yeah, I believe she really does want to go in the direction I want to go." Then

we take the steps. We can walk five steps and see how it is, whether it really fits. If not, then we see what else we want to do. The big problem in whether or not somebody continues to take your hand is whether or not your hand is sending dominating messages. As a therapist, I am a companion. I try to help people tune into their own wisdom. Of course, all this doesn't fit much of a psychotherapeutic theory.

Q: *You clearly prefer not to discuss therapy in a technical language. Whenever I have heard you speak, I have been impressed with the spiritual appeal you make to people. You speak the language of hope.*

SATIR: I think one of the most important things I do for people is give them some kind of hope for themselves. But it is not only in relation to me that they get their hope, it is in relation to seeing more clearly what they have.

Q: *What about your own spiritual beliefs? Many people think of you as a kind of apostle of the religion of human potential. Does it go beyond that for you?*

SATIR: I try to help people see what is right in front of their faces. What is obvious to me is that we did not create ourselves. Egg and sperm do that job. All we do is activate the opportunity for those two things to get together. Realizing that puts you in a place where you know that life is something inside of you. You did not create it. Once you understand that, you are in a spiritual realm. That does not mean "religion" in the usual sense. The physicists know about this. More and more, I am seeing that the physicists and the good theologians know what the basic life force is all about. It is something you can call "spirit," "soul," or whatever you want. In any case, it is there, and the only thing that really changes people is when they get in contact with their life force. That is the essence of self-worth.

Q: *So do you think these ideas about the "life force" are influencing the field of psychotherapy?*

SATIR: Oh, yes, especially in the current interest in the right brain and how it works. You see, a long

time ago, people knew there was access to a person though not through the usual channels. At one time it was called "mesmerism," then "hypnotism." That is where Freud started out. All those words really refer to accessing the right brain. Thanks to Buckminster Fuller and other people, we now know that the right brain is a residual for all the information that there is in life. Today hypnotherapists, parapsychologists, psychics, some physicists and those who are studying death are coming together in the knowledge that there are levels of knowing beyond our linear understanding.

One therapist who obviously used these ideas was Milton Erickson. He accessed the right brain all the time, which helped people to get to some new places. What was called "psychic phenomena" yesterday is the same as what many people call "hypnosis" today. It is not that there is something over here called "hypnotism," something over there called "biofeedback," and something called "out-of-body experiences." All these are manifestations of the same thing.

Q: *But would you ever refer to what you do in therapy as "hypnotic"?*

SATIR: No, but I know that it is. What am I doing? I am accessing the right brain when I ask somebody how they feel and when I help them to connect with parts of their body. I am engaging in what the hypnotists would call a "trance" or an altered state.

Q: *Even though* you *would not, I have heard Richard Bandler and John Grinder talk about your work as a form of powerful hypnosis. Supposedly you are one of the models for Neurolinguistic Programming (NLP). What do you think of NLP as a translation of what you do?*

SATIR: Let me put it this way. If I look at an orange, I have many ways of describing it. I can describe it in terms of its uses, its color, its form. I can also just eat the orange. With that analogy, what I think Richard and John did is make a left-brain

analysis of my work related to psycholinguistics. It was another level of looking at something. When I first met them, I was very excited about what they were doing. But I would not want to learn NLP, if you want to know the truth. I am not sure I could learn it. The part that bothers me about NLP is where practitioners take it as the end-all and be-all and forget the heart and soul of people involved. For me, anything that leaves out the heart and soul of an individual has got to reinforce what I consider the "scourge" in our society, which is that we touch the surface; we never touch the core.

Q: *You seem to have a curious position in the family therapy field today. While various surveys of practitioners cite you as one of the most influential forces on their work, you don't seem involved in the field any longer.*

SATIR: Some time ago, I decided to stop going to any of the big professional meetings. The competitiveness and the bullfights got to be too much for me. Listening to people talk, I began to feel as if it was not professional to care about people.

Q: *Would you talk about how your experience with your own children has affected your work?*

SATIR: I have two adopted children, who are now 40 and 41 years old. I adopted them when they were 10 and 11. They are natural sisters who came from a perfectly terrible environment. They actually presented themselves to me and asked if I could be their mother.

Q: *These were youngsters you were working with?*

SATIR: Yes. One of them was in an institution for delinquent girls. I thought, "Why not?" The oldest one said, "You know, I've never had any mother but you, really." So we made it legal. Judging from the difficulties of their past, I knew that there would be great difficulties ahead. There were. However, we survived them and learned from them.

When my children first came, they regarded food as the chief vehicle of love. In those days, $500 a month for groceries—which is what I spent—was a whole lot. Even though there was all this food in the

house, I would find food cached in many places. I just kept buying the food. It took about three months before they figured out that the food was not going to disappear. I understood that they could not directly relate on the nurturing level, they had to go through it by stages.

The other thing about my children was the fact that they were so much for the underdog. I mean, literally. I remember coming home one day and finding 26 dogs and five cats in the house. I will never forget that sight. One of my daughters had gone around the neighborhood and picked up all the homeless dogs. Twenty-six dogs and five cats on a rainy day in the house—you can imagine what that was like!

It was sort of hard to live through, but I finally got all that straightened out. These illustrations are some of what we went through at first, but I knew down deep that these kids had the potential and that they needed help for them to realize it.

That is one of the things that brought me to work with families. You see, I started my work with families whose members no one else wanted to work with. I knew that being able to change and grow had to do with how people felt about themselves. Of course, back then I had not developed the word "self-esteem." That was a fancy word I learned later.

Q: *There's no secret you are probably the prototype of the nurturing therapist. How is that different from being the mother of two daughters?*

SATIR: I think the difference comes in the fact that you are one step removed when you are doing therapy. When you are in it yourself, you have to work harder with yourself to keep your head straight, your heart straight and your emotions straight. When things came up in my own family, I really

benefited from my own awareness. If I would get angry with one of the kids for some reason or another, I did not go at them as I had seen other people do. Instead, I said, "Okay, Virginia, what's going on with you?" I would not take all of the responsibility myself, but I was straight. I would say, "You know I'm very angry, and this is what it's about." If you're a plumber, you use your plumbing ability to fix your own faucets. Why not use your insights and awarenesses to be whoever you are?

Q: *What did your children think about your career, your traveling and your being a public person?*

SATIR: I will give you a little example. There is a very strong bond between my children and myself. It has several dimensions. One of them is that they know that I have to do something in life that they cannot share. They also respect what I do. So we get together when we can. There was a big party for me about five years ago in Los Angeles; several hundred people were there from all over the world, among them my youngest daughter. People were talking about what I meant to them. My daughter got up and said, "I want to tell you how I feel about my mother. I think that some of you have had more of my mother than I have." Then she looked directly at me and said, "I want you to know, Mother, that I am sometimes so jealous that other people have what I didn't. That's one side of it." But then she added, "I also want to tell you how deeply I feel about the importance of what you're doing. Not only what you are doing for others, but what you have done for me." I felt that it was a beautiful statement of the kind of marriage that she had to make with what I do. I don't see my grandchildren as often as I would like, but that is part of the price I pay for how I live my life. ■

References

Behind the One-Way Mirror

Madanes, C. 1981. *Strategic family therapy.* San Francisco: Jossey-Bass.

Madanes, C. 1984. *Behind the one-way mirror.* San Francisco: Jossey-Bass.

Madanes, C. May 1986. Eros and violence. A presentation at the Eros and Violence Conference in Amsterdam.

Erickson's Way

Erickson, M. H. 1967. The use of symptoms as an integral part of hypnotherapy. In Haley, J. (Ed.) *Advanced techniques of hypnosis and therapy: Selected papers of Milton H. Erickson, M.D.* New York: Grune and Stratton.

Haley, J. 1981. *Reflections on therapy and other essays.* Chevy Chase, MD: Family Therapy Institute.

Haley, J. 1973. *Uncommon therapy.* New York: W. W. Norton.

Master, R. 1981. Milton H. Erickson: Remembrance and tribute. *Dromenon* 3, no. 3.

Rossi, E. *Healing through hypnosis.* New York: Irvington Publishers.

Schiff, N. 1980. Meeting a remarkable man: A visit with Milton H. Erickson, M.D. *Family Therapy Network Newsletter* 4, no. 3 (June-July).

Good-Bye Paradox, Hello Invariant Prescription

Anderson, C. M. 1986. The all-too-short trip from positive to negative connotation. *Journal of Marital and Family Therapy* 12, 351-354.

Selvini-Palazzoli, M., et al. 1978. *Paradox and counterparadox.* New York: Jason Aronson.

Selvini-Palazzoli, M. 1986. Towards a general model of psychotic family games. *Journal of Marital and Family Therapy* 12, 339-349.

ONE ON ONE

Conversations With the Shapers of Family Therapy

One on One: Conversations With the Shapers of Family Therapy is a special 10th anniversary collection of interviews from *The Family Therapy Networker*. You'll sit down with some of psychotherapy's most celebrated figures as they address the questions you've thought about but never had the chance to ask. In *One on One*, the masters in our field step down from the podium to share their frustrations as well as their triumphs, their doubts as well as their deepest convictions. It is a study of what it means to come of age as a clinician.

RICHARD SIMON, PH.D. is the founding editor of *The Family Therapy Networker*. He lives in Washington D.C.

Also available in hardcover.

The Evolving Therapist: *Ten Years of The Family Therapy Networker*
Edited by Richard Simon, Cindy Barrilleaux,
Mary Sykes Wylie and Laura M. Markowitz

A special 10th anniversary anthology from *The Family Therapy Networker* that captures the nuances of everyday practice and the uncertainties of the process of change. Whether you are looking for practical assistance on a difficult case or simply wish to enjoy some of the finest writing on the drama of the therapy room, *The Evolving Therapist* is an invaluable addition to your professional library.

Available in hardcover and paperback.

The Family Therapy Network · The Guilford Press

ISBN 0-89862-26⁵

9 780898 622690